DEDICATIC

This book is dedicated to two very special people.

Larry "Mellif" Lewis, who foretold the coming of this book long before it even began and continues to inspire from the Ancestral Realms.

Diane Destasio Haskins, who has always believed in and encouraged me and not allowed me to make excuses or put this work off.

I love you both beyond words . . . and bow in reverence to your love and roles in my life.

THE EVOLUTION OF THE SPIRIT OF MANKIND

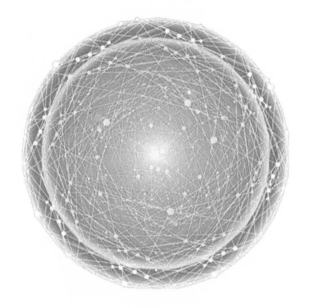

THE EIGHTY-SECOND REGIME OF LIGHT WORKERS

Through the Medium: Julie MacDonald

Foreword by Malidoma P. Somé, Ph.D.

Rowe Publishing

SOFTCOVER
ISBN 13: 978-1-939054-49-4
ISBN 10: 1-939054-49-4

HARDCOVER
ISBN 13: 978-1-939054-50-0
ISBN 10: 1-939054-50-8

Editing by All Ivy Writing Services
Original artwork concept by Angela Kaufman
Illustrations by Mike Batho

1 3 5 7 9 8 6 4 2

Printed in the United States of America
Published by

Rowe Publishing
www.rowepub.com
Stockton, Kansas

CONTENTS

ACKNOWLEDGMENTS

First and foremost, I offer my deepest thanks and gratitude to the Eighty-Second Regime of Light Workers for your granting to me the privilege of being a conduit for your words. My humblest thanks to the Source, the Ancestors and all of my spirit friends, teachers, loved ones, and companions for pushing me out of my comfort zone and helping me to begin to tap into the one thing that will never leave me, that which is my own light.

Of course, I have many humans to thank as well. Thanks to Kevin and the crew at All Ivy Editing for being willing to take on a project that was not easy to edit or even comprehend, but you have managed to breathe the intention of Spirit onto the written page, making the words and presence of the Eighty-Second Regime of Light Workers tangible and, most importantly, legible! My gratitude to Rowe Publishing for being such a great group to work with and for all of their suggestions, support and for giving me (well, the Eighty-Second Regime) the respect to publish this book without altering the integrity or content of the message.

This book would not have been at all possible without the help of my trusted friends and assistants, Yves Nazon and Patti Fasen, who were the backbone of this project from beginning to end.

Yves, you have been my motivator, my best friend, my confidant, my anchor, the thorn in my side, and the soft feather pillow to land upon during the trying times of the creation of this material. You have always been there and for this I am eternally grateful and extend to you great honor and deep abiding love and respect.

Patti, you have been transcriptionist, assistant, motivator, benefactor, sister, friend, and the stable rod to keep me walking forward along this topsy-turvy road. I bow to you in thankfulness and humility.

Thanks to you both for jumping whenever the "mood" struck me to sit for a session and for your encouragement, patience, love, and the occasional kick as needed!

Many thanks to my children, Michael and Samantha, who have always been cursed with having to suffer the consequences of the "call" of Spirit and the attention that it, at times, withdrew from them. Thank you both for your love and support in spite of the many challenges you have faced. I stand in awe of you both.

To my sisters, Catherine, Terri, and Beth, thank you for seeing what I did not always see, and for your unending support and encouragement all of these years.

To my dear friend Michael Kennedy, whose encouragement at the very height of my psychic unfoldment helped me embrace this connection with Spirit and dig deeper and farther than I thought I could.

My never-ending gratitude to Stephen Robinson, Charlene Robbins and Holistic Studies Institute for offering me a safe place to explore the world of Spirit when I first found myself in that world.

To Jun-san Yasuda, for your confidence and trust in me and for allowing me the opportunity to be of service to the Grafton Peace Pagoda and the mission of the Nipponzan Myohoji Buddhist order. You have provided me with more hope and inspiration than could ever be expressed in written form. You remain that which I strive to become.

To the many friends, family, students, clientele, and youth who have walked along the path with me, whether for a moment, hours, days, or years—each of you has touched me in your own unique way, and my life has been fuller because of it.

FOREWORD

When the familiar becomes new, and the journey to it is cut short by the gift of destination, the usual notion that lasting change must come as a sacrificial reward takes on a new meaning. We discover, much to our surprise, that what we went on a tedious quest for was always there with and in us. But a change like this still involves challenges. One of them is the daunting courage to bestow trust in something that comes at no cost to self; something we often say is too good to be true. There are countless voices that would utter disbelief, others that would invoke impossibility, and the rest would be quick to dismiss. Yet, the great question of the day is: what if this is the one and only bearable change available in our times? This contemplation is a mind- bending challenge to open up to possibilities never entertained before: change as a return to who we are.

The pages that follow are a rainbow waterfall of revelatory words from the other world with compelling colors like love, compassion, nurturing, humility and commitment. They are pouring through a special channel managed by entities that call themselves The Eighty-Second Regime of Light Workers. They flow down from an ascended place of awareness from which they can afford a bird eye view of the world and of us humans on a path riddled with so much pain and sorrow as we try to ascend to the very state and place where change concords with humanity's utmost aspirations. This mighty bunch, like an alarm that goes off, pour their gentle wisdom upon our longing souls. There is no tension in what they offer. In fact they encompass the essential things humans desire: Joy, compassion, love and connection to all things. Therefore there is no doubt that the revelations contained in these pages address everything essential to human ascension to consciousness. This is a gift of love.

When the human struggle to capture truth and meaning crashes over and over into the landscape of inquiry in a Sisyphean oxymoron, when confused minds wander aimlessly in a vast expanse littered with their failures, the utter distress of the soul translates into a stare in great bewilderment at the all elusive quest. The Eighty-Second Regime of Light Workers want us to invest in the belief that there is no such thing as failure; that all is informed by the specific learning modality we chose.

The revelations captured in this book are old and new at the same time because of their simple complexity. Sometimes it feels like these wisdom keepers are not teaching anything new, and sometimes what comes through is surprisingly simple. But these voices of truth seem to push up toward greater self-forgiveness and a deeper understanding of the profundity of the plain and simple. In the end, it all comes down to the timelessness of love as the unifying birthmark of humanity and of this planet

Reverend Julie MacDonald is a medium by birth, a professional psychic, and a spiritual activist at the cutting edge of consciousness. What comes through her is radical, credible and utterly compassionate to the plight of humanity. The gift of the message is a measure of the depth of her connection. It is a monumental synthesis of our relationship with who we are: spirits in search of ourselves. In this book are the blueprints of what it takes to get back to that zero point module that is us, and bow to this message with great reverence.

Malidoma P. Somé, Ph.D.
Dagara Elder

Malidoma P. Somé is author of *The Healing Wisdom of Africa, Ritual: Power, Healing and Community,* and *Of Water and the Spirit: Ritual, Magic and Initiation in the Life of an African Shaman.* He is a West African Elder, author and teacher, as representative of his village in Burkina Faso, West Africa, has come to the west to share the ancient wisdom and practices which have supported his people for thousands of years.

Editor's Note

There are many changes coming, and you must be prepared. There is nothing that you need to fear. There is nothing you have ever had; there is nothing you will ever lose . . . . We call to you from the beautiful places, the peaceful places; and we call to you from the hellacious war-torn places. We call to you always. Will you, shall you, dare you heed the call? We are of the Eighty-Second Regime of Light Workers, and we are here to serve you.

The communications contained in this book will seem both very familiar and very, very new. Readers will find threads of esoteric and Eastern religions, "New Age" movements, Christianity, positive thinking, the writings of A.J. Davis and other early Spiritualists, and the most pressing conversations going on in modern American culture. But where they will seem both most familiar and most challenging is that they speak to the deepest and most relevant questions of the human soul. Through the medium, the Eighty-Second Regime of Light Workers addresses our fiercest longings and desires and passionately exhorts us to change. This change is not a departure from who we are, but rather a potent and triumphant return.

In their own words, the Eighty-Second Regime is a sect or sub-sect of a group consciousness that is committed to assisting humanity's spiritual evolution through direct communication. This evolution covers a wide range of the human experience—work, religion, family, children, the environment, and society, to name a few—but the spirits are insistent to inform us that these divisions and spheres of the human experience are unified by their connection to the deeper work of the human soul. The Eighty-Second Regime is a collective consciousness made up of four different personalities: Rebecca, a playful, jovial spirit; the Compassionate One, a feminine energy full of love and empathy for human kind; the Grandfather, who speaks of the natural world both in terms of the environment and the ecology of the human experience; and the Uncle, a physically expressive spirit with connections to indigenous and related traditions. These four spirits come together in a group consciousness through the medium, presenting, in their own words, "a bigger vehicle toward the truth."

The book is divided into several chapters, each reflecting various sittings performed by the medium and one or two assistants. From the outset the spirits have intended for their communications to become this book, and they insist compellingly: "Mark our words that if you are reading this, you have put out that call. And so, all of this, every last piece of it, every nook and cranny of it, applies to you." Readers who take this statement seriously will soon realize the magnitude of the joyful work reading this book will compel them to undertake.

The first chapter, "Introduction to the Eighty-Second Regime of Light Workers," points out the hunger for religion in North America as evidenced by the increasing popularity of esoteric and Eastern traditions. This hunger, the spirits believe, comes from a lack of reverence people have for each other, the Earth, and the variety of the human condition. The spirits insist that anyone coming to the book to look for the one true answer should step away; they "do not wish this book to be used to *limit* anything." This openness, this sense of guidance, of raising questions rather than answering them, is perhaps one of the most important themes in the communication.

The next chapter, "Where the Eighty-Second Regime Resides," presents more of the ins and outs of the spirits and the nature of their communication. They speak of their world as interwoven with ours, injecting thoughts into the parts of the human brain that can receive it, their communication is filtered through the brain of the human. The information, they insist can also be diluted by limited human understanding. Their ability to communicate is made possible by and through the interconnected nature of all things, which is circular and expanding. This view speaks a great challenge to much of our current understanding, especially in regards to religion, and to one of the key themes of the book. Given individual perspectives, limited views or the inability to understand are not failures, but merely the nature of the particular sphere that the medium, reader, or even spirit dwells in. Confusion or mistakes are not failures, but simply the natural condition of souls that continue to make progress. This is a freeing and inspiring perspective that is further developed throughout the book.

After these introductory chapters, the spirits move on to discussing particular issues.

The spirits continue to explore humanity's growth in the next chapter, "The Principle of Karma." They explain that when a person incarnates on Earth, they have chosen a life plan based on what they feel they need to learn or give to others. They present the idea that "evil" people are not punished in the afterlife, but rather perhaps came to Earth to follow a goal of destruction that enables others to be more loving. This is a radical departure from a society based on punishment and retribution, even in our most esoteric or seemingly loving traditions. The spirits point out the retributory nature of humanity's understanding of karma and say that *gathering . . . pleasure from the idea that if someone has spurned [you], then that person will be spurned in return . . . in and of itself is incorrect. Because the spurning could have been for you to learn something you need to learn, and they have done you a favor. Therefore, they may get something "good" in return, and we use your word "good" only for your understanding.*

This wonderfully challenging idea exemplifies the nature of the communications you're about to read.

In the next chapter, "The Principle of Balance," the Eighty-Second Regime expresses the idea that natural disasters and societal ills are ways of nature to attempt to balance itself.

This idea is further explored in the subsequent three chapters, "Principles of Creation and Abundance," "Abundance Should Not Matter," and "More on Creation and Abundance." These sections go at the heart of capitalism and material gain in all its forms. The Eighty-Second Regime discusses the generative nature of thought, and how that thought energy extends throughout the universe. They are quick to point out, however, that unlike certain popular ideas today, such as those professed in other texts that discuss manifesting desires, prosperity and the creative power of thought are not necessarily linked. It is by wanting something, by creating in order to achieve a material or even spiritual gain, that the positive nature of thought is missed and misunderstood. In their own words, "When one can find . . . offer themselves out of the sincerest heart and not out of some ego-driven desire to be altruistic or to learn the 'secrets,' or to *master* the principles, then one will be achieving the highest good." Understanding that a lack of material abundance does not necessarily mean that one is performing poorly spiritually or even that one is in a bad situation can bring an immense amount of comfort and, more importantly, open up avenues for generosity regardless of one's situation. The Eighty-Second Regime exhorts us to "manifest more and then give it away! . . . Better yet, manifest love, compassion, and mercy, for that is your true nature."

The next chapter, "The Nature Connection," shows the links between the cycles of the season and the cycles of the spirit, and highlights the need for connections to the natural world. This is not simply the environment, but the ecological nature of the human condition and the life cycle's similarity to the cycles of nature.

"Dreamtime for Personal and Spiritual Growth" discusses what is communicated through dreams, how problems can be addressed through dreams, and the nature of meditation and lucid dreaming. The spirits highlight the importance of keeping a dream journal and manifesting positive and sincere intentions when going into dreams.

"The Common Threads Between the Various Religions" reintroduces the consequences of limited perspectives. The Eighty-Second Regime tells us that all religions have some core of the truth, but it is the shift of those truths from ways of being to becoming recorded and immutable laws that have turned them into a force for pain and suffering in the world. The

Eighty-Second Regime also reminds us that it is religionists' acquisitive tendencies, the desire for a payoff that turns religion into a negative force in the world. This is a potent statement for the world today.

The last chapter, "Meeting the Over Souls in the Forest," was one of the first communications channeled by the medium for this book. It discusses some of the nature of spirit communication and communication in general and is very personal to the medium and recorder. This chapter brings the text full circle in many ways. The book also features an epilogue and appendices that further detail some of the topics addressed by these entities.

In addition to its channeled messages, the book also contains details about the process of the communication sessions with the spirits and some background information into the medium and her assistants, both in the final chapter and throughout the text. The book gives an inside look at the medium's process of coming to know and communicate with these spirits, as well as the effect that these communications had on her life and practice. This is often not seen in similar books, and this information makes the text stand apart as more than just channeled messages, but a book *about* channeling as well.

Throughout this text, these entities remind us that anyone picking up this book has been specifically called to it for a purpose. Readers coming to it with openness, honesty, and a true commitment will find themselves faced with an exciting choice: the choice not to change into someone new, but to transform into exactly who they are.

Our mission, our contract, is not to serve you in ways to feed the ego, or to give you quick resolve, but to further you along the path of the unfoldment of the spirit made flesh . . . To bring you that much closer to the love that you are, that much closer to your own purpose here. When we say purpose, we do not mean your individual purpose, we mean the larger purpose. We are happy, for lack of a better word, to serve.

With love from the cosmos.

Author's Note

It has been more than eight years since I was first tasked with the compiling of the material for this book. Along the way, I have fought and resisted, and finally surrendered to it. Even now as I write the authors note I ask myself where this material came from. Did I just make it up? Have I been fooling myself, and am I fooling everyone else? For the most part, I do trust in my connection with Spirit and specifically my connection with those who call themselves the Eighty-Second Regime of Light Workers. However, I did not start this out with the same belief and conviction. The place that I have arrived at, within myself is that even if I am making it up, it is a good way to live. When I follow the advice of these writings, when I view the world through the glasses of this wisdom, I am more loving, compassionate, accepting, daring, and alive.

But I am getting ahead of myself. I suppose it would be important to start at the beginning of the journey that led me to this point. As a young child, I recall having "imaginary friends." Growing up in rural Vermont I often went into the woods and would "talk" to the people and little people I would encounter there. I don't recall ever feeling like it was unusual at the time.

As a teenager I experienced having the spirit of my grandfather visit me in the middle of the night before I had received word from my mother that he had died. There were others after that I had seen that were deceased; however, I had convinced myself that I had made them up. For some time, I believed that I had created these lies.

I recall getting "feelings" that something "bad" was going to happen. After a while, my mother would yell at me to "stop saying that." This was because whenever I would say it, inevitably, something viewed as "bad" would occur. On some level, I began to believe that I was making it happen by saying it, so I stopped saying it. I imagine that I also knew when "good" things were going to happen; however, the "bad" stayed with me longer.

Growing up in a poor household with an alcoholic father and an overwhelmed mother was challenging, to say the least. Over time, I began to numb myself, to numb my fears and feelings with alcohol and other substances. During this time, I also managed to numb my connection to Spirit and to "knowing things," though not always. I would still "feel" little things, such as what job to apply for, or what boy was going to be my next boyfriend by only seeing or hearing his name. Again, I was told that I had made these things happen because I had made a statement about them. Still, my connection was foggy at best due to my use.

However, upon my ceasing of the use of alcohol and drugs, it all came flooding back.

My connection began heightening when I began working with others in recovery. As a group facilitator in an in-patient rehabilitation facility, I would know things that clients had not told me. I would suddenly bring them up in the group as though I had already known them. I facilitated cathartic group sessions without having a clue what I was going to do in the group prior to walking through the door of the group room.

I specifically recall thinking that I was losing my vision because I would see shadows and colors around clients. The interesting thing was that the colors would change depending on the clients and their moods. I did not realize until a little later that I was seeing their auras.

As these connections and knowing began increasing at a rapid pace, I started looking into what was considered "New Age spirituality." Luckily, at that time, I had a mentor and friend who had gone through some of this herself and helped me realize I was not going crazy. One of the most frightening things to happen early on was that I was meditating, and I recall watching myself from above my own body (I later learned this was called astral projection). I did not, however, stay above my own body. I suddenly saw myself looking in a mirror as I stood beside a client that had recently been discharged from the program I was working in. This client had a gun to his head. I watched myself speak to him, and he handed me the gun. A short while later, I received a phone call from my officemate, who stated that this same client had just called the unit looking for me and had shared with her that he had been holding a gun to his head and that I had appeared to him. Needless to say, I was just a little freaked out by all of this, yet I knew, somewhere deep inside of me, that this was some important sign along the road of my life. I had no idea why, though.

There are many, too many, stories to tell about the unfoldment process that continued to occur at a pretty rapid pace; however, it would be important to note here that one of the things that occurred was while meditating, I became aware that, at times, when I would come out of meditation, I would have a sense that I had been "talking." I spoke with a friend about this, and we decided to conduct an experiment. I would go into meditation, and if I began speaking, she would then ask questions. We recorded that session (though I never saved the cassette), and to this day, I do not remember anything that was said; what I do remember is that there was a point where I was overwhelmed with love and peace and saw so many beautiful colors in my mind's eye. When I had shared my experience to my friend, she relayed that it had been then that she had asked the question, what is God?

Shortly thereafter, I dreamed that I met a man who said, "Follow me. I am your teacher now." The next day, without much thought, I called a holistic center that had psychic development classes and asked for an information packet. This packet included a picture of the same man that was in my dream. I enrolled that day. At the time, my decision to enroll was to be around others who were like me, or that was what I thought. Little did I know that it would completely change my life.

I began classes and, three years later, was teaching at the same institute and had enrolled in the seminary program to become a spiritualist minister, despite having been quite averse in the beginning of classes to what I considered "buying into a religion." I began regularly conducting séances and offering psychic readings to others.

In 2004, a gentleman was referred to me by a mutual friend for a consultation. What I knew about him prior to the consultation was that he was an engineer of sorts. I thought it interesting that someone who worked primarily with his left-brain would be seeking a psychic consultation. Upon his arrival and my introduction, I had a sense that this man was going to be an important part of my life. I felt inclined to invite him to the home circles that I was conducting even though I did not know him well. He began attending and became the official recorder of the circles. At some point, I also realized that he was the same man who had sat in a circle I had conducted at the center I was involved with.

I recalled that at the time, while seated in the dark, when I heard his voice, there was some strange draw to him. When the circle was over, the man that I had met did not match the voice that I had heard, so I discounted the feeling.

Three years later, it was this same man, Yves Nazon, who sat before me with a digital recorder as we entered our first official channeling session. At this time, I was still not aware that this information was being recorded for this book.

Over the course of a few months of holding these channeling sessions, Yves began to express that he felt the material would be great for a book. Being somewhat unsure still of this process, I discounted his suggestions. Eighteen months later, I could no longer deny what was supposed to be. We met and agreed that Spirit was pushing us to take down information to be compiled into the book that you are now reading.

As I release my hold on this material, I am also releasing my resistance to fully stand in the truth of who I am. A task that has over the years become less difficult to do than it is to not do. Occasionally, when left to my own thinking I do still wonder, is this real? Are these beings really speaking through me? Is it just an imagined thing? Regardless of these questions, one thing that is clear to me is that wherever this information comes from, this material is good, solid advice for living in peace, joy, and love. How do I know this? Because I have felt such things each and every time I followed the teachings.

MEET THE COSMIC FAMILY

The Eighty-Second Regime of Light Workers. To use "their" words, a sect or sub sect of a group consciousness (whom we refer to as 'The Collective') that has committed itself to assisting humanity in its spiritual evolution from the ethers through direct communication.

I am quite sure that one day I will find this "title" that they have dubbed themselves (for our own human need to associate "energy" with a label) to be a play on words. For this channel, although it is an awkward "name," I have managed to connect with it by imagining they represent the spiritual warriors, assisting us humans in fighting our divisive nature both within ourselves and toward others. It is important to note here that in 1995, when I first began "channeling" spontaneously through direct writing, the energies referenced themselves as being a part of the "Legion of Light." My feeling is that the Eighty-Second Regime "sect" is part of that legion.

Below you will see some separate identification of energies that are at times present with a persona of their own. However, we have been told that they are all part of this consciousness. When the consciousness comes through not as a seemingly distinct energy, there tends to be either no accent or much emotion, or you can hear dribs and drabs of each of these personas listed below commingled with many other energies. The voice and words sound most like my own when it is the collective consciousness that we are accessing.

Rebecca. A feminine energy that speaks with what seems to be a British accent. She informed us we could refer to her with the 'code name' Rebecca. She is quite charming and jovial and a favored persona of many. She also has a playful spirit about her and often jokes or teases the audience.

The Compassionate One (feminine energy). She has never identified herself by a name or a "code name." She has a very soft and fragile sounding voice. She shows quite a bit of love and empathy for humankind in her words.

The Grandfather. He speaks slowly, intentionally, and gently. He has a strong association with the Earth and often speaks to current earthly issues in both the physical environmental sense and the "climate" of people. He speaks often of the "old ways."

The Uncle. His speech is strong and has a hint of an accent on certain words based on his inflection. Quite expressive with his hands, his face becomes somewhat pinched when speaking. He is also the more directly challenging one of the group.

THE EVOLUTION OF THE SPIRIT OF MANKIND

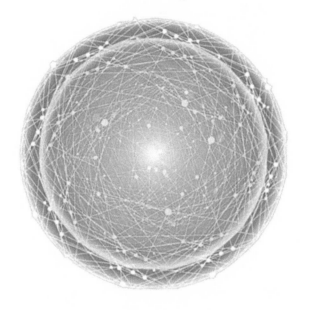

THE EIGHTY-SECOND REGIME OF LIGHT WORKERS

Introduction to the Eighty-Second Regime of Light Workers

August 22, 2007 – Yves was recording and directing questions. This session was seventy-five minutes in length. This was the first session that was recorded with the intention of being used for this book.

THE COLLECTIVE: Greetings. We would like to start out this evening really touching on what we refer to as pop spirituality culture—and understand that this would be our "disclaimer," so to speak, as we talk on this subject. There will be much more expansion on this at some point, but clearly we address this more for those who are ready to receive the expanded information of what is currently popular in your culture as a whole. There is a fad, in the masses currently that is good for a starting point of evolving; however, that which we are referencing has limitations, and it is getting people stuck in certain areas. Some will continue to stay stuck. But we would like to talk to you about the limitations of some of this current spirituality.

There are many wonderful things that are happening right now, especially on this

1

continent, because over the past fifty years, those in North America have been exposed to many different traditions. Whereas before, they might have known of them, it is now becoming more mainstream for people to begin to explore other practices. Meditation has become a popular thing that people are doing—yogic studies; different studies in Buddhism, Hinduism, and Sufism; and many other traditions, many of them Eastern thoughts, Eastern philosophies. However, what is happening often is that people are taking a piece of a philosophy, and they are getting only that one piece without having the broader perspective of the teachings. People are reaching for more because there is hunger. There is hunger right now because of what has been happening in the last one hundred years or more on this continent. People have been seeking for more. There has been a rapid shift, so to speak, in the culture: in intellectual pursuits, in material pursuits, and in all of those things. And as a response, people desire and see the need for spiritual connection. That pursuit is certainly elevating the consciousness of some of you here on Earth. However, there are many who are currently teaching some of these philosophies or practices who have honed in on only one angle, which is fine in and of itself, because perhaps that is what they are specializing in to teach. However, when it is only looked at in this small view . . . when you look at only one brick out of the whole building, you do not see the whole building. You cannot build the whole building with only that one brick, yes? Therefore, the purpose of us coming is to share with the world, additional information regarding these principles because it is important to help others "wake up further," so to speak.

You have, for instance, a practice in your popular culture that you call yoga. This yoga is a very good exercise. However, yoga means practice. The word yoga is equivalent to "practice." The purpose of yoga in its original context was to organize the various practices that one used as a whole for spiritual fulfillment and spiritual evolvement and for bringing the goodness or the light into their lives to share with others. So when you take one piece of a practice that was meant as a small part of a whole, you become very limited. There are many who are fooled into believing that as they are distorting their bodies, this is a spiritual practice. Perhaps compared to not distorting their bodies, it is. However, this is a physical exercise that is meant to fine-tune the physical body, to detoxify the body and keep it in good running order. All of the other yoga's or practices remain "behind the walls or veils," so to speak. There are those who practice them, there are those who know of them, but there are many who stay right here in this place of seeing how far they can stretch the human body because that often is easier than stretching the human mind, the human spirit, or the human heart, you see? It is important that people begin to practice something beyond their own self-improvement. That is, it is not only the physical body that will evolve—although it will, and we will talk about that at a later date—but also they need to evolve the spirit. And so, it is important that people begin to expand their awareness. One thing that is greatly, greatly lacking in your society here is reverence! *[Stated in a loud voice and quite passionately.]*

There is lack of reverence for each other, for the Earth, for the light, and even for what one would consider the dark. There are many churches, synagogues, mosques, and temples where people may don their finest clothing or their appropriate attire for these places where they go for their practice on a Sunday or a Saturday or any other day of the week. They may have their ideas about things or their rules about them from these religious places that they frequent, but so often, there is no true *reverence for the spirit of it.*

When we say "the spirit of it," we do not mean spirits such as those of us who are imparting information, and certainly we do not wish to be idolized as though we are God, for we are not. But even within the area of direct spirit communication, there is also oftentimes lack of reverence and lack of respect. People want information, people want messages, people want to hear from this one or that one, people want to know what to do now or how to have the best life, and there is lack of *recognition of the privilege* of what is being opened up in the universe for humanity to access.

YVES: Yes.

THE COLLECTIVE: This dissemination tonight is what you would refer to as the preface to the disseminations that are to occur, which will be grouped into certain categories, certain principles that we will discuss including how and where humanity is stuck within them; and when we say humanity, obviously, we are not speaking of all of humanity, but we are talking about the seeming trend right now, where most people are at and where they limit themselves. We will break down some of these universal principles and talk about their purpose, where each principle was derived from, the intention at the time, and how these same principles hold true or where they may interfere in evolution at this point in time. Obviously, there are so many different traditions and religions; we could not possibly touch on all of them without having to write a "twenty-five-volume set," if you will. *[Humor in tone.]* Besides, this vehicle probably will not be around long enough for that to be done, for that is very, very tedious and would take many decades of disseminating, and we would lose the readers' interest. For who is going to sit down and read twenty-five volumes except for your scholars?

5

So we will attempt to address different areas; we would like it to be clearly stated and emphasized that our purpose in going into these things is not to judge or to say, "This is right," or "This is wrong," but to say, "Here is an expanded view . . . here is a broader perspective . . . here is where the path can lead you to," if you should choose to seek further advancement, further evolution, and again not advancement of your personal self.

There are many wonderful teachings that have been disseminated over time, on your earthen plane. There are many wonderful things that come from some of these teachings, even within their limitations. Understand that even as we speak to you now, our ability to transmit the information is limited. Firstly, by the human vehicle, secondly, by your human capacity to understand, and thirdly, we may be at a certain place, but there is so much beyond us that is more refined, that has more information than what we have. There is information that even we do not have access to yet.

And so we are coming at it from the place where we are, in order to disseminate because even if we were to give you that information that is beyond us, even that which we can reach out and grab, it would not be possible for your current human brains to wrap (themselves) around it. Therefore we must meet the people where they are. We cannot ask you to jump into the ocean if you have not yet learned how to swim. So the imparting of the information will expand upon some of the more simplistic teachings of the principles. However, it will not be complete. It is very important to make clear that this is not at all a complete picture. This is not the be-all and end-all; this is one further piece or some further pieces of information that can be useful in getting you to the next place in your development. We will not give you the ancient secrets of all time or the "infallible word," as some people are looking for. It is out there—we will be honest, it is. However, none of you can reach it yet. There are some in distant places; many who do not walk amongst you have realized it, and because they have realized, it is very difficult for them to walk amongst you. Because the consumerism, the commercialism, and the level of vibration of the Earth right now or of those upon the Earth right now pull them back in to the illusion, and they begin to lose the realization.

So it is very difficult to bring the whole teachings. If the masses were to have the whole teachings, hysteria would result, you see? There would be massive chaos. Therefore, again we must meet the people where they are and bring them to the next place, then the next, and the next, and so on. This is what some of your religions do. This is what some of your teachings do.

Certainly, there are enough teachers out there who are bringing people farther in their awakening and understanding of spirituality, but there is not enough of it being spread out to the general population. You understand?

There are books that have been written where others have tapped into *universal wisdom*. They have used certain buzzwords to get people's attention. But even they themselves have begun to think that they have disseminated the be-all and end-all information. There is one who, at one time, expounded quite a bit but, even then, could not give all of the information. There are many ancient wise teachers who walked upon the Earth who told the truth; however, not everyone could hear the truth. Likewise, as we are sharing this information, some people will hear a small amount of it; some will hear much more of it, and we say unto you, "Let them who have eyes see, and those who have ears hear."

In all that we say, there is a deeper meaning and a deeper truth to what you are hearing because the human language barrier, you understand, makes it difficult, not only for you to absorb fully, but for us to fully impart.

There must be the necessary language available in this computer *[pointing to the area of the brain]* for us to use.

At times, we can and have come through with words or sayings in different languages; however, this personality, whose vehicle we are now using, carries those languages somewhere in the soul memory, and that is why they are accessible. Although when we are speaking, our energy is concentrated in the physical vehicle, there is a part of the personality of this person that remains, you see?

We do not necessarily take over completely. Therefore, we would not be able to speak in another language. Some of us have lived on your earthen plane at one time and spoken different languages; however, we cannot speak them unless they are accessible to us within this computer. The language that we speak now is not even a "language." *[Smiles.]* What we are is thought and vibration and form. We communicate through that, even as our energy gets concentrated into here, here, and here. *[Hands placed on top of head, forehead, and throat.]* We are still limited because when sending our thought forms to a human, it is picked up in words. In the ethers, when you are in between your lifetimes, you are not speaking to those of us who are around you. We are emanating! We are one thought. We are many pulses that make one pulse.

Some of this that we are saying now is introductory. We ask that as part of this project, you listen to these recordings after each session and you will devise questions to further us into the areas that we are discussing. The queries would be based on where the human race is currently in their development. Some of the obvious questions are how does this information get passed on, how is it accessed, and so forth.

One of the questions that Julie, had asked of us when we began pushing for this dissemination to be imparted beyond smaller circles was "Who am I to impart this?" "Who am I to do this?" Likewise, other people will be asking that very same thing. "Well, who is this? What are this person's qualifications?" What we say about that is, "She needs no qualifications, for it is not she that is speaking."

There will be, at times, information that is very simplistic in nature; at other times, there may be things that become more of what you refer to as scientific. At times, it may seem more obscure and difficult for understanding. And again, some will understand and some will not.

We will also say to you that we do not claim to come through as God! "God" is also a very limiting word. The Ultimate Supreme Power can—through watering down thoughts, watering down vibrations—it can and does trickle down to where we exist, and can then be passed into others, and finally to humans. However, make no mistake, the Ultimate Supreme Power, the Ultimate Supreme Force, cannot be put into words. In fact, it vibrates and pulsates at an immeasurable rate because the Ultimate Supreme Force is all. It is all things. Therefore, it cannot be condensed and made so small as to have a "direct line," so to speak. Yet you are all wired into it! You see? There is a wiring in, but it is so large and beyond comprehension that even our own comprehension here in the ethers is not complete. And yes, we may come before you and speak on spiritual matters just as others have done and will do from time to time—just as your great teachers that have walked upon the earthen plane have taught of spiritual matters. Some may even have a closer link to the truth than we. Yet they are not now, have never been, and would never be direct links to God. Your sacred scriptures are not, have never been, and will never be the ultimate word of God. Not one of those books, even the one that comes the closest to expounding upon a small glimpse of the truth of the many different realms of existence, can touch the truth. You cannot contain in a book or on a paper the magnitude, light, and love of Creation. *[Stated with much emphasis.]* It is an impossibility. So anyone who picks up this book looking for the answer or the path or the way might as well throw it back down now. For we do not wish this book to be used to *limit anything.*

There have been and continue to be, in your world, many horrific events, wars, fighting, breaking apart of nations, of friends, of families. All in the name of having the truth of the one God or the one idea of God, or being against someone's idea of God. And we will not be a part of that.

This is the "cocktail before dinner," if you will, something to whet the appetite. A brief overview, really, an introduction to the next phase of what humans are ready for now.

There are many pieces of truth, but they do not make the truth until all are woven together.

Just as it is with the work of artisans who weave, craft, or fashion things. The painter starts on a stark board and may start in one place of the painting to create. But the starting point is not the whole painting. The painter moves out from the starting point and oftentimes returns to the same starting point. Those who make your fancy quilts do so piece by piece by piece. The beauty and the usefulness of it only come after it is all woven together.

Likewise, the fabric of humanity needs all of these pieces, all of these different people, different cultures, and all of these different religions to move to the next place of being woven together to make it useful.

Many religions are more cultural practices than anything, based on where the practices originated and what the culture was at the time. Many religions and people who practice religion become fixated on teachings that were passed on during a time where certain things needed to be disseminated for that time period, for those current struggles. The struggles today are different, you see? If the human is to evolve, then the teachings must evolve. For the only way that some of those teachings are fully applicable is if you move humanity back to that time, place, and culture. Including the specific geographical places of existence from which they derived. There were certain practices that had to do with the area that people lived in, in order to survive, get along, or in order to move to the next place at the time, within the context of those specific circumstances of living.

People are now displaced to other geographical locations which differ from where they originated, and society has become what often is referred to as—although we would beg to differ—more civilized, more built up, and what is available and what is in those same places is different now than it was then.

If you were to attempt to take a horse-drawn carriage, down the same pathway that it once drove down, in your present geographical location, well, then it would bump into the buildings. So the teachings are the vehicles! They are the vehicles to evolution. There are some that, for lack of a better way of explaining it, are lesser vehicles and some that are greater vehicles. That is not a judgment; it just means that one has more horsepower than the other. Just as in your driving vehicles, you have economy vehicles, luxurious vehicles, racing vehicles, and many other types of vehicles. All may drive down the road; and some will get you there faster than others will, some will give you a wider and clearer view of things around you, some will keep you safer, and some will have the air or wind blowing in your hair and so on.

We will pause for a moment to see if you have a query based on what we have said thus far. Again, remembering of course that many of these little things we have touched on, we will go into at length within the confines of this book. In the meantime, we ask, do you feel the need for clarity within the context of this introduction?

YVES: No, everything is very clear. Just I'm anxious to get to more expanded parts of it. For example, you mentioned one of the religions is somewhat closer to the truth but not quite. I'd like to inquire about that . . .

THE COLLECTIVE: Let us correct that. It is not so much closer to the truth as much as it contains or is a bigger vehicle toward the truth, you see? We must state clearly that it is the teachings we speak of, not the religion. The teachings contain more places to explore and find the truth because you must understand, we are not here to say, "Follow this way, for this is the right way"—for there is no one *right* way.

It is important to reiterate that we will not, at any point in these teachings, claim to be saying to you that one is the truth.

There may be teachings that are a larger container for truth and others that are narrower. But again, just as we are limited, as we have mentioned, when we are using this body, similarly, all of your sacred scriptures were filtered through a human being (although there would be some in the world who believe differently). And so the filtering is filtered still—through the human mind and its own limitations, its own language barriers, its own comprehension, although, certainly, there are things that can occasionally come through the human body or voice or pen that go beyond what one thinks they had access to or what one thinks was available to them. Still, we spoke of this earlier: the program needs to be present in the computer (the human brain) in order to transmit. Therefore, any of these writings, *including this one*, has limitations.

What we hope to achieve, if nothing else, in these things that we will talk about is to begin to weave together some of these pieces of your religious practices to make them a whole practice that people may become more reverent. For when you become more reverent toward something, you also become more reverent toward others. All of you are a piece of God and if one can have reverence for God, *true reverence*, not reverence out of fear, not worship out of practice, but just reverence . . . reverence includes a love of, a desire for, a level of gratitude, and recognition of the beauty in all things, then they can see the possibility of all things. People show reverence by what they do, just as any gratitude they have is shown by what they do. These are not feelings for one to have. One may at times feel more peaceful, yes? Or they have moments of being reverent, but reverence is not a feeling. It is a state of being or a practice. Everything is a practice, you see? Everything! The sacred and the more mundane are all practices.

[Long pause.]

COMPASSIONATE ONE: The lack of reverence is that which has contributed to the death of the heart of humanity. With the death of the heart comes the death of the spirit. You pick and choose whom to honor, whom to respect. And yet we say to you that, truly, there is no one being who is worthy of more or less respect than the other. For each of you is a part of the greater whole, and each part is needed to help the greater whole. There are such atrocities, there is such suffering because you are all so afraid to look, really look, into each other's eyes. To see the divinity, or the spark of divinity that resides there. In some people, you may see that spark more present or prevalent. They may walk with it more apparent. While you should honor that, do not use it to make others less respectful.

Those who use their teachings or their religions to teach that this one thing should be more respected, or this one person, or this one religion, or that they perhaps should be more respected than others should, are doing a grave disservice to humanity. Many of them mean well, of course. However, let us be clear, there is not one of you who is not deserving of reverence.

In your world, there is such a loss of that. In this place, in this geographical location of the nation of America, there is almost nothing that is revered or sacred in the true meaning of sacredness. Food is bought and wasted;

trees and lands are destroyed with no thought because the only thought is, "How do I get what I want next?"

THE COLLECTIVE: This group of humanity that exists right now on this Earth, if it continues in its ways, will cave in upon itself, although not in your current lifetime. Yet we are here to tell you that this does not have to happen. There are those who say that it will happen because it must happen. This is not quite true. There is a sickness in the land; a sickness of hunger, and this hunger at times is filthy and vile. For even while there are some who are going without and have true physical hunger, many of you still are only hungering for more of what you already have—for a higher position, for more things to show the world that you have "succeeded." Yet the only thing you are successful at in this way of living is that you are becoming more and more irreverent. At times such as these, there may be the idea that in the conviction of which we speak, it may seem also a contradiction that we talk of all beings being the light and the hope for humanity. *But there is no hope if you do not look at the truth.*

Earlier, the physical being (Julie) stepped on a piece of glass, and the human body could have continued on its way with the piece of glass in it, correct? The glass could have then made its way farther into the skin. Well, there could have been infection, or the cut may not have become infected and the glass would have just sat in the cut for some time. We do not really know, but the point is there is an immediate recognition here in the physical body that says, "Oh, there is pain . . . there is something there I must remove." In the world of your spirit and the world of emotions, oftentimes you look to remove things just as quickly. In doing so, you say, "This is painful. I do not wish to see it, I do not wish to feel it, and therefore, I am going to rip it out," or "I am going to cover it up," or "I am going to get more such and such because, then, I will be okay, I will be happy. Once I get this, I will be happy. Once I find that, I will be happy. I will be happy once I find the right spiritual path, get a new car, get a new home, have children, when my children have grown . . ." You see, the search is constant; it is *constant*. There is nothing—not your houses or your cars, your fancy foods, your children or lack of children, your teachers, your books, or your religious texts —that will bring you happiness. Because even when you are experiencing happiness, it is human nature to want more of it. You are going to look farther; you are going to look deeper to amass more happiness, you see? Peacefulness is what brings joy. There is a difference between happiness and joy. But suffice it to say that part of the idea is that people are busy chasing happiness rather than experiencing the joy of the spirit made flesh. You understand? We have now nearly come to the end of our introduction. Most important of all, however, in this introduction, shall be the following:

We are most appreciative of the opportunity to serve in a different or larger way, and to any of you who pick up this book; we say to you that we have worked with you to get you this far. And we are available to continue to work with you that you may understand this on a grander scale, on a deeper level. We sit humbly before you as your servants of light. Our mission, our contract, is not to serve you in ways to feed the ego, or to give you quick resolve, but to further you along the path of the unfoldment of the spirit made flesh, to further you closer to the light that exists in all things. To bring you that much closer to the love that you are, that much closer to your own purpose here. When we say purpose, we do not mean your individual purpose, we mean the larger purpose. We are happy, for lack of a better word, to serve.

With love from the cosmos.

Where the Eighty-Second Regime Resides

August 28, 2007 – Yves was on recording device, directing inquiries. This session was seventy-nine minutes in length.

YVES: Greetings.

THE COLLECTIVE: This evening's session will not be a long, expanded session. There is one question, however, that you have posed for us to speak on this evening: *Who are we? And where are we speaking to you from?* We feel that these are important questions that will, perhaps, come up in the minds of many as they are sitting down to read this book. There is no exact way to impart to the reader a full and concrete understanding of who we are or where we are speaking to you from. However, we will do our best to explain it in terms as simple as possible so that the human mind can ingest it. Of course, there will be some human minds that will not be able to because, for some people, the answers are quite a stretch. Even us sitting here and speaking with you this evening is much too abstract for some, so we need to water it down to provide a more concrete understanding.

In the course of writing this book, at times, there will be a group consciousness that is speaking. At other times, there will seem to be more separate or distinct personalities that seem present as we send our thought forms. These thought forms are picked up by the vehicle (Julie as the medium) sent through the brain of the vehicle and then out of the vocal chords. So that is another reason it is somewhat difficult to clearly [smacking hands together for emphasis] state who we are. Therefore, our answers will be somewhat broad, and we shall go over it in a few different ways. Is this amenable to you?

YVES: Yes. Thank you.

THE COLLECTIVE: Where are we speaking to you from? Let us try and tackle that one first, shall we? For, again, that can be quite a stretch. Well, what we would really like to say is that as we speak to you now, currently through this vehicle, in truth, we are really right beside you. Not we as distinct personalities per se, next to Yves as a distinct personality. The film, which separates us from the physical, three-dimensional form is very thin. It is what you might refer to as a veil. Yet if we were to say that we speak to you from afar, that also could be true in terms of energy or frequency vibration. However, we are standing right beside you. Your world and ours are actually "interwoven,"

21

for lack of a better word. We move in and out of your world.

Second, who are we? There are some humans who believe that there are spirits who walk amongst the living. They are sometimes referred to as the undead, as the living dead, or as those who have not yet crossed all the way over. Certainly, there are and have been spirit entities that, upon leaving or transitioning from the physical body, hold on to the reality of the physical for a longer time. When we are walking among you, however, it is not because we are stuck among you, nor are we the living dead/undead. Understand? It is like when you look into your sky and see clouds of different hues and textures. At times, it may look as though you can just reach up and grab them. Or perhaps, like tonight, you have a beautiful full moon that moves so close that it may feel as though you can reach up and touch it, yes?

It is right there, nearly tangible, as if you could hold it; and yet, when you reach out to do just that, you cannot. Likewise, it is the same with us. We are very limited in our words. I am saying us, and yet even the word us, at times, gets you thinking in terms of physical bodies. Obviously, we are not.

We move among you, yet you cannot grab us, you cannot hold us. There are those of you who can see us and can feel us, who can even hold some of the energy of us in your hands, or direct the energy that we are made of when you are working on healing others. We are that same energy, you see? We are a pulse, we are a light, and we are a form, a different sort of substance or matter. Even in your scientific realms, humans have not come up with the correct word, because there is not a word that would capture who and what we are.

If we were to use descriptions of who we are in your terms, our energy is akin to a fine cotton ball that, at times, can also be sticky. It is like your spider webs. These textures of energy are part of what we are, but we are also a part of the very veil that is between our world and yours. We are able to move throughout both worlds. However, even those of you who are able to see us from time to time still do not always see us. To do so would shatter your reality of this illusion that you live in. It would do this in such a way that one would go insane—according to your societal norms.

In order to stay in the illusion, the human brain has to buy into certain ideas or certain realities, which are *not* real. It is all part of the trick, you see, part of the illusion. That is part of your being human. If you recall, following the time when you and this vehicle tapped into the over soul[1], when this vehicle released herself from the trance state, she was still hooked into the energy of us, and she had quite a reaction. Even then, there was a short (although, certainly, to the vehicle it did not seem short)

---

1 - See Chapter 15, Meeting the Over Souls in the Forest

period of time when the illusion was totally shattered. And this vehicle, this person that is Julie, was concerned that perhaps she would be stuck in that shattered awareness. She had some awareness about how difficult it would be to continue to walk through the world with that shattered awareness. Think of those objects that you refer to in your world as snow globes—in which is a little scenery, perhaps a snowman or a city street, and when you shake this ball, the snow comes down. It looks lovely as you are peering through the glass. However, when this globe is shattered, what happens? The snow falls away, the water rushes out—and no longer does that world exist, you see? Likewise, a human being could not possibly always see us, or the other realities, without being shattered themselves. The human psyche could not withstand that continuous vision of the other realities. The human psyche—in order to remain human—must believe in the illusion. Even though through practice you may come to a fuller understanding of us all being a part of a greater whole, you will never fully understand or conceive of our reality without a part of your illusion. This is because your physical eyes and your physical self that touches and feels still see's all of this, all of 'us' as separate from humans, you see? When the reality comes of observing and *totally* being one with everything, then you can no longer exist in this separate physical vehicle.

And so, for lack of a better way to describe it, the circuits of the brain would be "overloaded," if you will. When you overload circuitry, well, we all know what happens then, yes? In such a case, the mind and probably the physical body as well, would explode, more or less. As we say that, we chuckle, but we are really telling you the truth—the physical self could no longer contain itself, and so you absolutely could see it just break apart into shattered pieces.

So, again, as you can see in addressing this question, we are very limited in the words that we can use to do this. Each individual who reads this book will understand on a different level. This is because our plan is to give the information throughout this book in such a way that those who have not heard of any of this before will read it and understand what they need to understand, while a more complex part of the puzzle will also be available to those who are looking for a deeper understanding.

As a consciousness, although this is not the rule—we must say that you will find no rules here—anything you read here, in this book, or that we say to you, do not try to use to compare to something else we have said, for there are no rules. Everything moves and flows—nothing is static in our world. We again will speak in somewhat generalities here when we say to you that there are many who look for some identification. To clarify what we are, we must also address who or what we are not. Many humans get caught up in names of great teachers and those types of things, such as, is this an archangel? Is this the "Christ-ed One"? Is this a saint? And so on. What we will say to you about such questions, about "names," is that you will not have the experience of any *one* of those. However, we are a part of some of those consciousness's.

We are attempting to be as succinct as possible for your clearest understanding. The collective consciousness of this project—if it is to be referred to as anything or to put a label upon it—could best be labeled as the Eighty-Second Regime of Light Workers. We are a sect, or sub sect, of those of us who have contracted, when we are in the ethers, to assist humankind in their evolution by means of direct communication.

There are many sects and sub sects of those of us who have contracted. Many of us have stayed here in these realms of assistance, yet it is not always through the form of direct communication. And so, when we say the Eighty-Second Regime, it is difficult to describe with your words, but it is the best way to limit that which is limitless—at the risk of sounding like a bad riddle that we are asking you to solve. So trying to contain something that is unable to be contained is very difficult to do in attempting to keep it as broad as possible, yet make it as small as we can for you to understand. This is difficult to understand because, for many humans, it will be important to attach something to it—for instance, a name or label. In an effort to appease that need for the more material, then this label is what we would say that we, as a collective consciousness, would fit into this category of the Eighty-Second Regime of Light Workers. This does not mean that sometimes we will not reach out beyond our sect, or sub sect, and use other pieces of information or other thought forms to add to things in our contract to assist human evolution, or that we may not reach in to do that as well.

This is very difficult to put into words. If you were to envision, let us use the example of the clouds in the atmosphere of your Earth; you would see us as a cloud that is blown by the wind. Sometimes we move this way or that; sometimes we move up or down, or in or out— that is how this collective consciousness works. Sometimes the clouds are spread out thin across the entire sky (well, at least as far as the eyes can see), and at other times you may see small wisps of these clouds, which paint the landscape of the sky or of the heavens. Likewise, we are the same. At times, we may come in a more concentrated form, and at other times, we may come as the small wisps.

YVES: Yes.

THE COLLECTIVE: And so, if that is relatively clear, then we would like to talk a little bit about how this works, what we are doing right now. Since we do not often use your language, we do understand that we will never be able to make it completely or scientifically clear. However, if you feel that there is a need for more explanation or—

YVES: My understanding of it right now is this image that is used in the book where all the circular things are attached—and there's a myriad of them that are connected—your energy moves through these "channels" or tunnels. And there are hubs of intelligence with offshoots and so on . . . and I can understand the connection of all these energies as being somewhat representative of that. Would that interpretation be a somewhat limited understanding or limited analogy of where you are at as far as the different hubs and different energies' relationships are concerned?

THE COLLECTIVE: Yes, but we certainly would not be at the center of that collection of tunnels and tubes. The hub is at the center of that. We are connected to the hub. We had you create a diagram that shows the interconnectedness and the multilayered, multileveled things that, again, aren't really linear and don't go exactly horizontal, vertical, or any of that but are just one offshoot from another offshoot. As you look at the cones or spheres, each one is a conductor of sorts. We are connected to the hub or the centermost part of it. Yet our energy can shoot through one cone into another, into

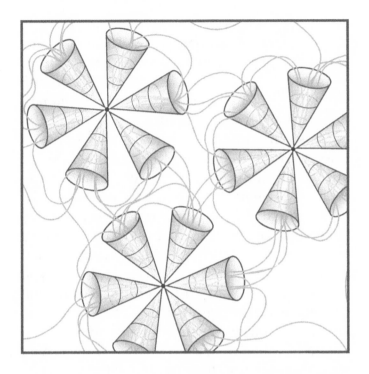

another, into another, and into another, you see? That exactly is what we are doing right now in using this physical vehicle to disseminate the information. We are going through these conductors then through this conductor [*tapping on the body*]. We are then using these vocal chords and this computer system [*touching Julie's head or area around the brain*].

There are many who ask questions when one is channeling information, about the personality that comes in, or if the person—the channel— becomes "possessed." We do not like that term. So we ask that you refrain from using that term. First and foremost, this is offensive to us and makes us seem as though we are something to be frightened of, or that we are hostile in some way—"to possess, to take over." *You humans* are those that try to possess. We spirits do not. Humans try to possess many things—money, driving vehicles, and homes. You even try to possess other humans. Humans try to possess love. They try to hold on to all of these things, but we do not—nor would we ever *attempt* to possess. Because quite frankly, if we were to be fooled into that practice of possessing anything, then we would have to fall back down to where you are. Most of us have already decided that we are done with that part of our evolution, you see, for good reason. Although those of us that do come in do, from time to time, enjoy the more tangible and tactile aspect of being in the physical body. When we use the physical vehicle, you may also see, from time to time, what you refer to as transfigurations of the human being or a change in posture. It is not because our separate distinct personality has come and sat inside of the body. Rather, those of us who are working with you still hold a certain consciousness, some of which we carry from our last lifetime or perhaps a very significant lifetime—and even though we are part of the collective consciousness, we still have our own personality, a sort of Spirit personality. So we do not come in separately, sit, and take over the body. When our different personalities separate and focus their energy more, our individual concentration sends stronger thought forms into this vehicle. The inflection of speech, the movements of the body, and the softness or the roughness may change; yet it is still this vehicle that is moving its own body, you see? It is merely *influenced* in various ways. This vehicle is already a very animated vehicle, even when its *physical body is hosting its own personality*. Correct? And so, this influence of one personality over another is part of what occurs. When our thought takes form and enters into the computer, then her mannerisms may be influenced, you see? When we come in as a collective, then you will see and hear, within the same sentence or within the same paragraph, shifts and changes. The body movements may become more fluid, or may become choppier, if you will. Again, there is a collective consciousness that consists of all of the pieces of our individual consciousness, you understand?

YVES: Yes. And so . . .

THE COLLECTIVE: As we have been addressing, how this occurs is that in the illustration that you spoke of, you have the hub of it, correct? Energies are shot through these cones; there are some of you who refer to them as portals, doorways, or wormholes. This information, or personalities, or pieces of our personalities, of the consciousness comes together, much like the many droplets of water that would be in a

snowflake. So each droplet of water that is frozen creates this snowflake; and each snowflake, is unique and different. There is not one snowflake that matches another one. And we are likewise, even though you will hear many similarities in intonation, in inflection, and much of what we say is maybe the same; this is because we are a consciousness. The truth of the matter is—hold on to your seats—that each time we come is a little different; it is like the snowflake. Even *that* is different because there are different amounts of the consciousness present at different times. That is, there are different concentrations of each of the thought forms that move into the mind self.

So we are not individuals that sit in the body and speak. We are sometimes singular, sometimes multiple, and sometimes a mass consciousness that injects thought form into the part of the brain that can receive it, then filters through the part of the brain that thinks and comes down to the voice box, which then speaks our words. Which is why this vehicle that is Julie, or the medium (that which is in between), often references images or pictures that she sees ahead of time before we get to the information. We, or this consciousness, are in the right brain filtering around to the left brain; so as it's becoming something tangible for the human to speak, there is still more information being imparted into the right brain. That is why she is able to "see ahead," if you will. No pun intended with this "seeing a head." That means that the information is constantly being inputted, inputted, and inputted. You understand? And so, as it is going in, it is coming down, and then it is coming out.

[Long pause]

YVES: The shift in the voice, the clearing, is that because too much information is coming through, or there is an adjustment of the frequency that is occurring?

REBECCA: Yes, what occurs in the voice at times is that there is so much energy that has been concentrated, and as it begins to come through the voice, it clears because the vocal chords are not meant for that much strain. Just as when you are at a concert or something and you begin screaming and you start to lose the voice, yes? So when there is that much force coming through with something, then there is a strain on the vocal chords at times. However, in this way, it passes very quickly; it is not something that stays with you. Whereas if you are at a concert, or what you call a football game or something, then it may stay with you for several days, yes? But it does not really happen in that way in these cases because the other thing that happens is that when the energies are changing and as the information, or thought form, is coming down, it also affects the throat chakra at times, which needs to be opened more for the energetic alignment. What is really quite amazing about all of this with the physical body is that because we come in only temporarily, whatever difficulty the physical body may go through, it recovers from it at a very fast rate, you see?

Also, when this vehicle becomes very tired from it, the voice begins to break or crack because another thing is occurring—perhaps there are many other toxins that begin to come up, and there is coughing, you see? There is a cleansing when these types of frequencies and energies are in the physical body, just as when you are doing your healing, yes? This energy, our energy, when coming in, begins to cleanse, and because this one (vehicle) tends to have a tendency to take in some toxic chemicals, some of that begins coming up. Even the coughing is somewhat of that cleansing or detoxifying. So again, you ask what seems to be a very simple question, and we apologize, but there really is not any one simple answer, you see? For instance, as she was clearing her throat on this occasion, it was because my energy was becoming more concentrated into this vehicle, so there was an energy fluctuation for her to adjust to. There is a more concentrated collective here this evening, so even my hold on her is not as strong as it had been before, you see? For we are what would you say—when you buy the bottle of juice and you also have the juice— concentrate. You see, you cannot just drink that concentrate; it is a little thicker. So because these thought forms, this energy, are a little more concentrated tonight, then it must be diluted, yes? Even my coming through, or any others who come through or the collective conscious- ness that comes through, is still going to have within it—you will *hear* "within it" as you are listening—several different tones perhaps that are reminiscent of several different beings that have spoken at different times.

The environment, as well as the energy frequency in your natural world, also affects the level or the concentration of that which comes through. For a simpler explanation, without getting too "scientific," water is a psychic conductor. Therefore, the energy frequency can become more concentrated. You may perhaps notice changes in the tides and the oceans as the lunar cycle changes, for example, during the full moon.

[Long pause and energy shift.]

THE COLLECTIVE: The veil between this world that we inhabit and this world that you inhabit is affected by the moon's cycles, by astrological influences. If everything is connected, then all of these things do influence each other. And although we are not here to write a book on astrological influences (there are those who have written very good books on that, we might add, very accurate ones), we do not wish to go too far or too deep into that currently. Suffice it to say that this also influences the amount of energy that is around. You understand? Also, as you are coming toward a change in season, there is also a thinning of the veil, of course. Much of that is because of practices that have occurred throughout the ages—you are coming upon, or close to, a time when the seasonal changes that have been honored, celebrated, and rituals have been performed as the Earth prepares to go into its dormant season, as things begin to seemingly die off. Much energy is raised with those rituals. It also is a time in many older traditions where the *seeming* dead or the ancestors are honored. And so, as the focus is concentrated on them, that focus of energy or attention gives them more permission to communicate, you see? That is why the veil thins during that time as well. You are coming upon a time when the veil becomes thinner, and so there are others who are milling about, who come and go, and are watching the process. Even if they are not disseminating, the energies are still around.

For instance, while you are sitting in this dwelling place there are other energies in other parts of this dwelling place that are humans, as well as humans that live in other parts of the apartment building as well. So we too are in a place where things are coming and going.

Another thing that you will begin to notice as we go further into the book is that although there will be times when our energy becomes more refined or more distinct, the flow of it will become more automatic because as we are working with the physical vehicle, it would be very difficult to impart this much information and to plug and unplug all of the time. You understand? So the more that we do this, the more wired we are becoming together. Therefore, the more this information will become readily available, accessible, and ready to be imparted.

[Long pause.]

Those of us that speak *only* come with an invitation; we only come with permission. We also only come with a willingness on the part of the individual to take what comes with it. When there is an honest sincerity, then there are many who will come, and yes, there are some who will come and infuse their energy who may not have access to the same amount of information because as we, again, are at the different cones, the different layers, and the different levels, from time to time, there will be some who, not even necessarily menacingly, will attempt to give information that is *not* helpful or is not for the higher good. *Not* because they are attempting to *mislead* or pull one astray but because they do not have access to the higher information and because they are still perhaps on a—for lack of a better word, and we almost hesitate to say—lower plane of existence, a less refined energy field of existence.

YVES: Would you say as you go out (using the analogy of the cone) that the farther out you are, the less information—not less information, less access you have to the information—and as you get in closer and closer, you have access

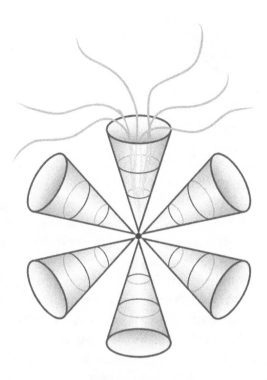

to more? Would that be somewhat of a correct analogy?

THE COLLECTIVE: If it is watered down, yes . . . but not exactly because, again, nothing is that static. These energies do not stay put, you see? You have the diagram; you have the sculpture; that sculpture is staying put. And each cone is not necessarily energy—it is the vehicle for the energy, you see? So as the energy becomes more refined, it can spread out farther and access further, although it still can reel itself back in again. You see?

When you have a liquid that is a very thick liquid, you pour that out, and then you pour out the same amount of a very thin liquid, such as water, they spread out differently. It reaches other fields, other points, and other places. As it touches each place, it not only touches the object, the object also touches it. And now it changes its constituency. You understand? Therefore, that is one of the reasons why, even though we are referencing this vehicle becoming more plugged in and not unplugging, it is also important to keep the physical vehicle clear and vibrating at a higher frequency, you see?

However, even well-meaning individuals who do this work or who, whether it's using their voice and energy systems or whether it is imparting information by viewing things, at times may be working with guides or those who are not able to access as much information and maybe accessing, in fact, things that are more material. In other words, if they are of a denser material, then they are still closer to the material world. Therefore, their answers or their direction may be more about the material world and the material things—and again, please understand, we are not saying by any means that we are way beyond all of that. Remember, it's just that we are contracted for a certain purpose. We are at a certain frequency for a certain purpose, and that is certainly, certainly to move the human race beyond the material—beyond that place of being separate and to move you to the next step of your spiritual evolution—so that those energies, that refinement that is beyond us, can then meet you there, you see?

Yet there are those who, again unwittingly, keep you attached to the material world. Those are the ones that you will find who often give you the information on how to best succeed in a materialistic way. They are focused on what is seen and viewed based on societal views, cultural views, religious views, and very often, limited views. They are attempting to be helpful—they are! And they are helpful, for some. Perhaps for those who are not prepared, to go farther. Some are at one place in their evolution and need such teachings or information to help them get to the next level of understanding. For even those that work from the materialistic planes confirms to others that life continues, you see? So we do not say this to condemn them, to be naysayers, or to say not to ever listen. What we are here to do is to teach from the next place of that, you see? Therefore, it is important for those who are looking to go to the next place beyond material success, earthly and worldly delights, that we are here. That does not mean that one cannot enjoy some of the earthly delights, for that is partly why you have come. Otherwise, you would be here with us taking up space in this vehicle's computer system here. Do we make ourselves clear?

In regard to what we were just referencing (and we will say to you over and over again that this information is available to all people), there are those of you humans who have also contracted to come and be the deliverers. While everyone can theoretically access this information, there are some of you who, by design, are better able to notice the subtle differences in energy fluctuations in order to discern the energies coming through. And because of a prior contract already, many of us in these various sects and sub sects have been working with these vehicles for many years *before* they started imparting this information. We do this in order to fine-tune the energy vibrations and to fine-tune their ability to pick up the energy vibrations in order to receive those of us who are here for this purpose.

We do not wish to leave anyone at the end of this chapter with ill feeling in their stomachs, but we wish to advise that we say to you, this information is available to all.

REBECCA: It is important that you do not attempt on your own to open your own physical vehicle up too much by yourself at once. For again *[long pause]*, there are those whose vehicles and whose ego selves are not prepared for this yet. And to introduce something like this could have many damaging effects, less likely to the physical vehicle than to the psyche, or even the ego, if not properly used. And while certainly there are those of us here now, who are with you now, who are what you would call savvy enough to not be a part of that or allow that to happen, that does not mean that there are other energies that will not, you see? And so, this type of thing can leave one with the feeling of power, and that is not bad; but if one is misled a little bit, if they are walking with energies that are less than refined, then that could create much bigger difficulties than what they would want.

We are preparing to take our leave. We feel that we have at least touched on and answered the questions of who we are and where we come from, unless you feel as though there is something further that needs to be—

YVES: No, I think you have explained as best as you could for us to understand. Thank you.

THE COLLECTIVE: So we bid you a fond evening and await our next sitting together; in the meantime, we shall continue to impart and direct this vehicle and to continue to align ourselves with you as well. We bid you adieu.

The Principle of Karma

April 13, 2010 – Yves was recording and asking questions. This section was broken into two separate channeling sessions. The first session lasted one hour and fifty-six minutes with no breaks.

THE COLLECTIVE: Greetings. You have prepared a query?

YVES: Yes, it has to do with humans who have committed atrocious acts in their lifetimes—a good example is Hitler. When he leaves this earthen plane, does he maintain the same persona, or does his form return to the love that is the universal love? Also in that respect, before he incarnated as Hitler, was there something that precipitated this? Did he decide to come and be such a "monster," so to speak?

THE COLLECTIVE: This is a good question, and we shall attempt to, as always, answer it as concisely as possible.

Let us begin by saying that when one incarnates on your earthen plane, it is important to remember that one chooses a life plan. Generally, "the identity of who they will be" is chosen after they have chosen what the next thing is that they must learn or must give to others.

There may be contracts they have that are outstanding and need to balance out, and we want to clearly stress *balance out*.

Oftentimes people get caught in the idea of "if something bad is done, something bad comes back," and at times they keep it linear—just in this lifetime—others stretch it out over many lifetimes. Some believe that it is linear in that you come back as something "good" if you did "good" in your life, and if you do something bad, you come back as something "bad."

The first thing that is the most important thing to say—as we have said before—is that there are no hard-and-fast "rules" about this. There is an order, yes. There is a general order to things, but there are no rules about "if one acts this way then . . ." because what you need to understand is that when one is acting a certain way or when someone comes in and does certain things that are deemed atrocious (and certainly from the point of view of human suffering, they are), one may in fact come in and *sacrifice* being someone who is looked up to in order to create an atmosphere that challenges other people to stand up and be better than who they are or who they would be.

So we will stay along the lines of this Adolf Hitler that you speak of, just for clarity's sake. One who comes in and riles people together in the name of hatred, in the name of that which is the very opposite of what we are here to teach, can create a large effect from that hatred. He gathered others around him that would also practice hatred, yes? What happened in the course of that is that others who may not have otherwise tapped into their compassion, who may not otherwise have reached out to help someone, who may have had even some of their own judgments about someone who is different than they are—what happens in scenarios such as this is that others can raise their vibration by "coming to the rescue," if you will, by standing up and by saying, "This is not okay. This is not how we should treat each other." Now, let us also clearly state that this does not mean this is always the case or always the plan because it is not.

Some people may come into this lifetime with a plan, and they may go "off course," so to speak.

REBECCA: There are times when one comes in and they wish to teach love—now we are not saying this is the case for Hitler. We are just going to use that to keep it as simple as possible because, again, this could get very complex.

Let us say, for example, that he was to come in to teach love, and yet somewhere along the way, he messes it up. Then it is possible that what happened is that although he did not teach love but instead hatred and intolerance, by being the exact opposite, love is still brought forth, through others. In other words, by being hateful, it allowed others to be more loving. So in some way, although it may seem warped, part of that intention has been achieved.

Each of you comes here with a "task list," if you will, a design. If your list is this long *[demonstrates with hands held apart widely]*, most people will accomplish about 5 percent or 10 percent of their list in a successful incarnation. That is your average human being. That is not to say they have not cleared up some of the balancing with other beings, but in terms of the bigger plan, this is often the case. Let us take it back a notch; you see, when you are not in your physical body and your spirit self or essence is in the etheric realms drifting about, you suddenly have all of this excitement about what you are going to do when you come back because you *remember* then. You remember better when you are in the ethers because when you are not bogged down with the distractions of things (as you are when in physical form), it is easier to see what needs to happen. Going back, let us clearly state that when we say you accomplish perhaps 5 to 10 percent of what your intention is, you need to also understand that if you are one piece of the many parts of you, it's not essential that you accomplish 100 percent. It is like you when you hand the ball off to your linebacker or what have you when you are playing your football.

Therefore, you see, this can be a very involved process to answer. That is why we are slowing down to be sure that everything is answered in a way that is understood by those who are perusing this text. There is no set amount really that you have to accomplish because you can keep doing it over and over and over again.

So let us say that this Hitler of yours came in with the intention to create chaos, to create havoc, to create destruction. There are those who come in to do exactly that! Mind you, it is not always that they come in to do "good," and they veered off the path. If they came in with the intention of creating that havoc and destruction in order to assist others to learn compassion or practice love, when it is *done* that way, there is no "karmic penance." There is no righting of the wrong because it was not wrong—it was a right! As you will see, you came in asking about the principle of karma, yes? As we have mentioned before, all of the principles lead to each other. They are all part of the cross sections of the roadways, the highways, and the byways of it. So when we are talking about one principle, we will also talk about others.

Now, understand you are not always grade A students that come to accomplish "good things." Sometimes you come in merely for fun and to experience your world in physical form. This sort of thing can go on forever, as there is no rush in terms of incarnating. No matter what else ceases to exist, the primal pulse will not.

So when this one, this Hitler, goes back to the place where this part of his spirit returns to in between incarnations, he may choose to come back and do something completely different. It will not necessarily be that he has to go through atrocities himself or be subjected to them to experience things that he did to others. He may choose that, but it is not necessary. He has come here to play a part, and he is one part of the greater whole. Are you ready for this? If all of you are smaller parts of the greater whole, then all of you are not only good but you are all also Hitler. All of you! So when we say that each of you is a mirror or a part of each other, this is not just some symbolic statement. In truth, in the most ultimate truth, it is what you are. In other words, you call it unto yourself.

The divine calls unto itself these challenges, these lessons, and this work to speed things up—to get a greater response. In your world, there are many who have served in the way (that Hitler did). Currently, because of the nature of things, because of all of the things that have been happening, the very man who leads your country right now (referencing President Obama) would not have ever set foot in that door had not all of these other awful things been occurring. It would not have happened for a very long time. People would not have allowed someone of his ethnic background to be president. However, because people became so tired, so fed up and worn out from the way the country was going, two things happened. There were those that became riled up by this man, yes? And there were others who thought, *Well, things could not get worse.* They were so tired that they just gave in to anything different. They gave in to any possibility of something different.

And so it is during times such as this, that you see that change can occur for the better. Of course, if you look through history, there are always times of chaos.

THE COLLECTIVE: This is not new. In the history of your world, these things happen all the time. People are often just not paying attention.

In various sections of the world, there are times when problems are amped up for the purpose of creating a response; for the purpose of pushing forward the mass evolution of consciousness. Otherwise, you would just be the fish in the sea floating around. Hence, without destruction, there is no creation. Conflict and chaos are a necessary part of your evolution.

Conflict and chaos are also necessary for the continuity of incarnation. For if everything became a smooth surface, if all beings evolved at the same time at the same moment, then the divine play would cease to exist. Because all would return to that one same vibration. It is all of these different vibrations that create all of the different life forms and lifestyles and life experiences. We will pause here to allow you to absorb what we have said and to redirect or ask for qualifications on those things that we have shared thus far.

YVES: So to put it simply, evil is a necessary evil . . . and the idea that most humans have that, eventually, everything will be okay, everybody will be the same, will not occur because if that would occur, then there will be no "existence," as you said, for this particular world because everyone will be in the same place . . .

THE COLLECTIVE: We will stop you there to answer; if that is amenable to you . . . the answer is your favorite answer, yes and no . . . *[Teasing Yves.]*
That is ultimately true that if everyone were to resonate at the same frequency, have this shift of consciousness to the same level as the divine consciousness, then yes. That is not to say, however, that you could not have periods of peace reigning. If you recall, there are many of you incarnating on different planes and different dimensions in different atmospheres and so on. So all of the "souls," so to speak, or spirits or consciousness pieces are not all incarnating in the same place at the same time. In other words, there are places where, even now, there is what you refer to as "ideal" conditions. But that is elsewhere, you see? That is *there*, *not here*, on your current earthen plane. Of course, there may be some other interference there that makes it not

quite as ideal again. However, there are other places, you see, where there is no ideal world.

Therefore, the chances of that instant simultaneous shift of consciousness occurring . . . well, we could not even guess. However, this is not to deter any of you from working toward that ideal world.

What we are saying is that we do not wish to deter people. We do not want to have them saying, "Well, if we were to do that, then we would no longer exist, so why bother doing it?" That is not the point of what we are saying.

What we are saying is; *of course*, respond to this call because of the havoc, because of the chaos and all of that—because *that* is the call to remember. The call is to remember how you are meant to work toward building that ideal world. Do not worry if enough of the rest of you will not be doing it correctly in the other places, you see?

And there is a plan—we wish to rephrase that—it could be a part of a plan . . . how do we say this . . . if one was to look at the different worlds and the beings there and the happenings there, then one could say that perhaps each little world is its own "pilot project," more or less.

Within that pilot project, there may be some proposed ideas on what could take place. So one of the ideas about what could take place with this project—on this earthen plane that you are seated upon—is that there should be a quickened raising of the frequencies of the beings here. That would create an evolution of a kind that perhaps some of you have read about in the history of ancient places that many people say never existed. Wherein even your physical bodies, although you may be human or in somewhat human form, the resonance of them will be such that you become more translucent—which is a very high frequency—but not quite completely "spirit." The idea being that you could use your energies here on the earthen plane (this has been done elsewhere before), and so you are experiencing yourselves still with flesh that is not quite flesh.

We understand that this can be quite confusing, but let us take, for example, the vehicle that sits before you now as Julie. If you could imagine that you were sitting across from her and looking at her, you would see the outline of her; however, it would be more energy than flesh, then you would be able at times to see through her. That is what we are talking about when we talk about the evolution. That is one of the plans.

There are others, and quite frankly, we would not be able to disclose much of that. Partly because we simply would not be allowed to; in addition, we do not necessarily have access to all of that information. We have some of the information about the many places and projects, but ultimately, all of that comes from a much higher source.

That small part was in response to the question that you had asked for clarification, so we wish to open for questioning again—because we believe, there were other parts to your question, yes?

YVES: Yes, thank you. Once a person dies and is in the ancestral realms, he or she then has the knowledge of what happened, and therefore, they get to come back and finish that long list of tasks. Yet you also mentioned that there are actually many selves in other places accomplishing a certain percentage of those tasks. My question is, is it possible that all the selves could complete the tasks within one incarnation, or does each individual have their own tasks to fill and they have to fulfill the whole thing? Do the other selves help?

THE COLLECTIVE: The tasks that we are referencing are not the tasks of subsequent incarnational cycles. For instance, when you came in as Yves, you had a list of tasks, of which X percent will be completed. Now, your other "selves" may have some of those same tasks. Let us go back to the over soul. The over soul has the larger task list, so when making your task list, you scan through it and decide what you want to experience and what you want to be different. How you are going to choose to get balance in one area or another. The part that is "Yves" is not necessarily aware of the other "you's" that are elsewhere. Some of you may at times have an awareness of that, but seldom— well actually, we should say seldom is there awareness that there is awareness.

So this list, this task list of "accomplish-ments" you wish to achieve, one or more of these can sometimes become unnecessary, so those get tossed to the side. We understand it can become quite confusing for the human brain to comprehend, so again, we are trying to keep this as clear and concise as possible, for if it is not understood, then of what use is it?

Let us go back to the 5 to 8 to 10 percent because we do not wish for the humans picking up the book to say, "If I am not going to accom-plish it, then why bother trying?" Most of you do not know what is on your list anyway! When we say that, it is because of the density that you forget when you are here. It is also because of the ways of your society.

Most of the people that are brought to these teachings, whether it is through something they have read or interactions with us through this vehicle, most are working on more than that percentage. Not because it is us, but because they are ready to hear the next pieces of infor-mation. There are other pieces being taught in other places and in other ways as well. It is not only our domain.

We do not wish to deter people, but what we are trying to get across is that it is difficult to remember these tasks when you are here on the earthen plane. Which is one of the reasons why it is important for people to continue to open themselves up. Continue to meditate and to let go of those things that keep you grounded in the false world, in the false reality that keeps your blinders on. This is in order to serve your spirit. To serve your higher self. The unfortunate fact is that most humans have not been doing that or have not even been aware that service to the higher self is the highest service.

The ways and means in which your world is conducted right now support the ways and means in which some of you humans continue to deceive yourselves. You must begin to let go of that deception, but again, it takes a radical shift for it to occur.

If you are standing and looking over your earthen plane and you are viewing it from where we are, looking down at the world, you would see pockets of chaos and destruction, of hatred, of materialism, and all of these things. You would see this sort of idea about whom you think you are—what makes you good, what does not make you good, and so on. We look at that, and in addition, we see the pockets springing up where people are reaching out to others, and people are learning more about the sameness of each other, the pockets where people are taking loving actions, they are taking risks and are casting off the chains and locks of this world that you live in.

When you are looking at your world in its totality, you would see that something has to occur. You would see that one of those things has to increase its momentum. In other words, if all of this chaos is happening to create a louder and a wider call, then if the response isn't big enough, what do you think would need to happen then? Then the call needs to get even louder, and how does that happen? Through more chaos, more destruction . . . so, you see, to get to the balance, there has to be an imbalance.

We will take more questions.

YVES: Regarding the task list again one does not get to complete within their own lifetime when they reincarnate, do they have a new list, or do they come back to finish out the previous list?

THE COLLECTIVE: This depends upon the soul's intent. You see, the generic answer to that would be they are still working on the list. However, there is always something added; the list is never ending, you see? Although again, there is no hard-and-fast rule. That is what needs to be understood because one could come in, and let us say, for example, that they want to practice compassion. They may very well come in and accomplish that; however, it does not mean it is checked off their list and then on to the next. There are those who come in time and time again to do the same certain things again and again. If you are a part of the bigger whole, then it is not just that one being or person who is continually doing it—again, remember, you are part of the "show."

There are those you refer to in your world as bodhisattvas that continue to make a commitment to return to the Earth to help others, and that is what they do over and over and over again. Therefore, they do not necessarily do it in one lifetime.

Some people take the karmic laws and base their belief in it regarding one individual lifetime. In other words, they believe if one is good in this lifetime, then they will be bad in the next, or they may think they will rise amongst the hierarchy of good beings. There isn't a place really where one could simply move upward and then not ever return from that place; there are cases of that, of course, but it is not the rule. Some of the cases of that are that as the energy is so much higher—and pardon our use of that word—it would need to take or form a lesser consciousness in order to come back and dense that consciousness down and down . . . but it is never really the case that they cannot.

Incarnation itself is a choice; you do not have to incarnate on this earthen plane either. There are other planes, however, for some of them; you have to be at a certain resonance to cross the boundaries and borders. You could also go to another dimension; you can go to another Earth. There are many options; additionally, you could not incarnate into physical form. In this case, remember, you are still a spirit, and there are still things you are doing in the etheric realms. You referenced the ancestors, yes? Well, we will not even limit it to ancestors. The Eighty-Second Regime and the many others who are out here in the ethers are still working in not only assisting others but also in assisting our own evolution. You do not need to incarnate to continue to evolve; this is but one option.

YVES: On the earthen plane, all life is related . . . meaning, from an ant to a cow to an eagle and a tree. What is the process in incarnating in deciding whether you come as an ant or a tree or anything in between?

THE COLLECTIVE: When you say process, are you asking how it is determined what one incarnates as and if there laws or rules regarding that? Well, you know how we feel about laws and rules—but again, there is an order to this, just as there is an order to energy. When you are here in the physical human body, you are resonating at a certain frequency. When you are no longer in the physical body, your frequency raises automatically.

Everything, yes, is a form of life, and everything that is on the Earth is a part of the energy of the Earth. We spoke earlier in this session, when you were referring to this Adolf Hitler; we were speaking of growth and all of that and of choices. We spoke of people coming in to create chaos, and had those things not occurred then, you would simply be like a sea of fishes now, yes? That is a different energy resonance. To incarnate as a human being, there is a certain not only vibration but—and this is where it could become complicated—there is a particular texture to the spirit. There are those who believe that if you do bad things (we will use that word because that is your word) on this Earth as a human, you will come back as an ant or you will come back as a swine or one of these things. This does not occur.

Now, can some of those energies evolve? Yes, they can; however, there is a condensing that needs to happen. Let us take the example of a goldfish: With the goldfish, there may be a more condensed energy in the ethers, but it is not really the same over soul directing the goldfish life or the goldfish choices. That, instead, is a natural thing. But in the more condensed version of the energy, it can, in a loose way, be deemed an over soul but not an overseer.

Now here is where it gets tricky. The goldfish—and let us say the ant or another type of fish—could combine energies with other energies. Similar to the human evolution of the body, the progression is the same in that it occurs over time, and there were other things that "morphed" it, so to speak. Now there are others who have questions such as there is talk of dolphins that have a much higher intelligence, and this is true. They are beings of great intelligence, and they are more spiritually evolved than the goldfish. This is not judgment on the goldfish; it is just the way it is. However, that does not mean that you become a dolphin.

But again, we want to stay on the ladder of the evolution of things, and when we say evolution of things, you must understand that when energy evolves to the place where the beings are able to make decisions beyond basic survival instincts, and begin to use reason and begin to intuit, then you are in a different classification of incarnational beings.

However, we are not at liberty at this time to delve completely into that except to say that there are those energies that incarnate as a higher level of being . . . there are interdimensional beings, otherworldly beings that can inhabit this world.

YVES: Interestingly, in relation to dolphins, the Dagara have a belief that dolphins are interdimensional because they can appear in places where you would not normally see a dolphin. Going back to your point, the human being cannot reincarnate as an ant?

THE COLLECTIVE: A human being does not reincarnate as an ant or as a cow, pig, or whatever due to the different frequencies of each. If it did, then it would not be evolution. Evolution could not then occur, including the evolution of the spirit. It would not happen even if one did do a lot of harm that was not their task list. This is the same idea as your heaven and hell. The idea of punishment, the idea that one would be punished by returning as an ant or a pig? This is not the case; it is not the way that the world works.

One would have to—well, I do not even know that we would even have that information to give you an example of exactly how that would occur. It would be more of some great "scientific experiment," if you will, for a human being to dilute its frequency enough to incarnate as an ant or a swine.

YVES: But an ant, a swine, or even a tiger can eventually evolve to be a human?

THE COLLECTIVE: Since there are no rules, we will agree that it can happen. However, that is not necessarily the order of things. We are trying to say that it is not necessarily the plan of all things—to become human—because, then, you would run out of all of the other things!

There are some things that are a part of the living, breathing Earth. The living, breathing Earth is its own incarnation. So you could look at the living, breathing Earth as the over soul of some of these other things. If this Earth were to explode, you would still exist, *its energy* would still exist, and it would find a way to create itself, or part of itself, or some pieces of itself or another self, elsewhere. So you see, this Earth is the over soul, and from that springs forth the bits and pieces that trickle down, trickle down, and trickle down into the smaller pieces of its self-expression. So the plants and the trees, the bugs and insects, and things such as those evolve out of the workings of the Earth. Again, we realize that for some people, this may not be a simple concept.

YVES: Again, with the law of karma and all these different life-forms, let us say, a mosquito, many times I smash this mosquito and apologize for taking the life of the mosquito . . . Are there repercussions for taking the life of the mosquito?

THE COLLECTIVE: You will become a swine! *[Humor in tone.]* That is the one rule when you become a swine . . . Of course we jest with you.

The repercussions, well, again if you are looking at this mosquito as a piece of the Earth —and mind you, we are not advocating that you are harmful when something is an annoyance to you—however, there is no more harm done to swat than there is when you walk upon the Earth. When you walk upon the Earth, you are stepping on the blades of grass, you are stepping on the soil, you are stepping on the rocks, you see?

So there is something valid behind the idea of not swatting and not harming. That is the respect of all things being life and of all things being one and connected. There are no repercussions. Now, karmically, will that be something that goes on your task list? Will you become a victim of fire ants in another lifetime? Probably not; however, if during your incarnation it was a goal of yours to not harm any life whatsoever and you were unable to sustain that goal, then perhaps you may decide to try it again or to try it in a different way. There is energy and there is soul . . . That is a deeper topic for another time: energy, spirit, soul, and the essence of things. Those will be good topics.

REBECCA: The important thing that we have gone over to keep in mind about karma is that it is a natural process of checks and balances. The teachings of karma stem from teachings in the East. In more modern thought of karma, in both the East and West, this idea of karma is being twisted. The original teaching of it was not as it is taught now. People have taken those teachings, and over the years, they have changed them. Again, this was to meet the people where they were at, at the time, because fear worked then.

It is important to begin to recognize that this is not a system of punishments and rewards; karma is merely checks and balances that you decide on.

Of course, there is what you would call the karmic implications in this lifetime. For instance, if you were someone who has not kept the confidences of your friends, then hopefully, ideally, during that lifetime, you would have the opportunity to experience what that is like yourself. If you do, then you have learned it then and there. You see, in the smaller day-to-day life ways, you are learning it. There are some sayings that would also encompass the idea of karma being the checks and balances. You have all heard the saying "What goes around comes around." However, it is not as small as you make it, and again, it is not punitive because it may come around in this lifetime or it may not.

The problem is people are deciding for themselves what that means. They are determining what that means. So even in their gathering of pleasure from the idea that if someone has spurned them, then that person will be spurned in return—well, that in and of itself is incorrect. Because the spurning could have been for you to learn something you need to learn, and they have done you a favor. Therefore, they may get something "good" in return, and we use your word "good" only for your understanding.

So again, it's very important that people try not to, as people often do, use principles to lash out at others or use them as an excuse, as in, "Oh, it must just be my karma," because you created that. You create your karma. So it may be your karma until that time, but your karma is also to change that, to change your way of viewing things, you see?

Also in the checks and balances of things, there is another saying, "What we resist persists," so as the law of balance is happening, if there is something that you are running from, it keeps coming back to you because you have called it to you. Your teacher, your Malidoma Somé (speaking directly to Yves to use an example) spoke of this before in relation to the animal kingdom. He spoke of how, in order to hunt, the animals must have prey that is moving for the hunt to occur. It is not necessary for the eating of the catch, but it is necessary for the hunt itself. Likewise, if you are running away from things, these things will continue to chase you, to hunt you. You have fallen prey to the very things that you are trying to avoid. This occurs so that when these things catch up to you, you can deal with them head-on.

You may notice that there will be times when we reference "laws," but we feel that "principles" is a better description since there are no rules. However, we use "laws" at times for your own ease of understanding; it is a term that is often used by you humans.

We have learned with you humans that we sometimes have to lure you slowly toward us. Just as when you put a worm upon the hook for fishing. You throw the line out and reel it in slowly, but surely, your dinner grabs onto the bait. Perhaps you humans are not too far from that goldfish after all *[humor in tone]*. We say this, of course, in jest.

We will prepare to take our leave this evening, but before we depart, we would like to ask you again if there are any remaining queries you have.

YVES: Yes. In the cycle of reincarnation, one comes in to accomplish certain tasks and leaves, and from there, part of it may ascend to another level, part of it may come back, so that implies or means some of it still resides in the "somewhere" in the ethers, so to speak. That being said, the Dagara of West Africa believe that you can call on the ancestors for assisting, but I want to take it to a bigger level in regard to Hitler. He has caused so much harm on this plane for whatever reason . . . in trying to ask for global consciousness like making an invocation for world peace . . . Is it good to call on this person who has caused so much harm to assist in trying to raise awareness and consciousness of the world?

THE COLLECTIVE: What you are doing here is that within that context, you are calling on that energy or name that carries with it a resonance, a frequency, and an Earth and cellular memory (although the being that was that energy may have evolved). Perhaps you know what we will say next; we would suggest that perhaps you not call upon the name of Hitler.

Words, names, and all of that have a frequency to it, and the frequency or energy signature is also burned as an imprint here on the Earth. Now this energy that you call as Hitler may in fact be the same. It may be out there in the ethers somewhere, still working it out. Remember, of course, that when we are talking of Hitler, we are talking also in generalities. Generalities about the laws of karma, and so, just as a person, let us use even one's ancestral lineage as another example. If one had a grandfather who was highly abusive, it is quite likely that they would not be calling on that grandfather until within the image or the idea of the grandfather, there was complete healing that took place. For to call on one that was abusive toward you is going to create something in you that is contradictory to the outcome that you are trying to create.

YVES: So in calling on an ancestor, you have to be sure which ancestors you are calling on because their signature on this earthen plane may still attract or bring back that same frequency?

THE COLLECTIVE: Again we are delving deeply now yes and no. Now, were Hitler a grandfather, for instance, his name might carry a different signature for his grandchildren. However, with this name in particular, there is energy to it (perhaps different from a grandfatherly-type energy) that spreads in the world all over.

Even in reading this text, there will be people who are very angry that we dare to say that Hitler is not being punished eternally because there are so many wounds. Those wounds are also why we will not (though it has been spoken of, in other writings and texts) say where the energy of this Hitler being is or who they are now. We will not do that, for it would serve no purpose other than idle human curiosity.

Your experience of an ancestor and another's experience of that same ancestor could be two different things. So what keeps you in line; what brings you power; what gives you hope, faith, and fortitude; and what brings you forward toward your intended path? Those are the things to keep in mind when you are determining whom to call upon. Therefore, while you can call upon anyone, and even though there may have been some clearing after they have crossed over into the ancestral realm, it does not mean necessarily that they are completely altruistic now.

You know of stories where ancestors have become angry and created chaos, yes? So remember, we do not become perfect celestial beings after death. Some of the trappings of the human ego is left behind just as our body is left behind, and there are times and places where a large part of that personality stays for some time.

YVES: So the thing is, know thy ancestor?

THE COLLECTIVE: This is helpful; how-ever, the other part of it is relevant in terms of what is your intention and what you are imaging and what you are calling forth other than just the ancestors. So in answering your question, it is more like knowing your inten-tions and being clear about it because if you are asking the ancestors to do something and they are not ready, then they would not do it anyway.

Remember when you are asking to ask for the highest good. Remember also that, ulti-mately, every being out there is an ancestor, and that you ultimately are your own ancestor. That perhaps could be a whole other book, but let us complete this one first!

April 17, 2010 – Second session on karma. Yves was recording and directing questions. This session was ninety minutes long. Julie entered the session after being quite worn out from the last session only a few days before. However, once she entered into a trance state, there were no concerns about her level of energy to complete this session.

THE COLLECTIVE: Greetings. We are pleased to be seated here with you again, on this evening. You have questions that you were to bring forth from the last session we had regarding karma?

YVES: Yes, thank you. When we are here on this earthen plane, it is easy for us to forget what we remembered before we arrived on this plane, and you mentioned that it is partly because of our society. What is it that keeps us grounded besides the density? What else keeps us in the illusion? How do we open ourselves, and what kind of society would help us remember what we are here to do?

THE COLLECTIVE: Part of what comes along with the density that we reference is that in your world, there is a certain necessity for the density, there is a certain necessity for the "forgetting," if you will, in order to be able to believe the illusion. Believing the illusion is partly what keeps you here in the physical dense body. Therefore, part of that is necessary. Another necessary part of that is seeing things as separate in order to maintain your separate body. So things that you see with the physical eyes, including other human beings as well as yourself, appear to be solid matter, but are not. Even physical structures such as buildings and other things, though they appear to be separate, are interconnected.

Now, one would not want to burst through that illusion all at once for more than a few moments at a time. It can and does occur, but again, there is a difference between blowing the illusion away and being aware of the illusion. Once you blow the illusion away, then you are no longer here on this earthen plane, yes?

However, there is awareness that comes not only from the mind but also from that inner part of yourself that what you see is not all that there is. All things that you see, even though they appear to be separate, are interconnected. There are parts of that belief of separateness that are absolutely necessary in order to come in this human form and work on those tasks. Because if you have something on your task list and you were to come in and remember exactly what you came to do, why then, you could get that done quite quickly, and the challenge would not be there. Then you are not really learning it because you are not going through the challenge or struggle of seeing things or others separate from you, or seeing things as outside forces. Ultimately, yes, it is about getting to the place where you see all of it, at the same time. However, if you were to recognize all of it when you came onto the earthen plane, then you lose the purpose of it all. To qualify, some of that is a "necessary evil," as you would say.

But what is it that can nurture that sense of awareness of remembering that you are all connected, of remembering that you have all come in the name of love? Because, ultimately, that is why you *have* come.

Part of the task list includes the ways that you go about getting to that place of coming in love, you see? Let us clarify; that statement does not mean that your list is comprised of ways in which you will act loving toward others; it may have some of that, but it may also have ways in which you will not act loving, which assists you in learning when love is not honoring the other person. The society that you all inhabit is certainly not that way, currently. However, that is not to say that is true across the board for all of the people in your society. There are places, people, and groups of individuals that are working toward this shift of consciousness that assists in bringing back that remembering. They are those that are beginning to notice that everything that you do is connected to everything else; likewise, everything that you do impacts everything else.

Ideally, the way to support and nurture this would be for your society to begin with your small children, in teaching them and modeling for them the way to walk through the world wherein you leave no "footprint," so to speak, you do no harm, you cause no damage. Now these ways, of course, are ideal and are difficult to do when you are in the human form.

The ways in which you would do that would be to begin when the child is very young, by nurturing their connection to the universe. You see, when your children first come in, they are connected to all of us in these other realms. They are blessed with not being able to speak and move about and understand the world around them, so they are able to maintain that connection. As they begin to grow and age, they will step more into the illusion. This is mostly because that is where you, the parents are, it is how you live, and therefore, you unknowingly bring them into that same illusion—well intentioned, of course. One problem is that your society is built on materialism and consumerism.

There are those of you who try to help others; you try to act loving in your interactions. There are those of you who are people of devout faith. Yet there is still the world of materialism that you buy into. Some of you will say that in order to stay in this world, you must! This is true if you wish to stay in the world—the way it is operating—in this society. One issue is when you do not buy into it; you become an outcast, so to speak. This is not, by any means, an easy task, to raise your children in this way (not buying into current societal norms) if you have not been raised this way. You may in fact have been raised in a very loving household, in a household that was involved in one religious sect or another and wanted to be better people. But again, remember that all of the religions set up the rules that were applicable to the time and the place. So now, we are in a different time and a different place.

The religious sects are also designed by politician types, so it wasn't just "This is what's best for you," but it was "This is what's best for us, and this is how we want to build this society, and what we politicians want to get out of it."

So going back to the small infant you bring into the world, it is important to dialogue with them about the other world. Oftentimes you will notice that when speaking to your infants and small children, they are often not looking at you but around you. They are seeing your energy field. Also, when small children are around someone who is nervous or someone who is angry, they will cry more. Because infants are more in tune, their body is a barometer of sorts. When you are in adulthood, your body is the main part and the spirit is the secondary part; it is the opposite when you are first born into this world.

The spirit, the soul, is overriding the physical body at the time of birth and in infancy, and it is the infant's mode of communication. If you were to never teach a child how to speak, if they were raised in this type of connected environment, they would hone those skills. They would hone other ways of communicating. You may notice a child may make a cry for whatever they need; that is the body's response to this spirit that is in it.

Therefore, the most ideal way to do it is to start with children, but it is very difficult because, then, the decisions that you make along the way are difficult. It may be simple in some ways in the beginning of the child's life, but when they go out into the world, they are surrounded by all of the other ways and means of doing things in this society. So the choices become, do you isolate your child from others, or do you send them out into the world knowing that the societal norms will begin to chip away at that which you have been building? Of course, in an ideal society or in the rebuilding of an ideal society, you would have these sorts of communities that exist, and you would be raising the children within them; then you are supporting that way of being (in the world in all ways). Even through their education.

Your society now is based on education that is centered on your marketability for financial and material wealth and success. So the learning is a different learning than the learning one receives from education of the spirit manifested in the human body, walking among the Earth and interacting with others.

Thus far, in terms of this that we have spoken, do you have other questions about that part of it?

YVES: No.

THE COLLECTIVE: So, ideally, you would start with the child. Most times, one feels pressured or pushed into having that child out in the society because you do not have the communal supports that are necessary to support that type of upbringing. It does not necessarily help the child if they are not in an environment that supports that way of moving through the world. If you are raising a child separate from the world, then they are not in the society wherein they can share what they are learning from where they are currently learning it. So then, parents are faced with the difficult task of figuring out how to put their child out into the society as it is now and continue to foster that connection at the same time. There are ways that will assist in supporting it, but again, they are going to lose that connection to some degree, yes?

One of the challenges in your society now, and has been for some time, is that because of the idea of wealth and success that you have attached yourselves to, parents are overly involved in attempting to model their children into something. Children need no molding; it is perhaps the adults that need some melting down and remolding. Of course, the argument could be, who will keep them safe? We understand that, and especially now, in this world, one could say, "It is a dangerous world." So one of the issues is that the way to go about it is so contrary to the way that this world works now. It is very difficult to bring this way of thinking into this world at this time; the precepts are not quite as powerful because they are fighting against this other system. You understand?

When allowed to be completely free, the child will blossom and grow and learn much more than from any formalized education, any structure or models or behavioral therapy and all of these wondrous things that society has created to try to get children to adapt to a maladaptive society. You are trying to normalize them in a world that is abnormal, and that becomes problematic.

We understand it is with your best intentions based on your current limited understanding, yet you are bringing these children out into a world that is insane, all the while thinking that you are doing things to make them sane. But how can you make them sane in this insane world that they are now becoming a part of? That same mentality that same belief system that tells you that the way to find happiness is through acquiring things or by having accomplishments listed on a wall. When in truth, the way to find happiness in your accomplishments is by doing what is real, what is pure, and what is automatic for a child . . . for a spirit . . . for divinity. And so, it is quite the conundrum, yes?

How do you attempt to begin doing that in a society that does not support it? And how do you do it in a way that creates the least amount of fallout? Without support systems in place, it is difficult to adhere to. Because the way that your world operates now is through that exchange of money and through all of these other things we have spoken of. To withdraw from that also means that there are a great deal of other struggles and challenges that come with it.

There was a time when exchanges were made that differed from using this monetary form. During that time, it was simpler to exchange or trade off, and really what it was, was a sharing. Just as when you have one of your potluck dinners and everyone brings a dish to share, you are giving and you are receiving.

Now some will say to you that using money is the same thing. They may say that you are giving money and you are receiving something in return. When boiled down in that simple way, that would hold to be a scientific truth, yes.

The problem is that greed has set in and that this almighty dollar has become that which is divine—it has become that which is all-powerful, all-knowing, all-everything. So it is no longer an equal exchange when people sell their souls for a dollar. When they compromise their integrity in the pursuit of this dollar. When they are no longer willing to walk in their truth in order to have financial security, for material wealth, or for status or recognition.

So it must begin in the smaller ways, for trying to just change it drastically, with this society being as warped, as it is, would not work out well. Many people start out that way, and then they give up and give in to the system. There is a saying in your language that if you cannot beat them, then you should join them, and that is often what occurs. Of course, the other issue is that children, at such a young age, are so brainwashed into this way of life, into this society. You see that in their cruelty to other children, in comparing what they have to what others have, and how they look versus how others look and so on.

REBECCA: So the smaller ways in which to do that is also a heavy responsibility on those that are ready to do it. Because, that is the "larger call." Those of you that are hearing the call need to step out even farther; you need to step out into demonstrating. Into "walking the talk" is, I believe, what you say, yes?

The way that you do that is to begin to let go of some of the control of your children, some of the control of the world around you.

As you are beginning to open up more to these truths, it is about really walking them fully because the truth is—and when we say this, we do not mean to sound harsh—somewhere in there as smaller children, when that "knowing" is still there, they know on some level that, basically, all of you are lying to them. You are lying. Not out of any malicious intent but out of your own self-deceit.

Therefore, the small ways in which you can assist is to back up from your control a little bit. Offer them your experience in life, have conversations with them about options of their lives, but try not to steer them or direct their course, for you cannot. Well, you can, in your society, but again, we are talking about how to begin to create an ideal society. For your children are not your toys or your dolls to mold into what you want them to be or what you think they should be. They are not yours to mold that others might say that you are a great parent because your child has done *x*, *y*, and *z*. Instead, it is about a contract, and remember, always a contract ultimately has to do with nurturing the spirit, helping the spirit to remember; and the ways you may do that in your world is through the opposite means than those you currently employ.

However, what you are doing now does not preclude you from doing it differently. In other words, what we are saying is it is not too late. You can teach an old dog new tricks. The question is, is the dog *willing* to jump through that hoop? Is she or he feeling it is too much to surmount? And what price are you willing to pay for that?

Those who will be reading this text at some point in the text will think to themselves, *I want to be different, I want to be a more spiritual person, and I want to move forward*; and we say, "Are you sure?" Because it means a lot more—as I am sure that both you (addressing Yves) and the vehicle seated here can attest to this that it means a lot more—than what you thought. Oftentimes, what draws people onto the spiritual path is the seeming power in it. You understand? So it is a little bit of a trick in order, again, to "lure" you along. Unfortunately, people sometimes stay caught in that desire for power, and they abuse those principles to obtain more power. They then attempt to rationalize it by saying, "It is a spiritual concept, or it is a spiritual principle . . ." or "I am a great minister . . ." "I am a great this or that . . . therefore, I deserve to have all of these riches all around me." Well, the minister does not deserve the riches any more than the CEO does or does not. It does not really matter "who" it is. There are many who may read this and say, "This is not me; I am not a rich person," but that is not what we are talking about. You do not need to be a wealthy person in terms of how your society defines wealth, you see? The question is, where do you place your priorities? What is it that you do in your day-to-day life and whether you have this much or this much or this much, what are you doing to try to hold on to all of it? Are you willing to have it with your hands off it? That is the question.

Now others may then ask, "Does this mean that money is bad or money is evil?" Money in and of itself is just a piece of paper; it is not anything. Like anything else, something only becomes a negative force or has evil outcome from it based on what you do with it. You can have someone who is an important religious leader, but it does not mean they are doing great things within that role, yes?

One of the other ways to nurture that connection in children (and in yourselves) is to show them ways to just be present for the world around them. You see, your world is so filled with all of this visual and physical external stimulation. There is so much noise as you watch your televisions, play your video games, and play around on your computers. You are so busy, busy, busy that your children never learn how to just be present!

When was the last time that any of you have just sat and been present with your children? And we do not even mean sitting and reading a book with them or helping them with their homework. We are saying, what if you just sat with your child? What if you just sat with another human being and communicated through this *[pointing to area of the heart]*? What if you communicated love without words, without sounds, even without touch! Just sit together without needing to fill in the empty spaces with something, which you are all so famous for.

The question is, what is it that you are all so afraid of? What if there is an empty space? Well, you might start listening a little more and realize that everything you have built up is a lie; it is a sham and a façade. We do not only mean in the bigger scheme of things, in terms of the illusion. So many people find so many ways to run away from themselves.

Now, because there is this thing occurring, this quickening (that we have talked about), and people are both listening and moving toward it, or they are running faster and farther away. They may even start toward it, then jump out and run away out of fear from the changes they may face. Of course, once you get caught up in the quickening, there will come a time when you will not be able to do that (to run away) anymore because you will not be able to fool yourselves anymore.

The problem that needs to be overcome is if one has been living a certain way for a certain amount of time, then to change that way disrupts the whole system. And it even disrupts the system in the smaller ways. For instance, in the system of your workforce and within your home life, it becomes problematic because it is a well-oiled machine that operates in a certain way and in a certain format. Therefore, when one begins to say, "Wait, maybe there is something more, something different, something else." So they begin to move this way a little bit, and then the machine or its conveyor belt cannot go that way, and it jams up or it starts going too fast for people to try to keep up with it, you see? Then what happens is that there is a backlash from that because people are trying to figure out, "How do we keep the conveyor belt going?" Their fear comes in, and then they try to redirect the conveyor belt or force someone back to it. So it is not by any stretch of the imagination an easy task at this time in your world.

Again, those of you who have been called forth and *for all of you who are reading this, there is a call to you right now*! So when you read this and you say, "Well, I do this, but I don't do that or all of that," we are saying to you, if you are reading this right now—and you may want to put the book down if you do not want to hear what we say next—you are reading it because we are calling to you, to *you*. That person right now who is counting the ways in which they already do this and think it does not apply. We are speaking *[whispering] especially to you*. Because you have asked us to; you may not have asked us directly, any one of the individual energies, but again at some point, either before coming in or during the course of your stay here on the earthen plane, you have put a call out to us. Some of you may be aware of that and some of you may not be. But mark our words that if you are reading this, you have put out that call. And so, all of this, every last piece of it, every nook and cranny of it, applies to you. It applies to all things you see.

We sometimes take a concept, an idea, and we package it up and put it in a compartment, yes? However, if it is a principle, if it is a truth, then it carries all the way across all things, right?

When you get into your driving vehicle, whether you are going north, south, east, or west, you do the same thing to start up the vehicle, yes? It does not take a different means of starting it if you are going to the desert or the forest. The mechanism of making the vehicle run remains the same. The mechanism for living a certain way, for walking in your truth, applies the same way in whatever environment you are in, in whatever situation you are looking at, and in whatever events that come up in your life. The principles do not change.

YVES: In reference to someone coming in to create havoc, there is a need for a cleansing to occur. Is the life that person is living part of the cleansing? Or does the cleansing occur afterward, when one returns to the place of in between incarnations?

THE COLLECTIVE: All people, whether they come here to wreak havoc or not, undergo a cleansing. Just as when you enter the physical body, there is a certain heaviness of the energy that needs to be created; when you leave, there is lightening up, there is a cleansing, there is a washing away of the chains that bind you to the earthen plane.

Just as when you come in and you are in the physical form, you maintain a connection to the spirit world; when you die, you maintain a connection to the earthly world. When you die, it does not mean that, all of a sudden, the lights go off and that you are now floating in the celestial realms. There is a process of disconnect. There is a process of washing away, of leaving behind some of the baggage that you perhaps carried into the world or picked up in the world. Cleansings prior to leaving the earthen plane would mostly be the cleansing of the mind-self to allow the soul to leave fully.

It is a tricky phrasing there because we could also say that that there is, ultimately, cleansing in the karmic realm with certain things even if one is accomplishing what they came to accomplish. So this holds true across the board. It is not only those who suffer a great deal or who create suffering that need to be cleansed. That may or may not take more time; however, someone could be a very loving person but still have strong attachments to this world. Also, the attachments that others have toward them can keep them, not necessarily stuck here on Earth, but certainly keep their energy focused here more than it needs to be. There is a way in the process of cleansing that they can take their place in the spirit realm and yet also still have a connection. Just as when a child is born here, they are still connected over there in the spirit realms.

So a good question is, how do you support that? The way is by maintaining that connection to those in the spirit world by acknowledging that connection. It is to continue to let that spirit do what it must there. So while you may ask for that spirit to be an intermediary at times or offer protection or to communicate with it at times, it is not helpful for you to create an unhealthy attachment that is going to keep them buckled to their human persona energy. To do so could detract from the washing away because if you are always calling on them, that could cause them to become overly involved. If the washing away occurs, they can be unbiased. As an example, if you have a parent who has moved into the astral realm, you may want their protection and their reassurance, and as a parent, they may still be coming from that place where they do not want you to hurt. Therefore, any action on their part might come from that place of parental protection and may not necessarily be the highest place to come from, or the place that is for your highest good. Of course, you will hurt in this lifetime.

YVES: So how do we assist them in that process so that they do not remain attached here? How do we help them move beyond this place and be able to assist from a less biased perspective?

THE COLLECTIVE: Many of your religions incorporate certain rituals, and they have certain practices that are all based on some of this idea, though they do it in different ways. It is based on the idea that you honor not only the person who was the human but also who they are now as spirit. And what you do is you assist them in the crossover.

Many traditions use "prayer." There is an old ritual where people would place coins on the eyes to pay the "ferrymen" who brought people across to the other side—to the side of the spirit world. In some religious practices, they stifle their grief because they feel it will keep their loved ones' spirits here. Yet, in other religions they may express their grief and practice the flowing of tears, for they believe that the spirits of their loved ones will float into the spirit world on their tears. This is another thing that can get somewhat sticky in the explanation. Let us say that you are steeped in a particular tradition, and the recently departed being was also steeped in that tradition, then the rituals for that tradition will work. It will work because this is what the deceased one was expecting. For instance, we spoke of the tradition of stifling grief. There is a practice in one of your larger religions currently on your earthen plane where grief is not shown during funerary rites. Women are not allowed to go to the cemetery; some say this comes from a belief that the grieving will call the spirit back. Now if this is what this person (who has transitioned to spirit) believes, then if there is grieving at the cemetery, what do you think will happen? *They will come back.* They will come back because that is what they believed. Whereas someone who is steeped in a tradition where to cry is a way to release the spirit, to cry is a way to lift them up so they can "sail into" the spirit world; then if no one is crying, they are waiting for *that to occur in order to leave or be lifted up. So they wait.*

For many of you now, there are not necessarily traditions that you are steeped in. It is also important to remember that there are many families, nowadays, whose members are steeped in *different* traditions. So if you have a parent in one tradition and a child in another in terms of assisting the parent, then you must go with *that parent's* belief system, even if it is not your own. Now, it does not mean that you cannot then do what it is that you believe will also assist. However, you must remember they are also watching for the signs, the rituals of what they were taught. That is what they will do. They will wait for them.

For those that have no formalized tradition or practice, a very good way for you to do this is to honor the person's life in whatever way you wish to do that. You might gather with others to honor through words what that being has brought to you, what they have taught you, because they *are* listening. They are hearing. It is helping them in making that transition by seeing that they have made a difference in the world, and they can give themselves permission to move on. It is also important to allow yourself to move with whatever you are compelled to do in this situation, whether it is to sob or comfort those that are. Most important is that whatever you do; it is for the upliftment of your loved one. There are also traditions that make "shrines," if you will, and that shrine is fed every day. In feeding them, you are nurturing them, not in a way to keep them here, but to honor them and to lift them up.

So you must believe in the effectiveness of those things because if you do not, then your heart is not in it. Your heart must move into that place because it is the heart energy that helps uplift the spirit of the deceased. Also, you can continue dialogues with this being—at times, they may come to you—there may be things they need to settle. There may be others that they need to assist, so they may come to you and ask you to do work on their behalf. So you need to listen for them also. When you suddenly think of them and see or feel them, pay attention. Greet them and ask them lovingly, "Why is it that you are here? What is it you have to say?"

YVES: Yes. Now, let us say that one has an ancestor who wasn't so kind to them, but that ancestor had a good relationship with other family members who helped them be uplifted in spirit and they are now in a place to be of assistance even to the one with whom they had the bad relationship with. Can the ancestor now be of assistance and help to the one on the Earth that had been mistreated by the ancestor if the one in this realm is still holding on to the pain?

THE COLLECTIVE: This is a good question. Of course, they are going to be able to assist the best, if the person is willing to let go of the issue and walk into healing. There are those who hold on to anger all of their lives, and often they do that across the board. They may hold anger and resentment against many people, so there may not be much walking into healing there.

From where the ancestor is, again remember that they are dealing also in universal energy, so they have ways and means (if it is within their purpose) to begin to wash away some of that pain in the human, by means of universal healing energy. Perhaps their spirit may come through someone and give a message to apologize. Maybe that is all the other person ever wanted or has been waiting for, if they never heard it from that person when they were on the earthen plane. Sometimes the way the ancestor is helping is not through direct mediation; however, they may have already helped while here, even though the person is still angry, by completing some karmic agreement.

It is important to redesign your understanding of the word healing and the word help. Because one may seem to help here on your earthen plane and another may seem to not help, but in the bigger scheme of things, they may be helping in other ways, you see? Similarly, you need to begin to view healing in that way also. We have spoken in the past about sickness and healing and how sometimes "healing" means leaving the body. That this is, at times complete healing.

Yet others sometimes look at healing as the person remaining in the physical body. Likewise, emotional healing also at times takes on different forms. In other words, it is not always the way in which the limited human brain understands it to be. That is because your society here and now is terrified of death. One of the reasons is that it is seen as the end of everything they have, everything they own, and that everything they worked so hard to amass and acquire cannot go with them. Do you understand?

YVES: We talked about when some healing has taken place, the ancestor has worked toward providing healing, and somehow the person may or may not be healed. So this thing about the frequency remaining with the person's name, if it remains. So if the person is healed on the other side—

THE COLLECTIVE: *[Interrupting.]* The difference is if the people here are not healed. That is where the frequency affects because you are calling on that being on the other side that is no longer resonating at that frequency (that they resonated at while here). It is the frequency that is left behind. If healing has not occurred across the board, for the most part, one is not going to call on someone that they are having anger and hatred toward any way, correct?

YVES: Switching subjects. We talked about when some people realize that they cannot accomplish the tasks, and so they depart early. Suicide is one form of leaving early. It seems to happen a lot in young people. What is the mind-set of someone so young realizing that they haven't even had time to begin the tasks, and yet they aren't going to accomplish them?

THE COLLECTIVE: Do not make the mistake in believing that suicide is always because someone has not, or cannot, complete his or her tasks. It may be that they have completed what they came here to complete, and sometimes, that very thing they have come here to complete may include the suicide. It may include something to stir people up. Of course, we cannot get into every reason that it might occur, for we would be here for weeks on end—in your time. It could be the accomplishment of them; it could be the non-accomplishment of them. What you most need to understand is that the human brain does not understand this because if the human brain did understand this, it would not opt out because it would say, "Oh well, if I understand this, then there is a way for me to accomplish these tasks."

So in suicide, the human being is suffering, beyond the suffering that most people can imagine. There is no light; there is no longer any hope of light to them. So they are not thinking, *I think I will leave because I cannot accomplish my tasks.* Although their thoughts might be saying that in other ways—*I might as well leave; there is no purpose for me here anymore*—again there is a cryptic coded message that they are receiving. So it is the spirit or the soul's overriding self that decides that. If it is the case of not completing and unable to complete for whatever reasons, whether they have veered off course too much or other people did not complete their part of the same contract, you need to understand that the human being is experiencing dreadful suffering. From here *[hands held out above the body into the astral field]*, the spirit-self or soul-self is overriding that. Again, it is like changing your clothes or saying, "Well, I am no longer at sea, so I must take off my wet suit and don something else." You see? Does this answer that?

YVES: Yes, it does. One more question: So you mentioned that one does not have to complete the list even though some are destined to accomplish so much. You mentioned something of a handoff, and I understand that to be that somehow, even unknowingly, there is a knowing of the other selves, so some of these tasks can be handed off to someone else. Can you elaborate on that, please?

[Much throat clearing.]

THE COLLECTIVE: It is not the individual that hands off; it is the over soul. So that is where the awareness is.

There are multidimensional lives and there are parallel lives—they are two different things. Let us clarify. Multidimensional lives—you are living in different dimensions all at the same time because there is no time. Parallel life means that you are working off the same "task list," so to speak. There are two ways that parallel lives occur, and we will try to keep this simple, although it can be quite complex for the human mind.

On the one hand, parallel lives mean just that. If you have an individual who has certain tasks to complete, if they need to bring healing to the world or healing to certain people they have contracted with, and then in another life, they have the same agreement. Now here and in the other life, they are wired in a little more to each other. Those are the ones you may tap into—those of you who can do that. You will see them reflecting each other sometimes; they will parallel each other, you see? So if one "drops the ball," so to speak, there is a signal sent off via the over soul for the other person to catch it. That may come in the form of sudden feeling as though you need to do something differently, or suddenly, feeling called to do something you had never felt called to do before. You see?

The other form of parallel lives (and again we could give you more specifics than that, but for simplicity's sake, we are not going to)—we have spoken before of the choices you make, and each choice carries energy, yes? When you take a turn in the road sometimes, there is a part of the essence of you that is left behind and creates something. So let us say that you were going to be a great politician, and you are on the road to becoming a great politician, and then you decided instead to be a great priest. The part of you that was moving toward being the politician, if you have put a lot of your energy toward it and a lot of your dreams and time, that would carry on in its own pocket, if you will. It may take a life of its own. When you are in a relationship with an individual, if that relationship ends, especially if there was karmic connection in it or deep feeling in it, then there is a place in which that relationship still exists even if it is not with your physical body. Of course, that connection may bring you back to that relationship again, but there are other times when it is not meant to, so it does not. So there is a place where it exists and moves forward, but it does not necessarily manifest in the physical realm.

However, if there was karmic completion that needed to be completed but was not, then you have another parallel life that is paralleling that one which would then pick it up, ideally, but that is not always the case.

We realize we are just skimming the surface, but believe us when we tell you that to go deeper into this could get complex and convoluted. For the purpose of where we are heading with this text, it would serve to "muddy the waters," so to speak.[2]

YVES: That is all of the questions that I have written down for now. We would like to begin the principle of balance.

THE COLLECTIVE: This principle, we will discuss in our next session, which will occur in two to three days from now. We will be preparing to take our leave, but before we do, we will inform you that she (Julie) will experience a slight headache this time, but she should get over this soon. We will assist in that. However, shortly, she will feel very tired, so if brought up, you can remind her that this is to be expected. And so, we prepare to take our leave, and we wish to thank you for your service in this purpose, and we look forward to meeting you again for our next session in two to three days.

We bid you a fond good evening.

---

[2] For further material on parallel lives and multidimensional selves, see Appendix A.

The Principle of Balance

April 22, 2010 – Two audience members were present. Yves was on the recording device. Yves and Patti were directing questions. Session was 125 minutes in length. Both participants reported feeling very trance-like during session and had difficulty staying alert for directing questions due to the level of energy in the room. This seemed to Julie to be the first time that Uncle completely manifested his personality, although Yves reported to have seen glimpses of this same persona in earlier sessions. It may have been the first time for "full contact," as Julie reported feeling her body change, and Patti reported seeing a man's face when looking at Julie while Uncle was speaking.

THE COLLECTIVE: We welcome you here this evening, and for your viewing pleasure, you may note that there will be times when the physical body seems to be moving or "twitching," if you will. What you are seeing here is—sort of—electronic pulsations as we play with the frequency to fine-tune and adjust the energies between our consciousness and the physical vehicle. There are also some other energies here with us that for the most part would be considered a part of our regime, but they are not always present. Again, they are of a somewhat different vibrational frequency, and so the body has to be prepared to receive that consciousness. At this point, their loose energies will be combined with ours as we work on adjusting her vibrational frequency. If it is able to manifest fully in this session, they may come in individually, but from where we stand at this point, it probably would not be during this session that they would. But there will be new characters added to the "plot," if you will, once the frequency is resonating at the appropriate level in order for the connection to be fully made and for the least amount of impact on the physical body. And so we will be working on that this evening. We know that we have given you instruction to come up with the next principle you would like us to speak about. Although we do know which one you would like us to address, we rather enjoy having you "kick it off," if you will.

YVES: Okay, the principle of balance. That is the one we would like to address.

THE COLLECTIVE: An important note here is that the principle of balance is also a part of cause and effect. It is not exactly the same, yet both principles can fall into each other's category. Again, these things meld into each other. There are no finite lines of division between these principles or "laws," as many on your earthen plane reference them. Therefore, you may see some of the information moving in and out of both principles. We will take pause as necessary for clarifying if it appears to become muddied.

Let us begin. There are several different things to address within balance. There is perceptional balance, which is that which applies within the illusion of this world in your humanness, and that will be the latter part of what we speak about. In addition, there is balance in the natural order of things. One mimics the other just as life mimics nature, so to speak, yes?

Therefore, in the natural universe or for the ease of simplifying, let us bring it to the Earth or rather the *entity* that is the Earth. There are many things that grow on the Earth, yes? We will take this a little farther; with individual planets, that is a good starting point. Dependent on the purpose of that planet and its uses, it will begin to evolve over time to strike its own balance and to correct and re-correct itself as things move out of balance. There was a time when much of this Earth was covered in water, yes? And there were influences from all of that water and from the Earth 's core itself. The universal energies around this Earth affected it in such a way that things began changing. Some of the water subsided, some land started coming up, and so forth. That was to create a homeostasis and a balance in order to allow for evolution, not only of the Earth itself, but also for the plan of the evolution of the animal kingdom, the plant kingdom, and the human being. You understand? Therefore, as these things changed over time, the Earth needed to change as well in order to strike its balance. If Earth were all water, it would be very difficult to have human beings living upon it. We could certainly go into long histories of the creation of things, the changes in the atmosphere, and in the land—and all of that would be very good if we were writing an anthropological, archaeological, or geological book. That, however, is not the book we are writing. Therefore, we will attempt to keep it as focused as possible on that which is meaningful in terms of balance.

So if one were to look at a time, let us start with when man (as you know man to be now) began to roam the Earth. There were things that began to change then, on the Earth. The foliage and other things that grow on the Earth were placed there for human consumption, for human medicine. Everything was present that needed to be present at the time.

As man began to procreate more and began to learn different things, it impacted the environment in a way that (and we are not talking about your current environment; we are still way back in the ages) the environment had to continually change and adapt in order for there to be a homeostasis or a balance between man and Earth. You have your sun and moon that are a part of what brings balance to that, which is on the Earth. Therefore, it is not just what is on the Earth but also the influences around the Earth.

When there was a natural order at one time, the Earth had an almost-seamless balance. Some of that can be seen in the different tragedies that occurred at different times. For instance, when an entire species of animal or an entire tribe of people was wiped out, that was the Earth balancing itself. There are times when that occurred because of things that were done that impacted the environment or the Earth in a negative way. When that occurred, there was a need for balancing in order for the Earth to sustain herself. It is the same as a dog that has fleas upon its back, yes? It scratches the fleas, and it shakes them away, and similarly, so does the Earth. *[Humor in tone.]* Not that we are comparing you human beings to fleas, mind you. This is merely what you would call a metaphor in your language. Therefore, all things start with balance, and all things return to balance.

A lot of what you have seen over time and what you are seeing now specifically is that what has happened is that humans have pro-created at such a high rate, your industry has built at such a large rate that the waters and air are being polluted. Then you have your larger cities where you are putting building on top of a building on top of a building, and people on top of people on top of people in this small place. And it is affecting the Earth! Although if one were to ask a scientist, perhaps they might say, "Well, the Earth balances itself in the center because it is round." Which, ultimately, in one sense of it, is true, but it is not just at the center that it balances. Sometimes it needs to shift; sometimes it needs to do other things in order to find a homeostasis.

So if you have in one place filled with so many people and buildings and in another place you have less and yet in another there are none, what's happening is that you have these various weight and the subsequent impact is unevenly distributed. Since the Earth is designed to be fully balanced, what begins to happen is that all of these things affect the Earth and the Earth's core. Then everything that is in or on the Earth also affects the atmosphere. It in turn affects the weather; the climate itself. Therefore, what you see that is beginning to happen more and more is that there are areas that are beginning to have storms that are not the usual storms that are experienced there. In areas where they do not generally have certain types of weather or certain types of storms, they are having them because, again, it is the Earth attempting to balance itself. So there is this other piece of a principle that fits into the part that is the "opposite," if you will. Many people talk about opposites in terms of a perspective of things; for instance, you have day and night, you have hot and cold. So it is that dualistic thing, and that creates a balance, you see? If it were daytime all of the time, well then, the trees would burn. There would be too much sunlight. Without the moon, the tides would not ebb and flow the same, and the oceans would dry up. On the other hand, if it were dark all of the time, then many of your plants would not be able to live, yes?

Therefore, within this principle of balance, the "cause and effect" of it creates a need to find that balance again, to find that homeostasis. Balance contains those opposites, the light and dark, the hot and cold, the rain and snow. Opposites also apply to what people would deem to be the good weather, the bad weather, yes? The good, the evil—all of that. And all of those opposites in nature are oftentimes translated into the human perspective, right? So you are mimicking nature when you talk about the light and dark of people or light and dark spirits or whatever. Everything starts from . . . *everything*, originates from nature. Every living thing. And let us also say that every thing is living. Everything comes from nature. *You* come from nature because nature is about what is natural. You understand? So we will pause for a moment to have you steer or direct as you see fit based on what we have shared thus far.

YVES: So far, so good. I do not have any questions.

THE COLLECTIVE: We would like to take this to another place, if we may.

REBECCA: We are going to go around the corner with this a little bit. Taking poetic license, so to speak. Many of you of late are being drawn to, called to, or pulled to more natural surroundings, correct? Part of that is because of your own need for the simplicity and the connection because your people are missing that, you see? Many people are walking around feeling dead inside. So much so that they no longer even recognize they are feeling it. However, there is a need for that connection; there is a need for balance to be struck for that relationship to be created with nature. So there is a natural ingrained part in the human being for connecting in that way, but for some of you, it is closed off. In addition, as you are moving forward on this path and you become connected with spirit, you become more connected with the Earth and with the natural rhythm and order of things. The other thing that is happening is that nature is calling you out. You understand? There is a need for this, as a part of nature's balancing.

You see, nature does not have only one way to balance. And it prefers not to destroy itself. Just as human beings have a natural survival instinct, the Earth does as well. And so this is its way to attempt to create that balance. To start out by getting you out there, having you connect more with it. As many of you can probably attest that the more of that you do, the harder it is to come back to this other world, yes? Because it seems so sterile, and at times it is as though you are standing at this subway station watching the trains and the people run by, and you feel as though you are just looking at a movie instead of being in it or a part of it. That is because even before you are aware of it, you begin to entrain yourself with the natural rhythms of nature. Therefore, it becomes more and more difficult for you to thrive in the hustle and bustle in these built-up places. There is also another need in calling you forth for this; it is also to begin balancing out the land. You understand? Ideally, the more of you that are doing this that then return to the busier world, the more people you reach and can, in turn, bring back with you to nature.

Then there is this whole movement of building more community that sustains itself, yes? A community sustains itself on the land that sustains itself through its relationships and that creates its own sort of "consciousness," if you will. That consciousness then assists in also "raising"—words are very limiting— not so much the consciousness of the land but awakening it in a louder way. You understand? Therefore now, we realize that for most people on this path, if this draw is there, it can create quite a conundrum at times. You cannot all just pack up and run away to the mountains; well, you could. Obviously, to do that right away can often be extreme, and you then create difficulty when it need not be there. What we mean by that is that you are developing this symbiotic relationship with nature, and the more that you feed that relationship, the more natural the transition would be. It would be as though you were moving from the desert to your Ice Age place, you see? It would be quite extreme, and your survival rate would be very low. Just as when we are working with all of you on this project, we certainly do not zap you all of a sudden with the energies, yes? Although at times, it may feel as though we are. However, there is a somewhat slow insertion after insertion after insertion of our energies; and similarly, that is what nature is doing. In addition, you also need to understand, it is not just nature merging into you, but it is you merging into nature. So there is an exchange that is occurring; there is this constant flow occurring between man and nature. Moreover, as you become more accustomed to it, then you will be able to listen more to what it needs in addition to what you need when out in nature.

However, sometimes well-meaning people that want to move out to the woods just begin to grab what they can to construct, yet they do not always listen to what the land wants. What does it want to offer, and how does it wish to offer that? And so as you are in nature more, you begin to develop a clearer understanding of the exchange between you and it, you see? Some people on your Earth still understand this exchange. And when we say nature, we are speaking also about the animal kingdom, yes?

Perhaps moving to a place that is filled with your favorite—bears may not be the best idea! [*Rebecca is teasing Patti, who has a bear phobia.*]

To begin with, if it is an area where there are so many of them, they are not accustomed to connecting with human beings anymore, you see? And so it is important to find the place where animal, plant, mineral, water, and human can live together in harmony, you see? There are some places in very small pockets of your world now where there are still some communities, or we believe your word is tribes, that still live in such a way that they are balancing the ecosystem. There is a balance in their living and getting what they need to live, but they do not annihilate other things in *order* to live. You understand? They do not take more than what they need. There is such a connection with the natural world that even when they are hungry, if there are certain animals whose population is dwindling down, they will not kill or hunt those animals, you see? This is something that has been learned over time because, again, they know that, ultimately, if the species were to become extinct, then in future generations; they would not be eating at all. Therefore, they come from a place of not only thinking about the now, although their day-to-day life may be filled with tasks for daily survival, they also think ahead. They think about what they are leaving behind for the future generations. Moreover, they act as stewards of the land. To protect it not only because it is sacred—all of life is sacred—but again, to protect it for generations to come. They understand the importance of working within the natural balance of the world. However, it happens in such small pockets that, unfortunately, what has occurred is that the Earth has to "shake its back," so to speak. It needs to cleanse itself, to clear itself. That is partly why you are seeing more or an increase in global climate change, as well as what you refer to as catastrophes in this world.

UNCLE: It is essential that those of you who are hearing the call really listen to it. We understand that these changes take time. However, some of you have already been chosen, have already contracted. Some of you may have contracted before coming into this incarnation of yours, and some of you may contract once you have gotten to a certain place in your growth here on the earthen plane. Therefore, you have a responsibility to heed that call. Just as you heed the call of what calls you spiritually. This is also a call. Eventually, for some of you, this call will become more a demand at some point. Again, we are not saying that you must go and live in a cave somewhere, although it could be of benefit in many ways, if some of you would like to. But there are not many cave dwellers in the Northeastern United States, where those of you seated before us currently reside. Really, this area is not set up well for cave dwelling; there are other types of climates that are far better for that. In the Northeast, you have mountainous regions, valleys, and all of that; and so living in nature would be designed differently.

We realize also that there may be what we would reference as human comforts that you might like. Spirit and nature are not necessarily averse to that. Perhaps building something to have shelter when you are in these more natural places would help assist you in going to that place more often. Becoming more connected with nature is now one of the necessary tasks for some of you humans. It is plan A, if you will, for the Earth to find its homeostasis again. Of course, it is not going to happen completely within your time of being here as the individuals that you are currently, yes? But over time, as you move back into this way of living, there is this opportunity for you to start—we like the word movement—to start a *movement* to return to that way of living. In other words—

GRANDFATHER: We do not wish for you to just go and hide away in the mountains, you see, because, then, when you die off, well, then, that will be the end of that! What we wish instead is that when you go into the mountains and the valleys, you still reach out to others to bring them with you. To teach them of the ways you have learned. Some of you will learn ways from different spiritual traditions. Others of you will learn from nature itself, from the spirit of nature.

UNCLE: Ultimately, all of these ways are useful, as long as they are respectful of the Earth, then it does not have to be one way or the other. You understand?

One thing that is also important to note is that the power of nature is much greater than the power of an individual human being. Therefore, it is best to subscribe to plan A. Not only because of the impact of that or the balancing that can occur from it, but for those of you who have offered yourselves in service to the universe, it is important to note that you cannot offer yourself in one way and then close the door on another, yes? So this is also the call for some of you.

Many of you nowadays reference this as advancement of civilization, and certainly, it has had its advantages from the human perspective. One problem of that is that people are living longer and population is increasing, more people that could not have children before are having children now. Therefore, *people* are interfering with the natural order. Therefore, nature has to "up the ante," so to speak, to attempt to protect itself, to protect others who are here, to be sure that people are able to have enough sustenance. Another problem is that because of this increase in population, and now your scientists, many of who deem themselves to be gods, are now creating and engineering foods to feed the increase in population, which is *not natural*.

THE COLLECTIVE: With the increase in the amount of people, there is an increase in food supply and demand, though the supply is not available everywhere. Farming is not natural anymore. And all of these things are affecting the Earth. All of these things affect the natural order of the animal kingdom. Some of your animals are not even fully naturally born animals; they are not born of nature. They are born of scientific experiments. When the animal kingdom is in nature, even that is part of its balance also, you see? Therefore, it has the *energy* of nature in it. It has the energy of the sun and the moon. In addition, when one that eats from the animal kingdom partakes of that when it is in its natural state, then it is a great offering. Then it is serving the body. However, because your bodies were also designed to live in harmony with nature with the animal and plant kingdoms, when you take something that is no longer in a natural state; you see your bodies become riddled with illness.

Illness, of course, has always existed; that too is a part of the natural order or the natural balance of things. But now you have created false medicines. All of the medicine that was needed for all of the disease was upon the Earth. But now, you see, now there are new diseases because there are new things being introduced;

however, nature, in its ultimate wisdom and balancing act, is also creating things to treat that which is new. However, many people are not looking for that; they are too busy in their sterile labs looking to create toxic chemicals to treat toxic things, and you see here again is where the opposites fit in: you cannot treat toxic with toxic. Where do the toxins go? Now you have doubled your toxins, and what becomes of that? Well, nature needs to do something else about it now so it re-forms into yet something else.

We will pause for a moment and see if you have queries about that which we have thus far shared in this small segment of our dissemination.

YVES: Again, so far, so good; everything is flowing quite naturally.

[Long pause.]

THE COLLECTIVE: Just as there are some species that are going "extinct," if you will— that is your term, yes, "extinct"—there are also other species that are rather overrun, yes? And that upsets the order or the balance of the Earth, and the universe.

[Pause.]

We spoke earlier of human perception and human behavior reflecting nature. We would like to touch on that a little bit at this point. Just as there is disorder within the natural order of things and the need—and again, let us also say that although there is an imbalance, there is enough of a balance attempting to work itself out currently. Nature is very powerful, much more powerful than human beings are. If it were that unbalanced, then we would not be sitting here with you now, and you would not be sitting before us. Perhaps we might be floating around in the ethers together, discovering other worlds. You understand? And while certainly we are not averse to that, for the time being, we will enjoy your company in this way.

We would now like to speak on that which we referenced about human perception and behavior reflecting nature. Because you live in a world within the illusion, there becomes a duality, you see? It is that duality that creates the balance. When you were children, perhaps you remember your teeter-totters or seesaws. When a child sits on one end and one child sits on another and it is meant to go up and down. One pushes off, one goes down, and one goes up and so on; and perhaps you would even try to find that center of balance and see how long you could stay there balanced. But when one moves just a little more or puts a little more weight on, then what happens is that it tips the other way. That is very much how not only nature but also human beings balance. Because the truth is that in order to have a full human experience of all things, you must walk through those opposites in order to find balance. We are attempting to find some different examples for full understanding for all of those who are reading this. There are some medicines, and we do not mean the herbs themselves, but more "medicinal teachings" that are taught that if something is cold, then one must introduce "medicine" that is warm, yes? So that that which is missing, you are inserting in.

There is a poet, a philosopher, who is a favorite of this vehicle who has written, "Your joy is your sorrow, unmasked" (Gibran, 1923). In other words, you cannot know the feeling of one without having experienced the other. There are many in the world now saying, "Well, it is about not experiencing either joy or sorrow." They have messed up the teaching a little bit. It is about being able to experience both and come back to the center. So it is not that one should not have; why, what would be the point in coming here, in your physical body, were you not to have the full experience, the tactical feelings of things, and the emotional rush of things? There would be no point! Again, you would just be floating out here with us. Even we, on the level that we are at—although we must say not quite as extremely as those of you—we may emote. What occurs with us is that the energy resonance changes—which is also what occurs with you, it just does so differently. When we have been of service, or when we are seeing that some of the things occurring are helping humankind, there is what you would call happiness or joy. It is not quite that, but what happens is that there is a—within our energy—frequency; there's a "starburst," if you will.

REBECCA: There are those of you who have walked a certain way through the world, there are many who turn around and walk back to their old ways, they return out of fear. It is then that our energy becomes dimmer. You understand? Therefore, that is really the same thing that happens within you, with your energy. However, the energy is moving through different "channels," so to speak. You understand? When one is expressing sadness or grief, it can be felt in your physical vehicle, yes? You may feel emptiness here *[gesturing to heart]* or here *[pointing to solar plexus]*, and you bend over from the pain of that. That is the sort of energy that is dwindling, you see? When you are filled with joy and love, you feel your heart start to palpitate. When you fall in love right, especially as children, when you fall in love and you see that person, you get those butterflies in your stomach, yes? So again, it is that surge, that "starburst" that occurs within your vibrational frequency.

We understand we are jumping back and forth, but it is a very difficult task to go in one straight line because everything blends into the other. You understand? And so going back to the idea of community and that when you are living and functioning as a community, the community takes it all on together, yes? There are community rituals often that are for joy, that are for grieving, that are for all of these different things. And so it magnifies the emotion initially, but what happens is it also helps it to cycle it through faster, you see, because there is a huge burst or there is a huge dwindling that then can be refueled or refilled by the universe.

Here is one very important thing that we need to say about the order or the balance in the human beings, and its reflection in nature. That is, nature is doing its own weeping or its own star-bursting. However, it is done in a different way. There is growth, and there is depletion. We do not wish to ever attempt to intentionally contradict, counteract, or speak lowly upon teachings because, again, all teachings have a purpose. All teachings are a piece of something that leads to the next thing. Whether it is in two days, two years, two months, two lifetimes. You understand? It all leads there. But the purpose of this book is to bring those of you that are ready to go to the next place in humankind's journey of the evolution of the spirit.

Do not *ever* believe that to have feelings—to have desires, to have any human emotion—is wrong or that it is not spiritual. Now, of course, here is where we get back to the balance of things in the natural world. If you were to have too many bears in the woods and very few people—why, the people would be eaten up! Likewise, if you have too much anger that you just hold on to, then it is going to block the joy, the exchange, or the compassion. Additionally, if you have desires that become your sole focus that keeps you from other things or harms other people because it has become greed, now *that* is a different story altogether. But if you are walking in them and finding a balance—and again, it doesn't mean that you must always have perfect balance—sometimes you go a little bit overboard here, right? Then you have to make up for it in other areas. So again, that brings us back into the principle of cause and effect, yes? "Feast or famine," if you will, that creates that balance. It is never an "exact science."

There are always ways that balance is being adjusted—just like with the Earth. These things must occur within the human and should be embraced and supported. You see, we will talk of the *[humor in tone]*—let us clearly state that it seems perhaps that we're always picking on the North American area here, and it is not because of anything other than . . . well . . . the truth. *[Laughter.]* That what has come to be is that there is too much removal from recognition of emotions and desires. That is part of being human . . . of being the spirit in flesh, you see? It seems to have been beaten out of you, if you will. For some of you, quite literally. You have become cold to one another, and you walk around trying not to notice the suffering of others, yes?

You often look away because it might touch on your own suffering. You like to think or pretend that there is no suffering. Because there is some honorable thing in your culture, in your society here, about pretending that everyone is happy. However, many more people need to take these toxic chemicals in order to keep pretending that they are happy, and if you look at them, it is as though you are looking at a stone wall.

[Long pause.]

There is a question that the mind of this vehicle (Julie) had spoken out loud to those of you seated here (after she had listened to a dissemination of ours), which was, "Why is it that now, if spirit has always been here and there has always been a call from spirit and nature, then why is the call different now? Why is that? If community is what is important, then why is it that people are being asked to leave everything behind to go elsewhere?" This is an example of that.

The answer is because that which they have become anchored to or attached to has become toxic to them as well. For many of you, this anchor was born out of your intention to have a stable foundation, a way to build your castle in the sky so to speak. When we reference your castle, we do not just mean buildings; we are talking about who you "are" and how you present yourself to the world. Who you have created yourself to be through your seeming successes based on current societal standards, which we might add is quite warped. What needs to happen at times is you have to be ripped out away from that. Because it is the only way, it is that leap, right? The leap off of the mountain, the dive into the water. For some of you these things need to be ripped away Otherwise, how do you demonstrate to others? The ripping away is painful, yes, and we are not asking you to not feel the pain of it or to not feel fear or anger sometimes.

[Humor in tone.] For we know you certainly do feel anger at times, even at those of us here in the ethers. We do not take that personally; the only thing that concerns us is that when your anger becomes fuel to keep yourselves separate from us, because, again, what we are referencing is true across the board, although we are making it perhaps at times a little more intimate with the audience here. So for anyone reading this text, or who is exposed to this, there is truth in here for *him* or *her* as well.

Now, in keeping with balance, another important thing is that *[humor in tone]* not all of the people could possibly just move out into the woods at this point, yes? Because, then, all of these other things would be left behind rotting, and there would not even be enough available space in the woods for all to reside there, yes?

[Long pause.]

COMPASSIONATE ONE: We will not stay in the body much longer this evening; however, we wish to say one final thing. There are those of you who are reading this book, now, that might have time to put the book down and say, "I will get to that one day, as soon as I have done this or as soon as I have done that." But there are some of you who do not have time to put the book down and wait. You do not have time to put the teaching down and wait. We do not speak of this only from a sense of what the world needs from you. But also in terms of what you need from yourself. How much longer will you clamor about and deny who you really are? How much longer will you allow your kicking and screaming to bury your feet in the mud? To those of you who have heard the louder call—and you will know who you are if you understand that sentence—do not tarry much longer in the place of "and when . . . yes, but . . . I would if . . ." because if you were supposed to wait for all of those things or if you were not supposed to do all of these things, you would not hear the louder call. For that call exists in a dimension, in a place that not everybody can access. Its voice is heard by those who are meant to hear. And, its voice is your voice. Therefore, you are only turning your back really on yourself! Yet you sink your feet down in believing that it is what you want to have, this way or that way. *[Speaking very softly.]* You made the call—so answer it. *Answer it.*

PRINCIPLES OF CREATION AND ABUNDANCE

September 5, 2007 – Yves was recording and directing questions. This session was seventy-five minutes in length with no breaks.

THE COLLECTIVE: In starting, we would like to talk a little bit about what happened the other evening. This should be included in the text.

On the other evening, when you were in the sacred environment [note: spirit is referencing the Grafton Peace Pagoda in Grafton, New York], there were experiences that this human (Julie) had regarding the seeing of energies around the physical hands. You were in an area where there was assistance that was given with that occurrence; however, what was being viewed was not only energy that is around the physical body but also energy that can be drawn on, to create, you see?

This was, more or less, for display purposes, to demonstrate the ability to move energy and the ability to create things. The physical demonstration was not only for this vehicle to experience, but also for us to be able to talk about during tonight's session.

There were also other lights and energies that were seen. She often refers to them as nature spirits or fairy folk. You were, in fact, in an area that had a little more of that type of energy around it because you were near the place where there are different herbs grown and used for consumption and medicines. Those types of magical beings and energies are around to assist with the "strength of the medicines," if you will. The lights of the fairy folk drew her attention and her focus in so that she would look at her hands and watch the movement of that energy.

This was to demonstrate to you all the boundless energy that exists, you see? It exists not only around the physical human body, but also it exists around you all the time. There is constant, continuous movement of these "atoms," if you will, of this light, this energy.

We have spoken before of how each thought creates, yes? Consider this physical demonstration that she was experiencing, of that which moves through the ethers. These particles, as they attach themselves to her hands, are the very vehicles, the very same things that attach themselves to thought forms. Thought forms carry their own energy as well. When the particles attach to the thought forms, they carry the thought forms forward. This is, in part, to give a more concrete explanation of what we mean when we say that thought creates things. Even when thoughts are creating things that only stay in the ethers, you see, it does not always manifest in the physical realms, dependent upon several influences.

One factor is the amount of thoughts that build into that, as well as the emotion that accompanies the thought. Emotion carries more power to create, yet can also weaken the actual thought form. Also, when emotion is released out into the ethers, it is met by your higher self in addition to other influences that may be working with your higher self. Therefore, whether or not it manifests itself physically, at times, it has to do with your path and whether or not this "intention" is meant to manifest now.

And so these particles surround and weave through the particles or the energy that is your own soul personality, or your "auric field," if you will. When we say "your," we are speaking in generalities regarding the human being. So these other creative energies or atoms or molecules are spinning around your own personal atoms or molecules all the time, you see? With any thought that you have, these particles sweep up that thought form and carry it. When there is another similar thought form, it sweeps it up again and brings it to the same destination. Now, let us say you have different thought forms or other fears that then get swept up in the energy and are "brought into the mix," so to speak.

So one of the other obvious principles that would come into effect is that if you have X amount of—or let us say, you have thirty-two billion thought forms of one thing and thirty-one billion thought forms of another—if they conflict, then it doesn't coalesce, and therefore, it doesn't come down into your physical reality. Because as this energy creation begins coming down to manifest, these others over there that are conflicting are trying to manifest at the same time, you see? You may see bits and pieces of the manifestations; however, it cannot manifest fully. If, for instance, one were to put forward thought forms around their wish to purchase a new home, they have put those thought forms out there and they are attempting to move toward that through physical action as well as creating it. However, if, on the other hand, they also wish to start a new business, and they then send the creative thought forms in that direction, then there are two different focuses, you see? It may seem as though outside things keep coming in and interfering in both of them; however, this is because so much energy is focused in two different places, you see? So many thought forms and it gets bigger and bigger and bigger on each side and yet neither can actually manifest. You understand?

YVES: Yes.

THE COLLECTIVE: Now, we are speaking of this manifestation because it is important to talk a little bit about this teaching or this very popular craze of "manifesting your desires."

There are many questions such as why it works for some and not for others. If you take into account the aforementioned details of energy, one of the very basic common reasons is, is it in the highest good, and has the person asked for the highest good? If, on the other hand, a person is not really interested in the highest good, then if it does not fall into the "highest good" category, so to speak, it may still be able to be created.

There are many who are teaching the principle of creation. Now this is the "newest installment," if you will, of one of the pieces of the teachings that are ancient and true. However, just as your hatha yoga, your exercise yoga, is but one aspect of yoga, this too is only one piece or aspect of sacred teachings. It is easier to accept a teaching such as this because it means for the human being that they can get something back, you see? We have talked about the state of affairs currently in your world, especially in North America; there is much greed and much amassing. And unfortunately, as this teaching is being brought in, on the one hand, it helps to serve to awaken more people to the reality of energy, thought forms, and the power of creation; on the other hand, people are getting stuck there in that one aspect of the teaching, you see? They are not getting the full teaching.

As with all else, we wish not to come across as being critical or judgmental, for there are those who are learning some of this doctrine that would otherwise not awaken at all. So in meeting people where they are, for some, this is the vehicle to get them to begin to recognize that there is more than just what they see with the physical eyes. To help them to understand there is more happening. Ideally, it will bring them to a place of recognizing that there are other influences, other powers, and other things that one might define as magical or miraculous, yet this is all part of "natural law," if you will. Magic and miracles do not really exist.

One of our concerns is that earlier civilizations also followed this type of teaching in terms of creating and amassing. They began to recognize their own inherent power, but they created without having the reverence, without love for humanity, without being able to move past their own self or their own small family or own small core. What happens is there becomes an abuse of power. And what happened is the society caved in upon itself.

REBECCA: And so as people are learning that they can create, as they're learning that they can influence their lives, what's happening is that they're amassing so much that it's beginning to take away from others, you see? The true purpose of it is being lost in the excitement of being able to have what they desire and have the life that they desire, when often, the life that you "desire" doesn't necessarily come from the place of your spirit, you see? It's coming from—and this again is not always true—the place of the human being who thinks that they need to have "things" to be successful, or to be important, or to have accomplished something in their lives. Because, again, they still believe that this life is the only one that matters, that this is the only thing that exists. Therefore, often-times, the creation itself comes from a place of fear or a feeling of lack, you see?

And so when you have a huge amount of people jumping on that bandwagon of "I can create my own destiny, and I can create abundance, and I can become rich if I will it," then here is this wagon with all of these people, and where are they going? They're going to this "special" place, and what of the rest that are left behind?

While these principles hold true, what is not being looked at enough is whether this limited understanding of the principle conflicts with the evolution of the spirit and the evolution of mankind. You understand? You see, it is not bringing the masses any farther than where they have already been. There were times when, if you go back in your history books, the stories that are told in them where there were the masses of those who in Roman times were in charge, and they knew some of these secrets, and they knew some of these things, and they would amass for themselves. And there were those who were here, meaning "upper classes," so to speak, and those who were the lower classes. And what you are seeing now is even more of a separation of that. So many of your people are feeling the separation of the classes now and wanting to have more for themselves because they believe that it will bring them happiness—you see—so they're reaching for that now as well. So rather than there being recognition of the divinity of all, they are reaching for higher so that they can feel as though they are closer to the truth or they are closer to the Creation or "closer to God," if you will. And then there are those here because it is not everyone's path, you see, to have, to amass. Yes, there is an abundance of all things that are available to all, but that is not only talking about finances or homes.

One of the prime principles that is being missed or ignored is that if abundance is available for all, why do not all have it? And you see, people are questioning and asking to the ethers. What you need to be doing is looking at each other and asking that question and responding. The reason that all do not have it is because of the continued selfishness and greed of mankind, and the fear. You understand? All do not have it because too many are trying to keep it for themselves. And they are pulling and pulling and creating and creating for themselves.

COMPASSIONATE ONE: Over here, over here, and over here is just thrown away and tossed aside as though it does not matter. Because as long as that one has what they need, and perhaps they can toss some here and there and feel as though they've done something, as long as that is happening, abundance will not be available to all. The purpose of you coming here is to recognize that you are god, to recognize the god in each other and, within that, have reverence for each other.

There is a continued denial of the rights of every human being, of the godliness of every human being. You continue to destroy each other; you continue to walk away from each other, to turn the other cheek and not look because it is easier that way. You say to one another, "Oh, I do not wish to know about that for it's too painful to hear," and yet we say only when the pain gets so great in each of you will you do anything to change it.

THE COLLECTIVE: There is an old saying in one of the religious texts, "That which you do to the least of your brothers, you do also to me." And what that ultimately means is you're doing it to yourself also, you see? If you are a part of all that, then the least of the brothers is also you. We spoke earlier in the inquiry of abundance about "God turning away from God"; do you recall that? This is what is happening in your world today, and has been for some time. It has always more or less happened in one way or another, in one shape or form in various parts in various continents, and that, however, it is becoming more and more so. You understand? Yes, did you have a question?

YVES: Yes, if those who are amassing and creating all this wealth or whatever it is that they want, if it is not for their highest good, how is it that they are able to create that?

THE COLLECTIVE: You have free will. Do not be mistaken into thinking that people are born here and that their whole life follows their highest good because it does not. People have free will, and they make choices that they perhaps may decide is their highest good, but that is only their highest service to their human self. That does not make it the highest good. If people were incarnated and followed their highest good, why, there would be no need for any of you to incarnate anymore. This would have been done eons ago, you see? The individual may decide, "This is a spiritual principle; therefore, it is in my highest good." Now granted, there are some for whom it is in their highest good (to amass wealth), for they may do good works with that, you see? Or perhaps they didn't even necessarily come for good works, but it's within their karmic path. But do not be fooled; do not ever be fooled into thinking that everything happens, as it should because that is an untruth! That is merely what the human being tells itself to substantiate walking away. You understand?

Therefore, again, we—and when we say we, we are talking about the larger we, not just this group of consciousness—we that stand at the gates and stand around and watch and at times assist you humans, remember we spoke before of that we cannot interfere. We, again, depending on the thought forms that have been sent out, can nudge; we can work to bring reminders in. Additionally, for some who continue to profess their intention to serve the highest good and to turn over their will, as *that* thought form becomes larger and stronger, we have a little more room for "nudging," if you will. However, we still cannot make them do anything. It is not within our capability or the will of infinite intelligence. Because, otherwise, you would all just be puppets, you see? There are some who believe that there is something written for their lifetime and that it is always achieved—this is not true. This is not true. If only it were so simple, but it is not.

When you attempt to filter the teachings, it does not give full benefit of what the teaching is meant for, which is assisting mankind on its "evolution," if you will. There are guiding principles, guiding forces to life, which make up the teachings. Now, let us say that to any of you who are reading this right now if you are waiting for the chapter that includes full disseminations on all of the teachings: it will not appear in this book. As we have said before, we can only impart what humanity is ready to receive, which does not necessarily mean that each person who reads this book will receive all of it. But we cannot impart principles that will create only more possibility of danger. You understand?

There seems to be some other questions or thoughts that are moving through your *[speaking to Yves]* mind as we speak.

YVES: You started talking that if we have so many thoughts of one thought form, and so many thoughts of another thought form, they will interfere with each other in manifesting it on this plane. If it were just two thoughts, it would be fine; but we humans have millions of thoughts, so then how is it that one can create a thought or manifest a thought that is in their highest good? You mentioned free will; free will can get in the way because the ego gets in the way, the ego-self gets in the way. How does one get past that and manifest something that is for their highest good so that they can evolve onto the next level? You also talked about—

THE COLLECTIVE: We shall address that first as best as we can. Well, that is an easy question and, believe it or not, has a very simple answer although not always so simple to do. How does one offer him or herself? Well, one does that by being willing. By being willing here [pointing to the heart], at whatever cost, to follow the highest good. For you see, highest good is not only for one. You spoke of "their" highest good; there is no such thing as only "one individual's highest good." When one moves away from "their" highest good, they are also moving away from the highest good for others as well, you see? Because if you are all interlinked and interwoven, if you are all connected, if you came here for certain purposes, to achieve certain things, and if you are not following "your" highest good, then those around you are being affected by that as well, which means that what is in "their" highest good is also being affected. When one can find a way to offer themselves out of the sincerest heart and not out of some ego-driven desire to be altruistic or to learn the "secrets," or to master the principles, then one will be achieving the highest good. Although they will veer from time to time, there is not one of you that follow a path perfectly, you see? You must also understand that what is to be accomplished or achieved isn't necessarily written out. There is a cause, a principle, a purpose, you see? There are certain things, yes, that would be necessary for that purpose, but at the same time, it does not mean that every step that you take is already "printed out," so to speak. Most of you still, oftentimes, are seeking spirituality for selfish reasons, and of course, that is what brings you there; so we have no complaints of that. For, again, whatever gets you to the doorway, correct? Even some of these abundance teachings get you to the doorway. That is why we do not wish to condemn this principle, but what we wish to say—to those of you who would hear—is that there are many other principles that walk in tandem with that one. You understand? When the pursuit of spirituality, the pursuit of a spiritual path, the pursuit of enlightenment, continues to come from a place of self-serving and a place of this ego-driven sense of importance, or trying to amass power, generally speaking, you will not be following the highest good. Unless that is your highest good in this lifetime. That could be so for some of you. Is that made clear for those who may be reading this text, the answer to your query regarding highest good?

YVES: Yes.

THE COLLECTIVE: And you have another?

YVES: Yes, we talked about those that are "here" and those that are "there," and how is it that they stay there?

THE COLLECTIVE: When you are referring to "those," could you be more specific for the readers?

YVES: We talked earlier about the disparity between certain masses of people, classes of people, the ones that are lower and the ones that appear to be higher. The ones that are higher are all amassing and creating, and the ones that are lower are not able to—they keep reaching up, but they are not able to manifest and create. How is that possible?

THE COLLECTIVE: We did not say that they are not able to manifest and create. What we said is that some of the purpose of this is so that those who learn to manifest and create will share. That is the problem. Because some of those that are "lower," as you say, choose to come in, believe it or not, and make certain sacrifices so that the others may remember and assist—to hold them up, you see? Now again, in the human body, they may not always be aware; the mind may not say, *Oh, I remember that I came here for this purpose.* It may be because they haven't been exposed to those types of teachings. They may only be exposed to the teachings that teach that you accept your life, which also is a true teaching, you see? So another reason that we cannot go into all of them in a book is that they will totally contradict each other. Because that is the divine universal law. Nothing is static, we spoke of that; everything is fluid, and so even rules, even principles, dependent upon where you are at, can change. And over time, over centuries, over worlds, they can change, you see? In some of these inner worlds or outer worlds or other dimensions, or whatever it is that you wish to call them—which we are not prepared to get into the specifics of those tonight—some of the principles are practiced more there (in other worlds) and some of them may be different.

They may differ due to the governing laws, the governing natural law of that specific universe, or world, and how it operates.

So if you were to look at a central pole, and off this central pole there are strings, with small metal balls tied at the bottom of the string—and let us say there are a dozen or so of those (just for the ease of counting them out for you)—all of these strings are attached to the pole, all of the metal balls at the bottom are the same, but the metal balls do not "recognize each other," so to speak. So if you were to take this pole and turn it upside down and shake it, then things could become tangled, or the balls might mash up against each other, you see? They may bang against each other—that is somewhat of a very poor description of what is happening in your world. The pole is the central piece that holds all of you to it. It is the guiding force; when *it* is held and turned upside down, everything moves, you see? If one string were to be pulled out and knocked one way, what would happen? It would swing, and in the process, it may hit others, yes? So that is how what you do affects other people. Therefore, in order to keep things flowing, if this begins spinning right, and to keep it flowing in motion, if this pole is turning in, let us say a clockwise direction, and then you were to take one to hit it in a counterclockwise position, what would happen? If it is still moving in a clockwise position and yet you pull one ball out and move it the other way, what will happen?

YVES: It would disrupt the flow and eventually go back, but it will be momentarily disrupted.

THE COLLECTIVE: Yes. And you see, that can happen because *it* has free will. Mankind is very much like a child in these aspects in many ways, in using this principle that we are discussing of creation and abundance. Because, so often, it is thrown into only one compartment. What of the abundance of love, the abundance of truth, the abundance of healing, the abundance of goodness and compassion? You see? There are those teachings, yes? Why are there so many who are jumping on the bandwagon of the abundance of finances?

[Directed toward Yves.] That is a question we are asking you.

YVES: Oh, I see. Oh, that's a human . . . a human trait of trying to amass physical things.

THE COLLECTIVE: Yes. And so, you see, there are all of these other sorts of "bandwagons," if you will, but this one is much heavier than all of the others. And as long as this one is much heavier, these others will continue to be lighter. Because if you have a set number of human beings, and if you—again, let us use a small number to make it simpler—if you have 1,200 human beings and 12 vehicles, and let us say that 1,100 are jumping on the amassing vehicle, "this is how I create, this is how I get what I want, this is how I never have to worry about money again, this is how I have all of my desires: I can live in a huge house, I can buy whatever I want, I can . . . " so on and on and on and on. Where does that leave the trucks of compassion and mercy, of faith and fortitude, of reverence and goodness? Where does that leave them? Much lighter, yes? So this is creating even more of a lack of balance in your world, you see?

Therefore, it is important that you humans begin to challenge yourselves. This is where the difficulty comes in; this is where we may, in fact, lose some of you. If you wish to learn how to manifest more, here is our challenge to you. Manifest more and then give it away! Do not keep it for yourselves; use it in its highest form. Better yet, manifest love, compassion, and mercy, for that is your true nature. You all spend so much foolish time running away from it, for you fear the vulnerability of it, because you believe that people can take advantage of you. But if you practice kindness, compassion, and mercy, then there is nothing that they have taken, you see? When you get to a place of honoring each other instead of fearing each other, there will be no need to separate yourselves by walls made of riches. The desire to amass more, the need to have more to be happy will dissipate. We are rather sad to report, however, that this will not happen for quite some time. Not in the larger population.

When it is decided to attempt to manifest things, first, ask yourselves, "Why is it that I wish to manifest this? What is underneath this desire if I wish to create more income for myself? What is the purpose of this income? If I wish to purchase a million-dollar home, what is the purpose of the million-dollar home? If I wish to buy a new, faster car, what is the purpose of the newer, faster car?" Most times you will find when you really look under your answer and lift up the next sheet of paper off it, the answer below that is fear. You are never going to manifest goodness through fear. Perhaps people will like you more if you have more, you'll feel more important if you have more, you'll be able to give more things to more people if you have more. But generally speaking, those more people are your closest family and friends, yes? Or perhaps you will be noticed for bequeathing a small token to some charity or another, and then your name is up and you look important and everyone says, "Oh, look at how thoughtful that human being is," and again, it's through this need to feel important. And if you were all to recognize, truly recognize, not just in some theory or philosophy, that you are god, that you are divine; there would be no need to be recognized by others. There would be no need to feel special, for you already are. So when you begin to recognize it in someone else, you see, that is when you begin to be able to recognize it in yourself. Not the other way around.

So when there are masses that are amassing, you are on an uneven slant, and the way to even the playing field is not to have everyone else suddenly amass because now you are all living in sheer terror, and the awakening takes longer. Because, then, everyone has amassed to do what? To do what? To play gods? Because that is what you are doing. "If I have enough money and enough power, I'm likened to a god." *Well, you already are! You already are!* So the playing field must be leveled, you see? It will not occur through the means that you are using. It will not occur through sticking with merely teachings of a vehicle that brings you to a place of amassing. You understand? There must be an understanding of the purpose of some of these teachings being revealed. And the purpose of these teachings being revealed is not for some to amass; it is for those who amass to begin to share.

YVES: Yes.

THE COLLECTIVE: One exercise that we would like to offer in order to get to that place of following your highest good toward becoming more willing to serve the highest good, in a more reverent, willing way. This exercise is to choose one day; we will make this simple

142

on you, although it won't be so simple to do. Choose one day wherein every person that you cross, you meet their eyes. And you look, not at their eyes, but into their eyes. Really look into their eyes, even if you are not conversing with them. If you are conversing with them, do not use too many words in your conversation. Let there be momentary pauses between. Some people will avert their eyes—it will make them very uncomfortable. You may automatically begin to avert your eyes, and we challenge you to keep them steady and forward. And if you do this, you will begin to feel a rise from time to time, a rise of love that is not explainable, of compassion. You see, many of you will stop midstream because you're still terrified of sacrifice or what you deem to be sacrifice. You think you sacrifice some things, but you really do it in order to avoid sacrificing others, you see? For the human being is a very smart vehicle here. It can trick and fool itself like it is playing poker with itself, you see? You say, "Oh, I have made this sacrifice for the betterment," and yet you have often made that sacrifice to avoid letting go of or releasing old ideas or old things, old habits, patterns, or lies that do not suit you anymore. You understand?

Some of you will stop midstream, for as you begin to have more love and compassion that may also mean that you begin to question some of the things that you do. And once you begin to question some of the things that you do, you begin to question some of the things that you have been taught, that you believe. And when you begin to question some of those, then your whole world becomes at stake of shattering before you, does it not? Most of you just won't be willing to do it, you see? However, it does not mean that you are not able; you are all able. And ultimately, you are all supposed to, if we are really talking the highest good of all, you see? *Let your lives shatter.*

COMPASSIONATE ONE: And you will see that you still live, and you still breathe, you still love, and we still exist. Only when you drop into the depths of the pits of what you think of as hell are you able to rise to the highest heights of what you think of as the heavens. For in your world, there is duality; you cannot experience one without the other. If you are not wet, you do not know dry; if you are not cold, you do not know warm; and if you are not scraped and bloodied, you do not know the tender mercy of the angelic ones.

COLLECTIVE CONSCIOUSNESS: Now, because your world is so dependent upon this way of operating, there is a somewhat larger price to pay for some of you initially when you begin to shed some of the "human comforts," if you will. For some of you, that's financial; for others, it is whatever you use to hide behind or run away to—perhaps it is the books that you read, or the work that you do, or the television set that you sit before, or the music that you listen to so that you don't have to think. The toys, the cars, the jobs, the wives, the husbands, or whatever it is that has helped create this false sense of who you are through these things. But if none of you stopped to break and shatter this illusion that your ego mind-self has created of what makes you safe, what makes you good, what makes you "okay," then we fear that you become doomed for much longer than what we had hoped and what you had hoped also. If only you could remember! While some of you have learned this "secret" of creating an abundance of wealth and what have you, which has spawned many followers, there needs to be more of you who are recognizing the other principles and practicing the other principles to spawn even more followers, you see? To balance out the bandwagons as we mentioned.

YVES: Yes.

REBECCA: The most important thing, if nothing else is learned from this, is that truly, truly you need nothing more than what you already are. Now it's true that in your world, it doesn't always pan out the way you wish because the rest of the world doesn't follow that principle or that philosophy. But how do you get back to it if you don't stop, you see? There is not a home, a car, a man, a woman, a child, a job that will bring you ultimate, complete happiness. Because when you have each of those things, you will always find the next part of it that you need in order to be happy. In other words, you will still *want* more.

Joy is a state of being; it is a way of living and embracing life that comes just out of innocence, love, and the excitement at life. It does not mean that you will not meet challenges, for that is part of why you are here. A lot of this you will not understand, so we leave you with some questions to ponder before you move on to the next part of the book. And we encourage you not to just turn the page and start reading some more but to take some time, perhaps a day or two, and ask yourselves, "Am I joyful? Am I happy?" Look at the happiness and what you believe brings it to you, for that same thing that brings you happiness is also the same thing that brings you sorrow when you either have it no more or when it doesn't behave as you think it should. Because whatever you have around you, you attempt to possess. You cannot possess; there is nothing that can be possessed. There is nothing that you can possess. It is all a trick. If you knew you were god, would you be busying yourself playing god and trying to find a way to have more power?

Here is one other question that we ask all of you to ponder. If you really knew that you were god, that nothing could ever really happen to you, regardless of what happens to the body that you now occupy, what would you do? What would you do if you knew that no one could really hurt you? If you knew that if you are a part of God and all others are a part of God that any choice that you made *toward being god* could not hurt another person, what would you do? What would your life look like? How would you be different right now? If you knew that everything really was available to you, everything was available to you, not just money but unlimited love, unlimited mercy and compassion, unlimited and unbounded joy, how would you live? What would you do today?

So imagine, if you must, if only for a moment. What would you do? *Now do it.*

We bid you a fond adieu.

Abundance Should
Not Matter

September 25, 2006 – This session was held prior to
the commencement of writing the book. The purpose of
this session was to ask some questions of Spirit during
a time when Julie was volunteering full-time as a minister at a local church and had no paid employment. Yves
was recording and directing questions. This material
is included in the book at the direction of the Eighty-
Second Regime. They felt it was important to share the
information within the session as the principles held
within it apply across the board. Also, they felt it was
important that the reader gets a glimpse of what challenges Julie faced in spite of being a vehicle for their
teachings. This was a rather stern session from Spirit,
as they appeared very adamant about getting these
ideas across clearly.

THE COLLECTIVE: Greetings. There were
questions regarding what you would refer to as
the teachings or the work, for lack of a better
word, that this woman, the vehicle that we are
using, has been embarking upon.

The first thing that must be said in this
regard is that the most important thing for her to

remember or recall is the teachings. Regarding the current energy exchange that you refer to as "money," there are certainly those here who understand the need for money in your world. I am not saying that there will never be money to be received for this purpose; however, what I am saying is that it is a separate issue, and there should not continue to be—and make this very clear—this "bargaining" with us when it comes to the teachings. There should not be a hold on to "If this does not happen, then I shall have to do that." For as long as that kind of thinking is being held on to, there is still resistance, and there are still reservations.

When one truly believes in the purpose, when one truly believes in the *philosophy* that she *professes* to believe in, there is not only the "either/or" of believing in the creation of abundance, but there is also the place of *being* where abundance does not matter! Where going without does not matter! For you see, it is not that the universe owes her anything. This work was something that came from her own sup-plications, from her own desires, from her own intentions. Until she releases the reservations, she will continue to struggle. This is not to say that she will not receive more finances, nor is it to say that she will. It does not and should not matter, not if she is truly doing this from a place of the truth of the heart and the higher purpose of her spirit.

Many of us, who came before her, suffered much greater iniquities than this. It does not mean that we did not feel the suffering at times, but one cannot put conditions on how they believe the suffering should occur, not if they are living in alignment with *divine law, universal law,* and the law of love, which holds no owning to payback.

I realize that this comes through in a seemingly cold, matter-of-fact way. It is not meant to be cold. It is coming through stronger because of the certain force of the energy—of my individual energy concentration—as well as the concentration of the many of us and the importance of the thoughts that we wish to impart on this issue.

While it is true that abundance is available to all, it does not mean that it is true or *not true* that she is meant to have it. That is the part where she is tripping; that is the part where there is no clarity because even her decision to create abundance is coming from a place of fear—a lack of faith that we shall carry her. She lacks the understanding that even in our carrying her, if she is raked across the rocks and mud and is bloodied, it does not mean that she was not carried. This must be made clear for anything else to come clearer.

[Long pause.]

COMPASSIONATE ONE: When one comes here with a specific purpose to reconnect with the love that exists in the universe, and with a responsibility to share that love, to share that compassion, one is not guaranteed that the way it will play out is the way that they dream of. Because that is the human part; the societal part begins to put twists and turns on it.

In many of your different religions and backgrounds and scriptures, there are those who have come for this reason. Some are referred to as the angelic ones who walk the Earth, the bodhisattvas who come and help all sentient beings. There are saints, sages, gurus, and all of the many different words and titles that you may wish to apply to the intention of an incarnation. However, all of that is simply a name that has been prescribed to something, and with those names come societal responses, and you pin on that what else you believe it means.

THE COLLECTIVE: There are those who have come into this life for this purpose, and they spend their entire life not doing it; and it can happen that the moment before they leave, there is one person, one, whose life they've changed—perhaps not even by what you would measure as a great deed. So you see, you have this human idea that you try to wrap around the soul's intent, and wrapping human ideas around a soul's intent has never worked. It goes against the very nature of the soul's intent.

The very nature of the soul's intent is to enter the human form, to come into the human environment, and to move forward through the muck and mire of the forgetting and still complete its purpose. How that purpose plays out from a soul level, though, you may have one idea of what it should be like. You may, in fact, see it to be something quite different. You do not see this because your limited views and your limited mind do not allow for the wider view and the larger picture of what needs to happen.

YVES: Yes, I am trying to. These concepts have been presented as a wider view, a much bigger view. And from a human's perspective, we tend to get stuck on what we think is important, which turns out to be inconsequential. Nevertheless, you have to understand that from our limited point of view, this is a big thing for us. Not having this, as you said, energy exchange, this monetary exchange, can make things better.

THE COLLECTIVE: And so you think that now you are educating me?

YVES: I'm sorry. Again, you see I do realize where I am. I do realize that I am nowhere near where you are. I do realize that and so . . .

THE COLLECTIVE: And so the way of getting there is to release and let go of these ideas because, again, you keep saying that in this world, you believe certain things, but that does not make them true. Therefore, rather than try to assist me in seeing it from your point of view, what I am asking is if you are willing to see it from the true point of view.

YVES: Yes.

THE COLLECTIVE: Then what is necessary, and granted we know that it is not always an easy task, is rather than saying—and this is common to many of you—"Well, Spirit needs to understand that while money is not important there, it is important here," what we are saying to you is no, it is not.

For part of the dive into deeper faith isn't trusting that you'll get more money, that you will acquire more things, but is entrusting that without any of these things, you *still exist*, you still survive. I do not mean survive only in the sense of staying alive in this world, for even if you lose everything and lose your life, the result of it is that you still exist and you still survive.

Walking on this path, you come up against ideas and ideals that you have held on to and that which society supports. And what we say to you is that society will continue to support them, and will never change any of them, if some of you do not show—if some of you do not prove—what is true. As long as you have this anchor over here that you believe keeps you safe—whether it's money, material possessions, jobs, or people in your life—and that, in your forgetting, you believe creates, "I am this and I am that, and I have this and I have that," the more you move away from what you *truly* have and who you *truly* are. Because all of that which you cling to must be knocked to the side. It is the same as when all the fancy jewels, pottery, gold, and silver had at one time been knocked to the side in the temples of those who claimed to be working for God and instead took from people.

We are not saying—again, let me make this clear to you—that we are professing or predicting that she will never have anything. What we are saying is that the outcome should not matter if she is walking *truly* on this path. All of this right now is about shaking the very core of her ego, the ego-self that seeks only to destroy the spirit-self so that it may say, "I am separate. I am a unique individual." She falsely believes that all that she is receiving from the universe is something that she is receiving personally from individuals. She believes she is taking from individuals, and her ego tells her she should not do this because it will make her a selfish person, a weak person, and many other things . . . We shall let you fill in the blanks. She worries that others may go without, and it will be her fault. However, within the situation she is in, she is offering others an opportunity to believe and to have faith in Spirit and in the flow of things.

She is not taking and they are not giving; it is universal flow. And again, as long as she stays in that place of feeling bad and of carrying guilt and shame, she is taking it much too personally and thinking she is much too important—that these people are actually doing this for her. She must realize that it is not for her, that she is insignificant in the bigger scheme of things. She as a separate individual in this life—as the person that she sees with the name of Julie—is insignificant. Because she is *not* Julie. She is not this individual entity. Therefore, it is not her refusing others; it is God turning away from God.

YVES: So to be one with the universe, you have to release all material attachments . . .

THE COLLECTIVE: You have to be willing to release whatever attachments stand in your way. That which is for her purpose, her intention, and for what she says each day about where she wants to get to in her spiritual growth. Then right now, yes—release! Because you see, the ego uses the idea that she has given up everything.

COMPASSIONATE ONE: But she has not given up everything. She still has shelter, she has clothing, she has sustenance, she has friends, she has warmth, and in the heat of the summer, she had cooling. It is important to notice the gifts that life gives unto all. When one is moving forward firmly in their intention, they bring to themselves reminders or bring to themselves something else to advance them further. And when they go into the mind-place and say, "Well, yes, I want to go farther, but first, I must be able to do *x*, *y*, and *z*," Spirit needs to show the mind-self that this is not so. This is how you, in your human self, shed another layer of the ego-self. Quite often, we have posed questions to you both regarding your willingness to move forward. Always the answer, although at times it may be delayed, is a resounding yes. Then when you walk away from the questions, as the moments go by, as the minutes in your world go by and things do not come in the way you wish they would or how your desire tells you they should, suddenly, you forget about that yes.

THE COLLECTIVE: Suddenly, you are believing that if you are doing spiritual things and making some sacrifices, things should then go your way. Well, if it goes your way, then you may not get to where you desire to go. Because your way is sometimes ego-driven. And when we say ego, let me make clear that we are not referring to someone who thinks only of him- or herself, is arrogant in their purpose and intention, thinks that they are almighty, and treats people like they are less than them. When we speak of ego, we are talking about the part of you that believes you are distinctly separate from all else. The part that tricks you, although we must say you need to be tricked in order to stay in the physical body, for once the full awareness comes, you resonate at such a high frequency that the physical body can no longer hold you in its density. So some of that is, of course, necessary. However, in order to also help the physical body evolve to a higher vibrational frequency as a whole, the ego slowly begins to shed itself. This is happening with many of you in the world right now. What is happening is that within the body's genetic code, you are preparing for the evolution of this physical body, in this density, in this dimension to rise to a higher frequency, which will also evolve the form that you are in—that the soul has entered.

YVES: So, to fully resonate with the One is a physical impossibility because the frequency is so high that the solid self cannot sustain that.

THE COLLECTIVE: Yes, well, it could explode! Not that it would really matter. You see, what we are working toward—and when I say we, I include you, here, in this place—is not only spiritual evolvement but also physical evolvement, that is, the capsule that carries the spirit. In one of your religious traditions, there are those who say that, one day, there will be paradise here on Earth. They see this paradise as being some *other* place that is descending as they are ascending. Then having risen to that place, they look down and see you still in your physical form. Now they did not get this idea from nowhere, yet it is distorted. Each of you, as the human beings that you currently are, has evolved physically before and will do so again. In that evolvement, you are working toward having a more etheric kind of body. However, there is much more that must happen before this can occur. So the paradise-on-Earth comes from a truth, but when put through the limited understanding of the human mind, it morphs into something else. Similarly, that is what we were speaking of earlier when you asked questions regarding financial compensation within the framework of what you know, what you believe, and what you hold on to. You take the premise of a belief, you take the idea of those things, and you filter it in a way that serves your interest—your ego's interest. However, your ego's interest is, of course, not necessarily the interest of the soul.

YVES: Are you saying that it is the ego speaking?

THE COLLECTIVE: I am saying that, yes, it is the ego speaking, because she is deciding for herself what the work should look like. She is using the work as a hook to hang certain ideas upon. This is not to say that she has not had time to have an unobstructed view of where she is headed. Some of her view may, in fact, be where she is headed. However, to be there and putting her spin on it is from the ego-self. The ego-self not meaning that she is intentionally thinking that she is great and especially deserving, but that ego-self does see itself as separate, and believes that this is the *one* view of it. However, her soul-self that is overriding the ego can indeed see the bigger picture, informing and inspiring on a level that she is not always aware of, even though she is much more open to viewing this than many on your earthen plane today. But it does not mean that she is capable of seeing all because she is not. For as long as her eye is set here on a "goal" of how to live her life or where to get to, well then, that is a limitation on the purpose of her soul. Moreover, as long as she has her own idea and buys into the rather twisted understanding of some of the New Age philosophies, that too will limit her ability to complete her soul's intent.

There is one to whom she refers as her model, her hero, if you will. This one receives always in gratitude and joy—never in guilt and shame. For she sees that the giving is not to her personally; she sees that she is not that important. Rather, she sees that the giving is to the purpose and that some of you come here and work in this way, giving up things so she might share the teachings. Everyone is in alignment, you see, and plays a part. There is not only the either/or; there are those who have contracted to directly support the mission, and they are those whose purpose is to bring offerings of many different kinds. That is *their* purpose—to do *that*. Not willingly receiving denies them their role and takes away their opportunity to serve in the way that *they* can serve in this lifetime.

We will accept no further questions, and we bid you a fond adieu.

MORE ON CREATION
AND ABUNDANCE

This session was conducted at the end of the dreamtime series as a means of sharing more information regarding the trendy spiritual practice of "creating the life of your dreams." Yves and Patti were present, directing questions. However, they mostly remained quiet throughout the session as the group seemed to have their own syllabus.

THE COLLECTIVE: We wish to expand upon an earlier session regarding abundance. Regarding the creation of abundance and the ability of humans to manifest their desires and so on. Now, let us first say that—as you are aware based on what we have been discussing—the spirit is able to do many things that the human is not aware of. It can call many things to it, so the idea that you can create, that you can manifest such things is correct. That is, the idea and principle of creation and manifestation is also correct, along with the idea of abundance, in so much as it means that there is enough available for all. We have spoken about this in a personal way during the session "Abundance Should Not Matter." By our stand on this, and when we say

161

"our," we do not mean only those of us whom we reference as members of the sect of the Eighty-Second Regime of Light Workers. When we say "our stand," we mean the perspective of those of us who are now not in a physical body and thus are not controlled by the human ego. There is truth to this principle; however, as we have stated before, a human twist has been added to it. This teaching has been taken—which is often the case where humans are involved—and redesigned or changed in order to serve the human interest or ego.

We ask that you understand, please, that we are speaking about this in reference to how it affects the evolution of the spirit.

We are not saying that we look down upon those who practice attempting to create all of their desires and make all of their dreams come true, for we do not. However, what we are saying is, if you are interested in assisting and bringing forward the evolution of the spirit of mankind, then it is important that you understand that attempting to create and manifest all of your dreams and desires comes from the ego and therefore keeps you more anchored in the ego, you see? It is seen as a spiritual teaching, and yet when practicing this principle in this vein, you miss the true teaching and the ensuing spiritual evolvement.

Now again, as we have said before, some of you may come here to acquire things; perhaps that is part of what you have decided to do.

However, if you have decided that you wish to become more loving, kind, and compassionate, then focusing on manifesting more money and all of your other "dreams and desires" serves only for you to lose your focus on mastering these other character traits. The reason for this is that you are not going any farther in your evolution if you are taking the principle and using it only to obtain more for yourself because in essence, it is stating that you still do not feel that you have "enough." You are still looking outside of yourself by thinking that when you have the right home, car, or amount of money, then you will be happy and you will be safe. When in actuality, if you truly believe in abundance, then you know that what it means is that you also believe that there is enough available for all. That being the case, you do not have to try to hoard it for yourself. You would then understand that what is available is that which was part of the original creation.

There has always been enough, but man's struggle has been to not try to own, to hold, or take. Because in taking for yourself, you are often taking from another. One could argue that because of etheric substances more and more money or other things you desire can always be created. And in theory, that is true, but we are talking about something else right now. We are talking about the balance of the universe and the true principle of abundance.

Allow us to use an example: the animal kingdom. There are animals that eat the leaves and berries on your trees and bushes. As these things grow, they are eaten; and within the cycle of nature, they grow back, yes? There is a natural rhythm to things while at times there may be some animals that go without food when it is scarce. During these times, it is quite possible that the larger animals take more of this food than the small animals.

However, overall, there is more of a balance because that is the natural cycle of things. What has happened overtime with human beings and their egos is that they have gotten away from the natural cycle of things; and because they have gotten away from the natural cycle of things, the cycle becomes imbalanced in some ways, you see? So, the cycle may not operate or function in the same way.

Another example would be that if there were a set number of human beings, let us say four people, in your household. You purchase your groceries for your four people, but when two of them need more of those groceries, then the others do not have quite as much to eat. There is an imbalance, yes? The solution, then, is not that the two people try to figure out how to obtain more groceries than the other two who first ate more because then that is all it ever becomes: taking, taking, taking, and feeling deprived. So you set up a pattern of taking because another "took," and on it goes.

The idea is that there needs to be a way for things to become balanced again. There needs to be a way for those who took more to get back to the practice of sharing. Now, this is not an easy thing to do; however, you are certainly not going to get there if people are jumping onto the bandwagon, stating that getting more and more for yourself is a spiritual pathway. If you are practicing the complete principle of creation and abundance, then you know that there is enough for you to be taken care of. Now, some of you will say, "Then why is there so much hunger and starvation in this world?" It is true that there are many who die of starvation. Something to remember is that for one, they do not really die; this is the illusion, and the spirit still exists. In addition, they may, in fact, die, that you might look at how you contributed to their lack. There is not one of you reading this book right now that does not contribute in some way, shape, or form. So when you say, "It is not I, because I do not take from people, I do not steal," or "I donate my money to my favorite charity every month," what we say to you is that this is good. However, if you are concerned with your spiritual growth and the evolution of the spirit of humanity, then it is not good enough.

The only way for human beings to begin to truly believe is through demonstration, through watching others in action. Just as people have been watching others in action accruing things and saying, "Hey, I can do that as well." What if instead they were to see some of you taking that ability to create and using it to create more things that are positive for all? Creating true brotherhood, sisterhood, family, and community; sharing with others; and being more loving and compassionate toward others. Many people feel so much suffering, even those who have amassed much still feel suffering, yet they do not understand where it comes from, so they believe they need more things. We guarantee you that if you were to spend a week around those who acquire things and then spend a week around those who have little, those who have little will have shared much more with you. Many of you will say, "Well, perhaps that is why they have little." Perhaps. However, what they really have is much more valuable because what they do "have" can be carried forth when they leave this Earth. You cannot carry forth possessions.

We have mentioned before that when incarnating, spirit brings with it a persona and its lessons. The spirit also carries its own vibrational frequency, which may be altered while living on the earthen plane. Therefore, when you die, you are resonating at a certain frequency. It will rise up overtime; however, if you are resonating at a frequency that is just associated with material things, then it will take much longer to rise. Let us be very clear because some of you reading this will be saying, "I am not materialistic, I do not have to have fancy things. I do not have to have a Rolls-Royce or fifteen different pairs of shoes." You must understand that it is not so much what you own or have; the error is in your judgment. It matters not *how* much money you have. It is about your attachment to what you do have, whether it is a Rolls-Royce or a Tootsie Roll. It is about your belief that this "thing" is your solution. If you look to some object or thing to bring you fulfillment, then you will never be fulfilled.

There are some who are very innocent in this and do not understand the errors of the current popular practice, and there are others still who are exploiting it and exploiting you. There are some who say, "There is so much available in the universe, and when you are truly spiritual, you are deserving of all of these things, and the universe wishes for you to have it." And we say to you, *why*? Why? Because that only gets you to the place, once again, of feeling you need to own something because you are "good." Well, you are good because you are good.

We have spoken about your system and how it does not work, and soon some of you will see more and more how it is not working. Therefore, of what use would your money be if money no longer has any value? What use will your properties be if your properties no longer have any value? Additionally, who is to say that you should own the Earth anyway? You cannot own such a thing. There was a time when there were many people who were used as slaves.

People bought and sold them. Many of you are up in arms about that still, as well, you should be. However, in many ways, you all still try to do that: You try to own property, you try to own people, and you try to own possessions. The owning of people is an extreme way to attempt to awaken you to attention. We are not saying that slavery happened for that reason; what we are saying is that it offers you potential for learning. As we have said, when you do not heed the call, the call must get louder in order to get your attention, yes?

For instance, if you are stuck in a traffic jam, if you fail to notice that the light has turned green, then the person behind you may say softly to you that the light has changed. If you do not hear them, then perhaps someone may begin to yell, or another may beep their horn. Now, if you happen to have your car stereo turned on, you still may not hear them; therefore, the honking must get louder and more frequent to get your attention. If it is still ignored or not noticed, the call or the sound must get louder; it must become more drastic. Not out of any punishment, if you will . . . it is just that it is a louder call, you see?

As you are moving into this age of the change in consciousness that has been predicted and is necessary, then the teachings of this acquiring and amassing is not helpful at all. When you are serving the self only, and, oh yes, of course, you can say to yourself, "Well, no of course, I shared with my family and my friends."

COMPASSIONATE ONE: And in turn, we say to you, who are your family and your friends? If you are all one, then there is not a one human being out there that is not your family. There is not one human being out there who is more or less deserving of what you have to offer. Yet you pick and choose. We are not saying that there are none of you who practice the teaching in its fuller form; however, if you do not demonstrate that, then what will happen when all of these other things are rendered meaningless, useless, and worthless? The only thing that you bring into this world and can take out of this world is love. However, somewhere between the coming in and the going out, many of you forget that. Many of you spend your entire lives moving away from that.

[Long pause. And then begins to speak very soft and quietly.]

Here is the real "secret": to use their word. There has never been a time when you as spirit have ever owned anything, ever lost anything, or ever gained anything. This is all part of that illusion. There has never been a time when what you need—and when we say *you*, we mean the global *you*—has not been available. We also mean the global spirit of you. The global spirit of you that was never born and will never die. That *is* everything already. There is so much jealousy and rage. It is as though you are all scampering and knocking each other down to get the prize at the end. When the prize at the end is the very thing that you carry within you.

THE COLLECTIVE: You carry it within you; it does not leave you. However, the more "things" that you are carrying, the more difficult it is to see around the stuff to see that, to feel, to know, and to remember that.

[Long pause.]

Getting more does not bring you closer to any god except your own ego. Yes, it is true that you do not have to clamor about and you do not have to suffer *if* you are operating within the law of balance. When you are not, there will be suffering. Therefore, rather than clamoring for more so that even more will suffer, if you would be willing to sacrifice a little, each of you, then it could balance itself out. Of course, right now, not everyone is willing to do that. So for some, it takes a louder call, a larger statement than just blowing the horn, yes?

So, we invite you, each of you (unless you have decided at this point to throw out this text because we are "rocking your world," as you would say, and asking a little too much). Let us remind you we are not asking for anything. We are talking to those of you who are asking the universe to show you the way; we are merely responding. So for those of you who are willing, we invite you to notice the ways in which you hold on to things, to notice the places where you are still materialistic. To notice the things that you need to have for your comfort, and ask yourselves why you need that comfort. Now we are not saying that all of you should now pick up and go live out in the desert with no water, but what we are saying is that you should shed anything that is in the way of your growth. Anything that keeps you caught in the idea that you need to have things or objects to be okay.

Of course, it is true in your world today, that it is difficult sometimes to have many of these "stressors," if you will, if you have financial burdens; and many of you state often, "Well, if we had less financial burdens, we could feel more freed up to help others." That is quite a good argument on your part. What we say to you about that is that perhaps you should realize that the idea of getting rid of the burdens is not about getting more money. Instead, perhaps it is the very thing that is burdening you. Let go, just let it go. We are not saying in any way that we look down on this; what we are saying is you look up to them too much. We are not saying that you cannot own something and be spiritual. What we are saying is it is more important that you own your spirituality. That you own your convictions, that you own your truest heart, and that you serve your truest heart rather than objects.

In many religions, they speak of idolatry, and there is a saying, *"Thou shall have no other Gods before me,"* yes? What do you think you are all doing now? It would be very easy if this twist on it were real. Of course, if you go to each of the religions that say their own version of that, then you would have quite a conundrum that you are in because each of their gods is the only one god. *[Stated very strongly.]* *"Thou shalt have no God before me," means do not look at objects and other things before your own sacred soul.* If you are a part of all the trickled-down version of the divine spark, the oneness, then anything that you look to, to bring you contentment, stability, joy, or safety—that thing is being put before God. In the United States, there is a saying on your money—what is that saying?

YVES: In God we trust.

THE COLLECTIVE: Yes, we dare say this is not so. Except for when it is convenient. It is the biggest illusion. It is a great magic trick actually, played on you by those who wish to have more and more power. They have gotten you to believe that this piece of paper holds something. That obtaining more of this piece of paper is worth trampling on others, forgetting about others. Again, we wish to state that we know there are those of you right now reading this text saying, "Oh, but I have never done such things." We challenge you in that because even if you do not directly say, "I shall step on the person's hands so they do not get this," there are other ways in which you have done that. Each time you drive through a place where you know that there are people who have not eaten and you have not stopped and fed them, then you have done it. Are there any questions or queries regarding this?

YVES: No.

THE COLLECTIVE: Then let us close by saying this: The universe is designed in perfect balance. Therefore, even with this thing that you call money, if it were still operating within its perfect balancing system, then you could have this money and all of your things and still be evolving in your spirit. However, only if it were in balance, only if it were equal.

Again, we ask you to go back and look in some of your sacred texts (and we have spoken before that in these writings, there were principles that were given, and then man twisted it to get what he wanted out of it). If you look in these sacred writings, you will find little pieces of these principles that we speak of, and that holds true. Of course, there is a lot of sorting to do and moving things out of the way to find them, but they are in all of them. Not all of them explain why; they may just have been written as rules, and they tell you there is punishment if you do not follow these rules. However, again, incorrect words were used. Even we do not have the exact words. However, the idea of punishment comes from the idea of the karmic balance of things. If principles are not followed, then things will fall apart. That, karmically, because balance needs to occur, there will be imbalance.

You have everything that you need right here and right now to correct all of this. *[In a very strong tone.] You could correct all of it in an instant.* However, too many of you are still too greedy, afraid, selfish, and doubtful. The balance of the universe means that a vacuum must be sealed off because it needs to circulate; it needs to move in constant motion. Life gives unto life, the universe gives unto the universe, and God gives unto God. So when you are turning away from one, you are stopped; it is an obstacle, and you are blocked. You are turning away from God. God is turning away from God, and how can you? Many of you claim that the world has turned away from you. If this is so, then the answer is not to turn away from the world. The answer is to turn around and face it so that when it comes back around, you might join it in the cycle, in the natural rhythm of things, and within *[stated very passionately] the absolute perfect design of balance.*

If there are no further queries, we shall take our leave and allow all of your vehicles to rest, yes? We thank you for your continued efforts on the behalf of this work, and those of you seated, we are asking that you take heed of the words we have spoken. Try them out, see for yourself if what we say is accurate; and when you see that it is, be sure that you pass this on to others—not our words, but your experience.

YVES: Yes, we will.

THE COLLECTIVE: We bid you a fond good evening.

THE NATURE CONNECTION

Session was held on September 26, 2007. Yves is present and recording. The session was 90 minutes in length. There had been a few weeks' gap between sessions due to scheduling issues.

THE COLLECTIVE: Greetings. We are pleased to be in your company this evening as it has been some time since we last sat together, so to speak. The time, however, in your world does not ever go without some valuable process. Some of this time has afforded an opportunity for "some of the meat," if you will, of the information to be better digested by both of you in terms of the teachings thus far. We wish to speak a little bit about that tonight, as well as about the lack of reverence in your world and how that originated. The origin of this lack of reverence was when the human race began moving away from following its own rhythms, which were in tune with the rhythms of nature. Earlier this evening, while looking at a picture in this dwelling place, you were referencing the beings that this vehicle (Julie) has access to—this picture and these beings are only a small part of the many different parts of nature that human beings have forgotten. Now, of course, there are many teachings from various traditions that teach different ways of getting in touch with these beings and with nature itself. One of the most important parts of doing that is allowing the rhythm—"the heartbeat," if you will—of the Earth to move through the physical body. Similar to the beat of a drum, where when one is beating on the drum, if you listen long enough, you feel yourself begin to move to that beat in response. Another example is when this vehicle sits down to channel our energies; there are times when her physical vehicle moves as our energy fluctuates. It is partly her physical body adjusting to the frequency, but it also is that it begins to move with the rhythm of the universe—because all of her other faculties are not in use; therefore, she is more open to it.

In this age of so-called advanced technology in your world, people have begun to use this technology as a guiding force; thereby, it has become more or less a higher power. Certainly, your technology has its benefits, but one of the downsides to this is that it has assisted you humans in moving away from the natural "technologies." For instance, the human body is much like its own instrument—you see—and at one time, one would know what was happening with the weather, the animals, even in its own tribe or area and what was forthcoming. The body was a fine-tuned machine that followed the rhythms of the universe and noticed the smallest of fluctuations or changes in the energy, which may have been caused by weather patterns or other things occurring, such as discord within the community and so forth. Your human race, at this point in time, is so caught up and relies so much on technology for its answers that it has shut down this gauge that it so often relied upon. When you are growing up, you are taught to shut those things down in various ways.

Your technological society, along with your religious societies, all squelch that human gauge, that human thermometer or barometer. In many religions, when you are young, you may question certain beliefs or practice out of a child's natural curiosity. A child is also, very often, much closer to the truth than the adult. When you begin to question things in many of your current popular religions, the standard answer is, "Well, we do not know the ways of God," yes? Therefore, you are being told and taught to stifle those questions, those questions that come from that place in you, that barometer, that gauge that is looking around and listening to information coming in and that knows that something is missing, you see? The child that likes to go out and play in the rain and is told, "Come in, you'll get wet," or, "You'll get sick," yes? Children are naturally attuned to the rhythms of nature, to the vibrations. Very small babies, even, will cry for seemingly no reason when there is tension in the household, yes? Because they can sense it even if they have not heard someone raising his or her voice. These are the very things that are "prewired," if you will, into the human body; so when you are born in human form, you are prepared to face the world. However, through conditioning and through exposure to current technologies and sciences, it slowly begins to become a smaller and smaller part of you, you see?

When this part of you *[pointing to the heart chakra area and making a closing or crushing motion]* is closed down, the heart chakra area begins to tighten and the heart itself begins to close down, the eyes begin to close down, the mind begins to close down. Everything follows suit.

Without an open heart, how could one possibly be reverent? When we say reverence, we wish to be clear that while the humans' current understanding of the word is equal to that of respect, they are misled in this. Respect doesn't even come close to what we mean when we are referencing reverence.

[Long pause, then speaking softly.]

There was a time when you did not see yourselves as separate, when the tribes or the community operated as one. When the animals in the forest or the plains were also the same, for when they would appear, you would understand they would reflect to you some teaching or some medicine, that which you needed to take in to help you along your path.

[Long pause, then speaking back in "normal" tone.]

On this continent, there were many who were killed, who were sacrificed for the seeming advancement of society, and with them were killed many of their ways of living. Here on this continent, you have so many people coming from so many different places, from so many different countries, because you must all come together. Yet because of this, you all have many different backgrounds and cultures; and in coming together, you and your teachings all clash. But eventually, you must come to a common ground, a common understanding.

All of your religions at one time followed the rhythm. You see bits and pieces of it in your various religions. Various religions hold festivals, holidays, or have religious days that were placed in relation to the old agricultural holidays, or the change-of-season holidays—again, all within the rhythm of nature. Many of you humans have forgotten this in their collective consciousness. Humans are so frightened and try so hard to control everything around them, that they do not allow themselves to feel the rhythms of nature because they do not want to allow the seasons of their lives to occur, you see? Life mimics the seasons of nature. In life, there is always a change that occurs, a shedding of things, a dormant season in preparation for rebirth, for the full blossom and so on. And yet, you all run from it with such fear, such trepidation. You wish to not have things change; you wish to hold on to things that are no longer useful to you—jobs, patterns of living, whatever, fill in the blanks. Because something about it tells you that it is safe because it is known. Yet we say to you that when it is so well known, seemingly, it becomes less safe *if* you are talking about the spirit of evolution of mankind, of course, yes? If everyone were to stay safe, then the evolution of the spirit would not occur. It *would not occur.* If only you were able to be like the trees whose branches blow in the wind. If only you would allow your leaves to drop when they must and to cover the ground or the floor of your life, so that you could sit in the quiet solitude, in the stillness, in the darkness, and embrace it. You do not see the tree reaching for its leaves to pin them back on. Some of the scientific minds may say, "Well, a tree is not a human." That is true; however, you know, and there are others that know, that a tree still has a spirit and energy and life, yes? If that tree were not to shed its leaves, if that tree were not to sit dormant, if its life's blood were not to freeze for a time (of course, we are talking in this geographical area), that tree would not be able to live. The spirit, the life force of that tree would be choked down, and it would die. You understand this, yes?

Yet, so many of you humans still fight to put your leaves back on, still run around to turn on all of the lights in the dormant, dark season. So many people are still hearing that same voice when they begin to question, the same voice that tells them to stop. You had a conversation earlier today, with the one who is referred to as Julie in this incarnation, regarding religions and belief systems and those who are afraid to question. Some have not yet come to a place of understanding that there is a question, you see? Others know, yet they are afraid. Others still, may have begun to question, try different things, and they move forward. All of these stages, you see, are the stages of the evolution. Just as the caterpillar, in the cocoon, comes out and then becomes a butterfly. Similarly, we will attempt to explain this as best as possible for your understanding and for the understanding of the readers. While certainly there are some of you who have come here in this lifetime to move forward in that evolution, this time—this time around—some of you will do it, some of you will not.

There are others who have come, not necessarily to evolve in that way, but they are moving forward toward evolution; but it may be in smaller increments, you see? If you are all a part of each other, then the evolution does not necessarily count on every single being, being at a certain place at the same time. If you are all one, then each person is representing a part of that evolution. There are those who are here in the larvae stage, the cocoon, the caterpillar, and the butterfly, or the moth or that which has wings, you see? So all of that together makes a cycle.

Now, what does that mean? Does that mean that, as some people say, you should just all go about your business and let everyone fend for himself or herself and be on their way, and eventually it will happen? While this is true to a certain degree, there is still a certain amount of responsibility to love others enough to open up the doorway or the window for them to view what else is available to them. Therefore, if you turn your head away, then you are not truly fulfilling that part of human destiny. It is important for you—and when we say *you*, we are speaking of human beings in general—to begin to become more in tune with yourselves, first because, of course, if you cannot go at all into yourselves, then you cannot at all be in tune with nature. Of course, people who live in settings that are more natural have a little bit of a jump-start in terms of being in tune with nature. Your people, who still work in agriculture, your farmers and such people, often still can at least predict weather and those types of things, you see?

So often in your world, many of you just turn your heads because you do not want to look because you do not want to see. Because if you stop to help, maybe you will be late for your appointment, or maybe something will be taken from you. In talking of helping others, we are not necessarily talking about proselytizing so much as just being the door attendant, you see?

Being the door attendant can sometimes mean being loving or kind or compassionate toward someone who perhaps you do not wish to be that way toward. Sadly, most of what is revered in your life today is what kind of job one has, what kind of home one has, what kind of car one has, how well one's children are doing in their jobs, or if they have found a good spouse, and so on. And what of those who did not find a good spouse? Do they deserve less reverence, less respect, less love, less understanding? Your measuring sticks, your weighing machines are way off base. Again, we say this—and we wish to reiterate for the readers that when we say *this*, we are saying this not to judge you but these teachings are regarding the ways toward evolution of the spirit. In terms of that, then yes; the way that you measure success, the things that you measure as important are off base. Allow us also to explain that many times, when we hesitate, tonight as well, it's because we are carefully injecting only enough energy for the information and the words to come through without as much emotional impact to the vehicle as what she has experienced in the past. You understand? For if we were to show the bigger picture of it and put all of the energy into it right now, this physical vehicle would have difficulty getting the words translated out because it would immediately be having an emotional response. You understand, yes? Therefore, forgive us our jumping around this evening.

Are there questions that you have regarding anything we have spoken of thus far or that you feel needs clarity or more explanation?

YVES: A question that I have is how, in an environment that is not in nature, like in the urban city environment, one nurtures that essence that is within a child and keep it going, knowing that society itself will try to squelch it from one who understands that aspect of it? How does one nurture that essence in a child? Or even, well, yes, in a child, or maybe even in an adult; but the child, if you can keep it in a child, then it will be . . . it will grow.

THE COLLECTIVE: Yes, well, of course, the first thing is that the adult must be sure that that is harnessed in themselves, for otherwise, they will not know how to support that child, to nurture that connection, and to keep it stabilized. So the first responsibility of the adult, or adults, really—because it is up to all of you to do this with all of your children and each other's children—is to clear your own blockages, to feel your own rhythms, to *really* feel them, not just to know that they exist, you see? That is number one. We could tell you—and it would be wise advice—however, we realize all of you cannot move out of the urban setting and out into the country (for, of course, that would be the easiest way, yes, for there is less distraction). Again, the most important piece is if the adults around the child are tuned in, because if they are not, then how could they possibly nurture that which they do not even know? A child shows natural curiosity and wonderment. Allow the child to be curious, allow the child to explore, allow the child to question authority. Do not discipline the child who questions. In your world, again, you may say, "Oh, yes, you can question religion, but do not question me for I am your mother, and I know best," you see? So there is a little bit of a contradiction that occurs. If children are allowed to question out of their own curiosity, out of their own need to understand when they are small, they will be less likely to question in the more contrary ways when they get older. If they are taught through demonstration that their questions are valuable and valid, then they begin to build that confidence, you see? You cannot—well, if you are staying in the urban setting—for the most part, keep the child from the influences of your "average society," so to speak. But that is okay, because, you see, society is not going to change overnight even if you are nurturing this in a child. So they must learn how to negotiate this being in touch with things as well as being out in the world that is not in touch with things. You understand? When children say things about friends or angels or ghosts or this or that or whatever name they use, do not push it away as though it is nothing. For many parents do that. "Oh, that's nice," they would say. They see that as supporting as opposed to saying there is nobody there. But it is not supporting the children. To support them, move into that world with them, for they are the closest to us, you see? For they have just left us. Even if you do not see what they are seeing, be a part of that world with them as well. Ask *them* questions, nurture that connection in them. Bring them out to nature, for even in your urban areas, there is always a place to go to where a more natural setting is available. Allow them to run barefoot on the grass, in the mud puddles. Allow them to get dirty. Allow them to climb trees. Talk to them about the trees. Talk to them about the spirits of the water and all of these things. Talk to them about Mother Earth. Take them out under the night sky, and let them explore that too. No one of you will be able to do all things, but there is no one single thing, you see? There is much that must be done. You must understand when there was a time when you were all connected—everyone around was connected, so the child was brought in, and one did not even have to think about how to keep the child connected. It just was. So it needs to be a normal part of life, not a special thing, you see? It needs to be worked into day-to-day, minute-to-minute, living—and not just to the child because, again, children can see all. So if you are only attempting to teach the child but you are not living this way in your life, then what example are you really setting? Their conflict would then become even greater.

Now for those of you who are reading this book and who are saying, "Well, I am trying to get there, that is why I am reading this book, but I am not quite there yet. Does that mean I need to wait until I am there to teach my child?" Why, no, you do not have to. You can go on this journey together. You can learn together. Even that is a wonderful gift to give to a child. To say, "Hey, I don't know either. Let us look together. Let us explore this together. Let us go out and feel the Earth beneath our feet together." For this is also a statement to the child that you too are willing to be open, to be connected, to take risks.

Perhaps you have heard the saying *"to walk gently upon the Earth,"* yes? Yes. And that saying carries much more weight than what it is often given. Because walking gently upon the Earth means recognizing and respecting and having reverence for the circle of life, the rhythm of life, the rhythm of nature. It means bringing *love* in to every area and to each person that you meet. Love, as we have said before in many other sittings with you, is not an emotion. Love is an action, it is a decision, it is a way of being, a state of grace. Yet so many of you pick and choose who you will love, who deserves love, who has done enough for you to "get" your love. Well, the love isn't yours—it isn't yours! Love is the pulse of the universe. Love is the beginning and the end, the alpha and the omega. Love is the supreme guiding force.

In a later sitting, we will talk more about love and the ways that that has taken form in your world and the ways that have misled you, or the many of you in search of love, in a quest for love, or in your understanding of love.

And so one last thing that we wish to leave you all with, from this part of the teachings, is we ask you that as you go through your day, be it your seeming tomorrow or next day or on a weekend day of yours to take the time to go out to a place where there is nature and to not busy yourselves with a function in nature, such as taking a walk or a hike or planting a garden—all of which are very productive things—but for this exercise, we wish to encourage you to just find a place to go to and sit there and to be with nature. Do not attempt to make anything happen or to look for anything in particular. Just be there with nature; just sit and breathe. Anything that happens, allow it to happen. Even if suddenly a storm comes in and you begin to get drenched, allow that to happen too. Alternatively, perhaps the sun will be hot where you are sitting; allow yourself to be hot. Perhaps the greater challenge for some of you is there may be bugs swarming, yes? Allow them to swarm for they too are a part of nature. Allow yourself to feel them around you. Take note of whatever is happening there, whatever your experience is in that place—just take note of it. Notice how you feel, notice what the mind tells you about how you feel or why you feel that way. Notice when there is stillness and when there is chatter. Notice when you convince yourself you must go, and when you have done this, then sit down again and stay longer because you are right at that place, right at the doorway of truly hearing, seeing, or feeling. Then, do it again.

Are there any further questions for this evening?

YVES: No

THE COLLECTIVE: We bid you a fond adieu.

DREAMTIME FOR PERSONAL AND SPIRITUAL GROWTH

June 19, 2010 – Yves was present and on the recorder and directing inquiries. This was the first of our "marathon" sessions at the direction of the group. The reason they gave us for this was to assist us in getting the rest of the material done, in quick order, for the book. Additionally, they wanted Julie to become more accustomed to rapid entry and departure of the energies. This was a difficult session for her, and she complained of quite a bit of discomfort from a headache during the first break. Her headache continued for some time, even after the session was over; however, the Eighty-Second Regime advised us both that this would not last as it was merely a reaction to the rapid change in her own vibrational frequency. This session was three hours in length not including breaks.

YVES: Welcome. We are here and ready to participate in this first marathon session, and we understand that you have your own agenda for this session that you will address, and so we are ready to listen.

THE COLLECTIVE: We are pleased to be seated before you once again. Tonight, we will be talking about dreamtime and what happens when one is dreaming.

We will cover different standard scenarios of what occurs during the dreamtime. Such as what is happening with the consciousness; what it does, where it goes, how it reads and interprets dreams; and so on.

We will also be talking about the ways in which human beings can utilize dreamtime to become more aware during dreamtime. We may even give some pointers on ways to direct your dreamtime. So that is our loose syllabus—if you will.

We do understand that during our discourse, you may have queries regarding those things that we speak on. We ask that if you have a query about anything we have spoken of, if it is not clear, you ask it then when we pause. If there are queries that come out of other ideas of things, then we would ask that you jot that down and come back with that after the "commercial break," if you will.

Dreamtime is a very sacred and important time, just as waking time is a very sacred and important time. And pardon us, we will perhaps use the word *time* a lot right now in an effort to be more efficient, but we will not keep repeating "although time does not exist," as we often do. This phrase is used for your own understanding. There are a few different scenarios in dreamtime that we will cover.

There is your average "mundane" dreamtime; others have talked about it, as well, but they tend to give it less importance than "astral traveling" dreamtime. However, we wish to talk about it because it is important to understand what is occurring. It is in dreamtime that most people (who are what you would call your "average Joe," for lack of a better word) would recall more of these dreams than other dreams. This does not mean that more of them occur, specifically; however, it could mean just that, depending on where they are in their spiritual or life path. These are the dreams that your scientists often refer to. They are the chicken stew of the odds and ends of your day. The things you are concerned about. There may be pieces of things, and none of it makes sense. It is often referred to as a time when the psyche is working through things. Some say it is a time when there are just random flashes of the day's events. Now, the human brain—let us start with the human/earthen aspect—is like a machine, a computer, and it does not do anything without reason. Signals are sent, things occur, so when you are having these "mixed platters"—if you will—of bits and pieces of things that do not seem to add up or make sense, what is happening is that you are processing things that have occurred. You are processing them not only in a physical way but also, and this is important, as an "observer."

So, it is as though you are watching things unfold. The reason for this—we will attempt to be as succinct as possible—is that it assists the human being in seeing things clearly.

Now some of you reading this book might say, "The dreams do not seem very clear." You may have a dream about putting a cookie in your dryer, which may seem quite an interesting thing to do in your world, wouldn't it? What we would say is that there may be bits and pieces that are being released, but you need to observe them as they are released. The part of your consciousness that is your "waking consciousness" gets a bit "numbed," so to speak, when you go to sleep. Mostly because your physical eyes are not open, so you are blocking out other distractions. Another important thing to remember is that when you are dreaming or during those times that are referenced as REM sleep, the time continuum is different; even your scientists have discovered this. Meaning, as things move through your psyche during dreamtime, they move at a much more rapid pace than in the normal waking hours. This is one of the reasons your dreams seem to be a mishmash. Oftentimes, you do not bring the awareness of all of it back with you, but it is not always the case. At times, it is the letting go of that which you are still holding on to that should be released. Now the human being does not necessarily wake up and say, "Well, gee, I have learned so much about myself this evening," but they have begun the process of letting go. These types of dreams are common in most of your nights because they are the preliminary dreams, especially for those who are not adept at more controlled or lucid dreaming. Just as you are beginning to fall asleep, the mind is still working, so you are releasing thoughts and stress just like in meditation. In order for the mind to relax and let go of stressors, you must first allow the distressing or distracting thoughts to be present as they arise. This type of dreaming is another level or layer where things can be released. Therefore, as you move through the evening's sleep, your other consciousness (the part connected in the ethers) becomes more awakened; and then it sets out on a course of action. This first part is more con- voluted and difficult to explain than the other parts of dreamtime that we will discuss. So for the ease of the readers, is there a need for clarification?

So then, we will be moving along to other aspects of dreamtime. If that was clear?

YVES: Yes

THE COLLECTIVE: There are times when your consciousness—and we wish to use the word consciousness for the ease of your under- standing. One could insert the word spirit in there, but it would not be true that it is 100 percent of your spirit. The consciousness, as it closes down its waking self, the part of it that is—unbeknownst to you—the driving force in many things you do, wakes up more.

Now there may be times when this consciousness will just be lingering about near the body, and it may be picking up on things (because it is not trapped within the body). Some of you may have the experience of hearing someone calling your name, or you may hear a conversation as you are falling asleep, and you bolt awake, thinking people are in the room. What is happening then is that you are opening up to the other things that are occurring all the time, which you often do not notice during your normal waking state. Some of it could just be as similar to as if you were hanging out in one of your coffee shops and other people are nearby and you overhear them. It is not that you are intentionally listening; you just happen to be seated there. Also, there are times when your consciousness—your spirit—needs a reminder, so to speak, or needs an energetic cleansing. (We spoke of this, how at the end of the human life, when the spirit leaves the body, there is a cleansing, and the energy it provides is like cleansing raindrops.) Similarly, there are times when your consciousness or a part of your spirit will leave and return—for lack of a better word—home. Now home, as we reference it, would be based on that individual consciousness, perhaps it's out into the ethers, or, for some of you, it may be coming-around spirits that have worked with you or into the bubble of soul groups. There is a refreshing that occurs—just as when you meditate to de-stress your human self, the spirit also needs that. It is something likened to an oil change—if you will. It helps to keep it running at full capacity.

Also, there is a homesickness that occurs that the spirit part can tap into, but for many of you in waking life, you cannot do so because you do not always remember that "home," so to speak. Now we are just digging deeper holes here with you. So you may go home or go to any number of these other places, or you may just be flying out in the ethers. You may, in fact, meet up in the ethers. Not only with us or with other spirits, but even with people who walk on the earthen plane.

This may be a place where people talk things out or work out problems that they do not necessarily know they have brought back with them. Some of you may, some of you may not. This may be a place where people go if there are difficult conversations that need to be had; this (dreamtime) is where you have the first conversation.

Because even if they are not lucid dreamers, it is one part of your higher self reminding the other part that now is the time, so that experience begins to trickle into the subconscious and prepares the human self. Just like how it goes for some of you reading this text—there may have been times when you have spoken to a spirit, or we may have even sent other messengers to prepare you for reading this text! Therefore, when it (the manuscript) is out there, you may not know how you stumbled upon it, you may not know why you walked into that bookstore and walked down the third aisle to the left, but you did! Some of you may know, and some of you may even say, "I need to go into this bookstore to the third aisle and to the left." Many of you will not. You might say, "Well, I just happened to be in there, and this book fell off of the shelf. Some of you may have felt "drawn" there—so to speak. So dreamtime is one of the places where these things can occur.

Dreamtime is an ideal place to go if one were to have an argument with a best friend; and if they were not sure how to patch things up, then it is a good place to start! There may be times when you do that naturally anyway, and later in the session, we will give you some pointers on how to do this, as well as some warnings about it. Because always, there are risks when the human ego gets involved. You understand? So there are some preferred parameters—so to speak.

Some of you have what you refer to as "partners" or "significant others." Oftentimes, you find each other because your higher selves have put the call out—out here—*[gesturing toward the ethers]* during dreamtime. You have heard stories of how people who may have grown up in the same town but never met until later when they were living across the country from each other. They were somehow brought together;

so you see, some of these things begin to occur out here, *in the ethers during dreamtime*. It is the place where the over soul that oversees the other parts of you exists. Therefore, this is the place where you are reminded—so to speak—of what you have come here to do. Most people, much of the time, will not remember the exact things that occur. They may instead say, "I had this dream last night that I don't remember, but it seemed really important." This may be one of those things that have occurred. Questions?

YVES: This place where the spirit or consciousness of individuals that meet to resolve things, is that a conscious effort to go there and resolve these issues? If it is, how do we use that?

THE COLLECTIVE: As we have said, we will get into instructions later on how to use that and what to use it for. So yes, it can be created, consciously. When we say consciously, we mean the waking mind. However, oftentimes, what the human being does not want to do, the spirit is willing to do. So at times, you may not even be thinking about how to make an apology to "Uncle Joe," so to speak; but some of that healing—if it needs to occur—for the over soul, may begin to happen or occur in that place. So it can be conscious, but it also does happen without you being conscious of it.

It can, at times, fall into the category of prophetic dreaming, though not always. You may, however, have a sense of something that is going to occur. Or perhaps, you did have a problem—a relational problem with "Uncle Joe"—and you have a sudden sense that he is somehow closer. That perhaps he will call, or that you should call him and just reach out without even knowing what to say. So you see, it may be seemingly prophetic. In fact, you may have brought a small amount of awareness back with you. Therefore, for all intents and purposes, it is prophetic but is more a result of the work you have done in the ethers. In other words, negotiations can be made while you are wandering about out there in the ethers.

For some of you, this may also be the place where you meet up with your ancestors. You may come back with dreams about seeing a parent or a grandfather who has passed on.

Since you do not have all the physical senses interfering during dreamtime, you are more open to interaction (with departed loved ones). After loved ones have transitioned into this world of ours, many people will talk of having had a dream that their loved one was still alive. They often speak of how they looked younger or had a "glow" about them. That is because while that spirit or consciousness is out there, it is remembering, interacting with that loved one. Images, remember, have to be interpreted through this computer that you call the brain, so you may come into the ethers and see that the loved one is still alive. If their energy has been cleansed, then it may be more vibrant, yes? So in seeing this, you interpret it as "Oh, they looked so much younger." Or "They did not look sick anymore."

However, this does not mean that a loved one is still suffering out there (in the ethers) if you see them and they appear very sick. This is a very important point to make; again, *your* human brain is going to decide how to interpret it. You may be out there with them, but if you are still holding on to the fact that they were so sick, then that is the image that is created by your mind. (We have, on occasion, also said that when you see a spirit or a loved one with your eyes or with theirs closed, oftentimes, it does not mean that they actually keep their former body; but you recognize their energetic imprint, so it triggers that image. Because it taps into the program in the "brain-computer," and, likewise, this can occur during dreamtime.)

There may also be times when the computer uses what it knows. In other words, you may have what you may call a prophetic dream, but it is oftentimes the consciousness preparing the self for something. The images in your dream may not be exact images of what is to occur, or with whom. It may be more of the "flavor" of it. We have spoken before about, for instance, the fact that we use Julie's words that are in *her* brain. They must be already stored there for us to use. So, let us say if it were someone you were to meet, if you were to meet your soul mate out

there in the ethers and bring back some awareness of that, chances are, if you have not ever
met them before in that human form, you would
not see them in that way. You might see them
quite differently (because we are talking about
being in ethers and bringing the awareness
back). Their personality or their looks might be
similar to that of someone you know; and when
you meet the actual person, you may think, *Oh,
but I thought I was going to meet this person that
I saw in my dream.* Now that is not to say that
one cannot ever see the actual person, but generally, it is only those who are more accustomed
to moving through the ethers and dimensions,
and interpreting can do so. Do you have questions about that?

YVES: Are you saying that since you have
never seen this person you will not recognize
them when you encounter their energy in the
ethers? Instead, you may "see" a picture of
someone that you already know whose personality attributes may be similar to this person
you haven't met, and that this is how you then
view him or her.

THE COLLECTIVE: Yes. In other words, you
may have a dream about your best friend that
you are walking down the street with your best
friend, when suddenly; you are holding hands
and having romantic feelings for each other.
When you wake up, you think, *Well, I have never*

had those feelings for my best friend. And then, lo and behold, overtime, it may be that this new person that you have not met yet may look like your best friend or have some of the same personality traits. So, because you are used to seeing your best friend on a regular basis, that is who you see in the dream. In the ethers, this person you have not met has revealed himself or herself to you, but you do not know how to translate it if you have not seen them with physical eyes. However, this is not always the case. There are those whose vehicles are more used to translating "energetic codes," so to speak, so that they may see the actual person in dreamtime.

Likewise, other vehicles may describe people in spirit exactly as they look because they see them. There are other times that one may know that a grandfather is there because, out of nowhere, they think of their own grand-father, you see?

As with everything else, there are no hard-and-fast rules to it. Part of it depends on the vehicle (the person), where the vehicle is at in their opening up to all that is out there in the ethers.

We will move on to other occurrences in dreamtime. Now, here is where it can get a little slippery for some. We spoke only a moment ago about these symbols you have of people. About the human part of you that knows those people. On the other hand, your spirit-self has been exposed to many other spirits than just those you know in your waking consciousness. There may be times when you are in the ethers that you get called on to assist others that you may not know here (while awake), but you know them out there. You may come back from dreamtime and say, "I had this crazy dream . . . I was at this scene of a car accident." Or "I was at a pickling company" (we are making up random examples), and you may go on to describe a situation that occurred and for which you were there to assist in some way. Now, it could be that it was literal—that you did see what you saw. It could also be your interpretation of the assisting. There are some of you who spend much of your time out there assisting others, and you are not even aware of that. There are those of you who have a commitment to assist others, and this is the place you are doing it. You may also just happen upon random things while you are flitting about in the ethers—because you can!

There are stories of stranded motorists or accidents where people talk of angels who come and assist them. Now, for the purpose of this book, we will describe angels as "energy beings," which would mean that everyone is an angel, yes? Certainly, you have your sects and sub sects of energy beings; we have spoken about that. However, for this case, let us say that ultimately, everyone is an angel. Everyone is an energy being. So, there may be times when discarnate beings assist others in saving their life if it is not yet time for them to move on. Nevertheless, there may also be times when they may not be discarnate beings; they may, in fact, be disembodied consciousness. So while you are out there in the ethers, you may be the one assisting. You must understand that consciousness, when free, is no different from us. Your entire consciousness is not even in your vehicle. It will not fit! We have referenced the layers or levels of energy resonance before, and while we, in Spirit, may not be in the same place as your consciousness, your consciousness can still move about freely. You may experience it when you "space out" for a moment—it might be when you have suddenly realized that you have been staring at the wall for ten minutes. These are the times when your consciousness (or conscious awareness) is leaving the physical plane and going somewhere else, or is perhaps just jumping out for a break. As a point of reference (because this could get into a whole other talk), let us say that even when you are awake, you can visit the dreamtime places if you practice. It is easier to do with people you are close to. For instance, perhaps you are sitting at your office desk, and suddenly, you feel someone—a family member or someone that you care deeply for. You feel them as though they are right next to you; you can even smell them. That is when the consciousness of that person has traveled to you. It could also be that you both have traveled and met out in the ethers, and there is recognition of it on some level. Again, there are ways to do this intentionally, and we may get into that later on as we get into the other parts of the dreams.

[There was a twenty-minute break after which Julie came out of the first part of the session with a headache. She was relatively sure it was from the quick immersion and then exit of energy during the break.]

YVES: Okay, we are back.

THE COLLECTIVE: Many of the concepts that we wish to talk about will be a stretch for some. However, the information is important to share since we are talking about dreamtime.

During your dreamtime, not only are you sometimes processing things or observing things from your daily mundane life, but you are also out traveling in the ethers, you are meeting people, and you are helping them. You are working through things, and you are seeing things to come. But because—if you remember what we said—the consciousness, when it is not bogged down by the density of being in the physical human body, can move about in different areas. However, there are some areas that it cannot visit because it may not resonate with the correct vibrational frequencies. You may at times lower your resonance some and go into some not-so-fun places, and we will get to that as well. So you are able to move about freely, and as such, you are able to move through tunnels, or "wormholes," if you will. You do this, that you might visit other places, other worlds, and other you's.

We have also spoken of parallel lives and multidimensional selves, and this is another place where meetings can occur. Some of that may be because there is a magnetizing to the other self. You are out floating about and somewhere in your consciousness; you know where the other pieces of you might be. Therefore, there may just be a draw to that same energy. We spoke earlier of negotiations or bargaining. You can also use this time to go to other places to negotiate or bargain with your "other selves." Now, it is not as frequent as the other types of dreamtimes unless you are an avid "ethereal world traveler," so to speak *[laughter]*. That again depends upon your path and how much of it you are following or not following. Therefore, it could call for more visits to your other selves. When awaking from these types of dreams, you may say, "Well, I had this dream, and I was with these people, and I felt like I knew them; but if I think about their faces, I don't know them." It might register on you that there is something known. More than anything, it is because when interacting with your other self, your other self *does* know those people who are there. So again, we are attempting to keep this as elementary as possible for everyone's understanding. Of course, with all things we share with you, there are many levels and layers of it, yes?

You may also go to these other worlds just to visit with your other selves. It may just be perhaps you have been there before; and again, when we say "before," we apologize because of our lack of appropriate words to use in your language, because *before* would also be *now*, would it not? We do try to stay as linear as we can in our explanations, for that is the only way for the human mind to begin to grasp the concepts; otherwise, there would be no point in us speaking if we were to give you the whole shot of truth, so to speak, as to how these things operate. Remember, we are coming and meeting the people where they are to bring them forward. So you may visit these other places. You may do it out of curiosity, you may do it because you happen to accidentally slip through a wormhole, or you may do it because there is a call there.

There are some of you that may have certain practices that teach that dreamtime, and any other time that is spent out in the ethers, is being of equal value and validity and realness as waking time. In some of these practices, dreamtime can be a time for also doing some of your energetic medicine work. This is also a place where you may meet up with the great teachers who have, at one time, walked upon your earthen plane. As well as being indoctrinated or taught by some of the many great teachers who are scattered about our realms (and many of them exist in these different worlds now), you may also meet them in the other worlds where they now exist. Some of you may come back with a memory of that. To be clear, when we say "other worlds," we are also including worlds such as the animal kingdom and the nature kingdom itself. What we mean by that is that this is a place where you go to communicate with, or to commune with, these beings that exist here on Earth and are known as the four-legged's. They too, as we have said, have spirits. Their characteristics carry good medicine, yes? Dreamtime is where you may go at times to get some of that medicine. Because medicine is not always given in a physical *[smacking-hands-together to emphasize physical]* way, yes? Even if you have a physical malady, energetically, it still has to connect with you. And so, there may be times when you are communing with that animal kingdom, or perhaps, some of those same teachers or other teachers may take on an animal form to teach you or to give you the medicine. We believe you call them "shape-shifters," if you will, and it is in these other realms where they can introduce the "medicine" to you, do you see? These are not realms for which we are going to give you instructions on how to go about maneuvering through because *that* perhaps is best saved for the masters of that practice to teach you. We know of this, and we are familiar with it. There are some of us here who sit before you who obviously, in some way, are shape-shifters—as in we are able to introduce part of our consciousness into Julie's physical body and use her voice and her brain, yes? So while we are familiar with it, for most of us, it has not been our main practice; and therefore again, when you get into some of these other teachings or other practices, it is better to stick with those who know how to "navigate the waters," so to speak.

Many of those who read this book may not necessarily have psychic experiences or prophetic dreams. They do not necessarily know much about their other selves, and so let us explain it in another way. For instance, one who is an avid gardener may travel into this other world, the natural world. The world of the plant and mineral kingdom. They may visit and not remember; but perhaps the next day, they will go out into their gardens, and suddenly they know exactly what to do to make something grow better. Or they suddenly decide they are going to plant something different, move something, or do something else new in their garden. That is because they have been instructed, so to speak—again, it's a limiting word—they've been picking up the thought forms in the other world of the nature energies in order to accomplish that. Most who are avid gardeners, for instance, would be able to say that they have all had experiences where suddenly they found a solution, perhaps, to their weed problem or to their gopher problem or what have you. They may even just start spending more time in the garden and so on.

Before we go farther, since we understand that some of this information can be quite heavy for the readers, we would offer you an opportunity to pose any queries that you have about that which we have spoken of thus far for clarification purposes.

YVES: It is very clear so far, thank you.

[Long pause.]

THE COLLECTIVE: And so we take our leave now. Our next session will cover instructions on how to move through dreamtime. Yes? And there was some conversation earlier regarding the amount of break time between these sessions; you may take whatever is necessary to prepare your physical and emotional bodies for the "next chapter," so to speak. We bid you a fond adieu.

YVES: Thank you.

Session 2 – June 23, 2010 – Yves was present and recording. Yves and Patti were directing questions. This session wasn't quite as difficult on Julie's body. It was a long session lasting about four hours, including our breaks. They even went on to more materials to be inserted in the book following the completion of their discourse on dreamtime.

THE COLLECTIVE: Greetings. We are pleased to be seated with you both on this evening. We would like to open the session for any questions or clarifications that you have noted from either our last session or questions that again would fit within the context of the two sections that we have covered thus far.

YVES: You mentioned there was a difference between spirit and consciousness. Can you elaborate on that, the consciousness of the vehicle (or being) as opposed to the spirit of the being?

THE COLLECTIVE: We were referencing when the consciousness leaves the body during dreamtime, is that correct?

YVES: Yes.

THE COLLECTIVE: When we say the "spirit" of a being, we mean that would encompass the spirit in its entirety, the sum total of all of the parts and pieces or levels of its con-sciousness. With consciousness, the levels are often separate. For instance, we have spoken of the waking consciousness as that which oper-ates through the human brain, or the human computer system (the machine). Then there is the "unconscious mind" level—that which is the more intuitive part of you and operates and functions in that way. Lastly, you have what some refer to as the super conscious mind. This level of consciousness is more connected to the ethereal realm, and therefore connected to other energies around it as well as the over soul or overseer that we have spoken of. Let us not get caught up in the rules of it; we are not going to go through a dissertation about this. This is merely for the ease of explanation. The con-sciousness that leaves during dreamtime would be a piece or a part of the spirit. The spirit of the being is all-inclusive. This would be similar to what you would see if you were communi-cating with someone who has just departed your earthen plane, when you see his or her "spirit." The truth is, it likely may not be their entire spirit, but when they leave their body, their entire spirit goes. There is no bit of it left.

The entire spirit cannot leave the body during dreamtime because—well, then someone would come in during the morning, and you would just be lying there [humor in tone], and you would not return from dreamtime. There is a need for that essence to remain in the physical body in order for the physical body to work. It would be much like the batteries in one of your robotic beings. You understand? If the batteries are taken out, then it is rendered useless; and likewise, if the entire spirit were to leave to go on travels, well then, it would not make it back in again.

YVES: At some other point, you mentioned that sometimes discarnate beings come in to assist, in case of an accident, and that sometimes, disembodied consciousness assists as well. When you say the disembodied consciousness assists, are you saying that this consciousness can physically interact in the case of an accident on this earthen plane, to assist and help?

THE COLLECTIVE: Yes, that is correct. So once again, this could get very deep for some human minds; however, part of this also depends on the level of skill, or, rather, on how adept one is at controlling their travels in the ethers. You are not limited in what you can do because the part of your consciousness that is out there can, and does, interact with other beings that are in plain spirit form or spirits occupying a physical body. You do this in the same way as you communicate with others during dreamtime. Those people are not always asleep when you communicate with them. Allow us to give you an example:

You may go to the scene of an accident or perhaps another type of traumatic event such as an Earthquake, a hurricane, or other things of that nature. People may have stories of suddenly seeing someone or something, helping them out, or directing them somewhere; and suddenly, that person is gone. Energy consciousness still carries an imprint. Your energy consciousness carries your imprint, you see? While they may not see you as Yves, per se, for as we spoke about earlier in this session, they may not know Yves. However, your energy imprint will create in their mind, or brain (which needs to make sense out of something), an image. This may be likened to someone else that they know or something that they would assume would be helpful. They make that into that image because it is the only way to understand it. The brain has to comprehend; the brain cannot do anything else—that is what it is there for. It takes signals, and it interprets them. You understand? And so, it (the brain) may see this being or man that appeared and then suddenly disappeared. That does not mean that you have manifested or acquired another physical vehicle; it is just that that was how they have interpreted the event.

And our understanding is that our guest had some queries?

PATTI: Yes. Insomnia seems to be a very common problem now. Can you speak about how that affects the aspect of dreamtime when consciousness leaves the physical body? Does this then affect the physical body in a detrimental way if they are not able to do this?

THE COLLECTIVE: When you say insomnia, are you referring to when human beings do not get enough sleep? Well, the first order of business to understand is that human beings get way too much sleep. Much more than is necessary, or in much longer sorts of "parcels," if you will, than is necessary. For prime operating condition, proper rest is perhaps one-quarter or one-third of the time your average human being spends sleeping. Now, of course, there is more than one answer to this question. If one is not getting enough physical rest and their consciousness is not able to go out in dreamtime, then yes, ultimately, there will be an impact on the body. Many of the symptoms that someone exhibits from lack of sleep is actually due to a lack of opportunity for the consciousness to do what it needs to do during the dreamtime.

Interestingly enough, here is one thing that you may hear that people speak of that occurs when someone is saying that the body is not getting enough sleep. You may have heard of people hallucinating; yes, so what begins to happen is that the consciousness just starts traveling on its own. There is what you might call a split of the consciousness. Because it needs to travel—that is what it does. It connects with the higher self; it connects with other things on the physical body. The eyes and the ears are your main sensory organs that take in data to be interpreted through the brain, correct? Now, when the body is either undergoing extreme stress or is not getting enough sleep (there are many other reasons, but we won't go into that for the purpose of this text), then the separation between the conscious waking self and the sub- or super-conscious does not occur. You understand? So the travels create a need for the brain to interpret what it is experiencing. At the same time, the main physical sensory organs are taking in data that it then sends to the brain. What happens is that the two meet in the brain, and the interpretation can be mixed up, you see? To some, that is where these hallucinations come from, from the lack of the separation of those differing parcels of data. We will leave it at that for now. Is that clear?

PATTI: Yes. Thank you.

THE COLLECTIVE: One thing to point out is that one of the reasons we have spoken about dreamtime is that for most humans, it is the easiest way to establish that the consciousness is traveling. Most often, it is easier for you to be aware of it that way.

However, the consciousness can, and does, leave the physical body at other times as well; and it's not only when one goes to sleep. For instance, on this afternoon, you and the vehicle were feeling what you refer as "spacey." There is no mistake there, for you were partly flying out in space! Also, we were working with your energy vibrations and frequencies to harmonize them to allow for a smooth session with us this evening. While that is occurring in the physical body, the consciousness responds, and there is an ease of transition. You may not even be aware of what its travels were, but that was occurring. So that can occur . . . that does occur with all human beings, actually, but not necessarily to the degree that it should.

PATTI: Do the same effects apply also to those who are taking sleeping pills?

THE COLLECTIVE: The effect of that is not so much on the super-consciousness; however, any substance that is introduced into the body to have the body do something by this artificial means—that substance itself—will obviously affect not only the body but the being's ability to follow the super-consciousness or its spirit-self. This could then affect the ability of the super-conscious to work as it usually does during dreamtime. Again, we do understand that not everybody wakes up in the morning and remembers their dreamtime anyway. However, that is not always the case, nor does it have to be the case. But rather, it's because sensory pieces of the brain and body are "numbed," so to speak, by this artificial substance, to the point that the super-consciousness is unable to communicate what is needed to your unconscious. And are there other queries?

PATTI: No, no other queries.

THE COLLECTIVE: So, then, this is a good time to take a short break. This way, we can continue monitoring the body and not overload it so that we can get through the entire session this evening. And so, if you would please take a short ten- to fifteen-minute break to get refreshments or what have you.

YVES: We are ready to continue whenever you are.

THE COLLECTIVE: First, what we would like to talk about before the "pointers," so to speak, is the "benefits," if you will, in becoming more active, lucid dreamers. As well as the benefits of using dreamtime for your inspirations or answers, for intentional communion and communication with guides, ancestors, other selves, so on. Now, of course, as we spoke of this, we see it is something that assists the spirit-self; the consciousness comes back after having ventured out there and assists the spirit-self to incorporate the knowledge or the memory of your purpose here on an unconscious level. There are many of you who are, sort of—what is your popular phrase today? —"walking on the path," what

219

you call the "spiritual path." And many of you create goals toward becoming more in touch with your spirit-self and the drive of the spirit versus the drive of the human being, is that correct?

YVES: Yes.

THE COLLECTIVE: And so, because during dreamtime, these other faculties [gesturing to eyes and ears] are also numbed, it is easier to move your consciousness about to find your answers. Now, let us be clear when we say your answers; again, we are talking in regard to those of you looking to accelerate the evolution of your individual spirit, yes? Ultimately, as all of you are doing this, it assists in the evolution of the spirit of man itself as a whole. So if you are on a path such as that, that is, looking to do that—the rest of you perhaps can skip this next part [*humor in tone*].

When speaking through this vehicle, we often point to the solar plexus or the heart area of the body. We consider this as the place of knowing, the place where the spirit knows. The human mind and the human ego can easily override that—you understand—so when you are utilizing dreamtime with the intention of moving farther along this path, it assists you in staying truer to the spirit, and its calling. Because there you are, finding your answers based on what the over soul or overseer is calling for, and you bring it back *that* way. Then, even if you don't remember or you are not so sure, it gets programmed in a different way, you see. It gets programmed in memory in your cells and the tissues instead of just programming in the brain.

This is helpful, and here is an example of why. You may sit across from a friend of yours or another being that you know in your waking time, have conversations about this and that; and oftentimes, the human ego does not allow you to see some of your own obstacles that you place in front of yourself that become the tripping blocks to your growth or your movement forward. Therefore, the ego stalls your growth along the way. Are you following us?

When you spend more time with intentional dreaming, with "intentional communion through dreamtime," so to speak, you are obtaining that information outside of the place of the ego. This makes it easier to integrate it into yourself and then assists in awakening that part of you that begins to notice and understand that there is much more to the path than what you see with your eyes or hear with your ears. We have spoken often and always include, when appropriate, that *everything* is the work, yes? Everything, everything—we cannot say that word enough—every place you go, every person you speak to, every thought you have, every action you take. It is not just when you are in dreamtime, it is not just when you are meditating, and it is not just when you are sitting in

221

your ceremonial places, yes? You see, the ceremonies and all of those things are merely a path *to* that place. They are a vehicle or a means to get to the place of listening and living through the spirit. In other words, these are tools to get you there; these are *not* "the work." They are tools to get you to notice and acknowledge that you are not confined to your physical body.

Very often, there is a mistake made, although it could be a quite innocent mistake in believing that this over here is your practice and over here is the rest of your life. There is an old saying, "Your life is your prayer." And what that means is that how you live attests to what you believe. How you live attests to where you are in your development and who you really believe you are. So, when you begin to make those connections in more places and in more ways, it begins to create this unshakable conviction. An *immovable* force, although, you will still trip and fall, because you are still in your human vehicle. *[Humor in tone as the next sentence implies a joke being directed toward Patti, who is accident-prone.]* We know it may happen more times for some of you than it may happen for others, but we mean in the spiritual sense of tripping and falling. Of course, that happens less often; and you put up fewer obstacles, and then the evolution can occur more, for lack of a better word, rapidly. We do not like that word so much, but for now, we will use it.

So we encourage you, when you are worried about things or when you feel burdened by things, before you go to bed at night, you sit first and you make a decision to find out your answers. Before you do that, however, be sure, be absolutely sure, that you sincerely mean—with all your heart—that you want the truth. If you do not mean it sincerely, your brain will interpret it in some other way—you understand—as brains can do that. You ask for that, and then you program yourself for it. Perhaps you might say something such as an invocation or a prayer that you are asking that your guides or your ancestors or whoever you meet during your dreamtime, that they assist you in knowing the right action to take, or fill in the blank with what you are looking for. Some of you may come back with a very strong understanding and knowledge about what to do; some of you may not bring it back in the form of an "idea." One very good practice is to, upon awakening, ask yourself that same question that you asked yourself before you slept. Ask it before you have time to think, before your feet hit the floor, you see? And *you will* know what that answer is.

YVES: Yes.

PATTI: Yes.

THE COLLECTIVE: There are many techniques for moving about in dreamtime. One good way is to begin to practice first in the smaller ways. Make a decision to have a dream about something. Then think about that dream that you want to have when you are going to sleep. However, do not force it. Do so just as you would in meditation. You cannot force these things. You can do this as a guided meditation. You can program yourself to move toward the dream, and of course, you can say within your mind-self, *I am now walking down this path. I get to the door, and as I open the door, I notice that blah, blah, blah, blah, blah . . .*

It is important that you not struggle or fight within this, for when you do that, similarly, as we have said about meditation, that only keeps it away more. Allow it to take you because for some of you, you may be able to go directly there. For others, as we spoke about earlier in the dissemination, you have to release those things, those thoughts. Therefore, for some of you, you may need to do that first. So, it is important not to attempt to force it; you should just be gently "nudging," if you will, yes? Then you just begin to move that into the intended dream. You can ask to, perhaps, meet with your ancestors.

Many people keep a dream journal, and this is a good thing to do. If you do that, especially in beginning if you are not familiar with dream travel or directing the course of your dreams, then it is good. Because when these dreams begin happening, or when you begin seeing things, you can go back to that and notice that it is working. Doing that, of course, builds up your awareness that something is really happening. Once you do that, then it opens up more, and you open up more.

Do not just keep a dream journal and throw it in the drawer. Go back and read it every couple of days to monitor things and see if there is anything that stands out. You may then see that perhaps something has occurred, or that perhaps you just knew something. One of the best places to begin to practice is with those exercises, in terms of learning how to move your consciousness during this time, and do not choose the more difficult tasks first. Start instead with the simpler ones.

So, wherever your energy is most drawn, that is where you may want to decide to visit. Perhaps it is drawn to a certain country or a place that you have always wanted to visit but have not. Or perhaps you would like to go back and visit somewhere that you have already been, where there is already a connection. You may want to connect with an ancestor or a guide or another human being in your life with whom you have a connection, someone you interact with. These are the easier things to do because those energies recognize each other, so it is easier to get there in the beginning. This can be very helpful for moving along your path. Again, we would like to reiterate that what that means is this can help in every aspect of your life, really.

We take a little risk here; we will say a little more about some things, but again, we spoke earlier of negotiations, and that dreamtime is a place where you can negotiate with others. This is also a place where you can negotiate many things, not just when you are having a problem. Those of you seated before us tonight, for instance, can negotiate this text that we are compiling. You can negotiate contacts, you can negotiate with editors and publishers and other such people. You can begin to go out and plant the seed, even if they do not remember it. When the manuscript comes across the desk, there is going to be something about this manuscript that will make someone feel like "it speaks to me." This would be a very good practice for all of you because again, it just helps in opening things up.

Are there any questions thus far on what we have shared with you regarding some of these benefits?

YVES: Not at this time, no.

THE COLLECTIVE: Going back to negotiating, perhaps you have difficulty with a boss and perhaps you—well, perhaps you just can't stand your boss, so to speak. Yet in the waking part of the day, there is not a way to connect with that boss because their ego, or perhaps your ego, is interfering, yes? You can utilize dreamtime to find a place to meet with that boss and to honor them and their spirit, and in this way, to commune with it. Then you will see that they will still be your boss, and they may tell you things you do not wish to do or what have you, but that strain will be eased. It is very important when you are practicing these things; however, let us make this perfectly clear that when we speak of negotiating, we do not mean manipulating. We do not—we are not, in any way, advocating that you attempt to use this to mess with the free will of others. There are those who do this, and that is why we will not get into the exact science of some of it. However, we do believe that if any of you would even try to do that, it is out of innocence. Because if you are reading this text, then obviously, you are looking for something more than how to manipulate people. However, oftentimes, your ego-self, because it wants things to be certain ways, may believe that it is the right thing to do.

To use another example, earlier in this day, the vehicle (Julie) was communing with a spirit friend who had a request from her. Therefore, we would like to use them in an example of dreamtime to talk about the negotiating and all of that which occurs and how that occurred for them while her friend was still in his vehicle.

This friend and the vehicle were often able to communicate in dreamtime, while he was alive on the earthen plane. This was a somewhat tumultuous relationship they had at times. However, many of their issues or problems were actually worked out during dreamtime. There was enough done and accomplished in dreamtime because their spirit-selves knew that it would need to be so. When this friend was ill and dying, he needed her assistance. Since they were already accustomed to communicating in dreamtime, it made it easier for him to come to her in this way and ask for her help for he could no longer use his voice box to talk. Although they did not know it when they first came together, their karma was such that she was meant to assist him in this way. It was through images as well as through more direct communication, although there were some twists and turns within the dream itself. Through dreamtime, he came and asked for her help and said, "I am dying. I need you, I need your help. I'm sick. I have nowhere to go, and I am . . ." and so forth. Therefore, because she trusted this, she responded and, out of that, searched for him, and she did find him. Now, within her ego-self, you see, she was frightened to go because she thought to herself, *What if my dream was wrong? What will this person's reaction be to my showing up?* You understand? Yet she listened. She listened enough and understood that what needed to occur in that process of things, in walking through that dying process with him, occurred because she listened. She did not allow the ego to interfere. However, there were earlier times when she had other dreams regarding the same person; however, she did not listen because she allowed her ego, her fear, to override her intuition. So this is one way that there were negotiations done over time during dreamtime that led to that point where they could meet in dreamtime and that arrangement could be made. Had that not happened prior to that time, then her ego due to her own feelings of anger or betrayal or loss or grief or any of that, in addition to his own pride, would have interfered. Any further queries regarding any of this?

YVES: The point to remember, then, in using dreamtime is that this should be for the highest good in terms of whatever one is seeking. Not for personal gain and not from the place of the ego but from the place of the higher self, is that right?

THE COLLECTIVE: Yes. Of course, it is the ego that makes a decision that one wants to get to a higher place as well, so it gets a little mixed up there. However, oftentimes, it is the ego that fuels you to find a path or to find a practice because you may be looking to gain skills. You may be looking to be even more connected. Many times, it is that ego-self that initiated this, and we use that to our advantage, actually, if you must know the truth about that. Your higher self does this as well.

So, when you are coming from a place of sincerity, when you are coming from a place of love, then it is important to be sure to put that out there about that. Use the "qualifiers," if you will, adding on "in the highest good," or saying, "assist me to see how to manage this in terms of moving it forward, for everyone's benefit." There will be times when you seek out information due to the ego because obviously, if the ego was not involved, you would have no need for the information because you would just be "riding the wave," so to speak. Very few of you do that often. Well, not much at all, really. You have the desire to do it, and you may do so in bits and pieces. Understand that we do not mean this in a negative or judgmental way. That is just how the ego operates when the spirit takes on a human form. Of course, there are those who desire to be more selfless; but you have to start somewhere. You understand? You do not become selfless overnight, unless, of course, you were born as the Buddha or someone such as that. We, of course, mean the character of the Buddha.

The more that you are consciously attempting to connect with your higher self, with the overseer or the over soul, the more you are exposed to the way of understanding and the way of compassion. As you do this, you will notice that your questions begin to change as you are again—to use your phrasing—walking along the path. As you get farther up that path, the questions change. Ideally, the questions begin to lessen because you begin to know and to trust that next step, that next place, that next opening, that next shedding, that next shaking away of the ego. It becomes clearer, and it becomes more important for you to be loving and kind and giving than it is for you to become enlightened.

Enlightenment is often a very selfish pursuit fueled by the ego. Many people begin this "path to enlightenment" because they do not wish to suffer, because they do not wish to feel, and they do not wish to hurt. When you begin not hurting others, when you begin being loving toward others, when you begin embracing others, when you begin not judging others, then you are enlightened! Then, when you begin to see others as you and you as them, that is when the spirit begins to be lifted. It is only lifted if you are lifting others up with it. You cannot go alone. Is that clear?

YVES: Yes.

[Long pause.]

THE COLLECTIVE: Meditation also assists with this because, again, when you meditate, you are doing the same as when you are dreaming. Yes, different ways, perhaps, but it is all the same. Of course, there are many methods for learning meditation; there are many fine books with different techniques.

What we will say about that is that each human is an individual person; and perhaps for some, one technique will work better than for others. You understand? It is important that you find the technique that works for you. Now when we say "you" find the technique, when you say, "Well, my lying down and closing my eyes and drifting off to sleep is my meditation," we must clarify: This is not meditation; it is going to sleep.

Meditation is more of a conscious letting go, a conscious allowing of things to come in, and it allows you to leave the body sometimes as well. Therefore, it is more a closing off of faculties that feed the brain and allow your awareness to expand outward while also allowing things to come inward. So it assists not only in the technique of learning how to utilize dreamtime and being more in control of where you go and what you do. It also assists you in washing away some of the other gunk that happens with the human beings. It brings you closer to the place of recognizing others and you as one. Of becoming more loving, more kind, more giving, more compassionate and less self centered, less self-serving, less greedy, less materialistic, and so on and so forth. You understand?

Here is yet another exercise: You can talk with a friend of yours and make an agreement to meet in dreamtime. You can decide on an area where you will meet. You don't necessarily have to decide on the area, but you can. Some of you may have at times said to a friend, "I feel like I was with you last night, but I don't quite know what it was," or "I think I felt like my father's spirit was around, but I couldn't tell . . . I don't quite remember." Well, if you felt like that happened, then it happened. You ask, "I believe that spirit was speaking to me and told me thus and thus, did that really occur?" Having the question itself means that it really occurred. You understand? So make an agreement to meet your friend and see what happens. Then perhaps maybe you want to make another agreement and meet your friend in a particular place. Now, again, remember that even if you do not choose a particular place, some of you (depending on how connected you are) may wind up in the same place and have the same description. However, some of you may not.

Remember, we spoke earlier that the consciousness has an experience and your brain interprets it based on your own frame of reference. So, it may have been an interaction with this friend that was a very moving, wonderful, warm interaction. Now your image experience of that may have been that you were on a beach because that is how a beach feels to you. On the other hand, your friend may then say, "I guess we did not meet because in my dream, we're on a mountaintop." Perhaps the mountaintop is what represents those same feelings for them. It is less about the details and more about the substance of it. Quite frankly, the human mind will often screw it up. And we do not say this to judge the human mind; we will say it is very limited. Of course, it must be for you to remain as this seemingly separate individual and for you to have this experience in humanness. As we have said before, were you to have this enlightenment and awareness and all of that to happen all at once, then you would no longer need to be here. Are there any questions on that which we have already spoken of?

YVES: No question on what you have spoken about, but you had mentioned earlier that in venturing out during dreamtime, there are boundaries where the consciousness cannot go, is that correct?

THE COLLECTIVE: There are places that the consciousness cannot go because it cannot reach there. It cannot because its frequency will not fit in or resonate with the frequency that is occurring in some of those other places. Also, another reason why that may occur is if the human is very fearful of certain things, or of certain truths even. Although they may begin to go somewhere, they may not be able to make it all the way there because even while sleeping, that fear can override the consciousness and pull it back. Are there other questions regarding techniques, pointers, things such as that?

YVES: No, that is clear.

THE COLLECTIVE: We do wish to emphasize again, when we speak of dreamtime, that we are speaking more loosely than just when the body is sleeping if we're talking about traveling through the ethers or allowing your consciousness to move. Ah, yes, let us go back for a moment. In terms of this practice, hopefully, you ultimately become so adept that you do not need to be in dreamtime to do some of this. You can do it in waking time. As you are making negotiations or searching for answers while in dreamtime and out, the ultimate goal is for you to no longer have to do that. The goal is that your consciousness that is more often out (in the etheric realms) begins to reside within you. Then those things that perhaps cannot be negotiated, other than in dreamtime, can now be done so because you have become different. You change, and your ego does not get in the way. Therefore, reparations and things such as that or negotiations or what have you become easier. They become second nature, and even the need to make reparations become less because you do less damage, because your actions are more loving.

YVES: How does the negotiation occur in waking time? Is it just through the practice of doing it in dreamtime that you begin to apply the same technique in waking time, or are there specific things that are done with a waking consciousness or in a waking environment?

THE COLLECTIVE: We need to ask for clarification. Are you asking how the dreamtime negotiation affects real time, or are you asking how, in waking time, we get our consciousness to leave and use it to create the negotiation?

YVES: Yes, the latter, is what I meant.

THE COLLECTIVE: There are ways to do this in waking time without you having to move your consciousness. These will help your consciousness to move itself. There is a popular word of yours—*bilocation*, which means that the self is in two locations at one time. Not the physical body, right; but the physical body is here and another, bigger, part of the consciousness is elsewhere. Now, often, that occurs when people go out and look around and get information about things or what have you. Some people are quite adept at that, and some can project their consciousness to a person so that the person feels as though they are standing right next to them. We touched on this a little, yes? We spoke of how you might smell the person suddenly. Perhaps, you may suddenly just start thinking about them. When you think about a person, you see, you are already doing that. Some of your consciousness is going toward them; it is going up into the ethers into the place where the connection exists. In this place is where the energies meet, and again, we use *ethers* somewhat loosely. However, it is the best way to describe the etheric substance that is outside of you yet is you. That can get rather deep as a well. So, when you even have a thought about someone, there is a part of your consciousness that goes out toward that energy that is his or hers, you see? Perhaps some of you have had the experience of thinking about a friend that you have not heard from in a while, and suddenly, that same friend calls you on the telephone. Most of you still say that this is a "coincidence," yes? These are ways that you can do this in the "waking time," so to speak. Also, you can practice imagining yourself going and standing near someone and check in with him or her later. They may say, "I was thinking of you earlier today," or perhaps they suddenly call you anyway. Again, when you are just embarking on this, it is very good to keep notes so that you can check later because you may not always have time, in your day, to do this. *[Smacking hands together.]* Human beings want solid proof. They are so physical that they demand proof. And so this is a good way to provide that for yourselves. Now, there will be times when you say to a friend, "I thought of you at one fifteen," and the friend says, "Oh, I did not think of you until one twenty-five." And you say, "Oh, then it must not have worked," or "My consciousness was slow." This differ-ence in time experience is because you have time in your world. We in the ethers do not. So there are times when, again, pardon our use of the word, there are "times" when you may jump the space-time continuum in such a way that there is a "delayed response," if you will. Or perhaps, they are what you would call just a little thick skulled, and it takes a little while longer! These exercises can be of great benefit to humans. Even those of you who are involved in the many modalities of energy healing have methods for sending healing, yes? Some of you may send it out toward a person or place. Others may use symbols, and some of you may just travel to the person and do it. It does not matter which way you do it; whatever way works. So, many of you have done it already. It is just a matter of allowing things to carry over, you see? If you can do it in one place, then you can do it in another, and another. This goes back to the idea or the principle that everything that you do affects everything that you do. You understand? The principle of cause and effect and the principle of creation. It is important to remember that in all that we are sharing, we are talking about spiritual growth. Remember that, that is what we are talking about. *[Stating emphatically.]* The whole purpose of this book, and everything that we speak of in this book, has to do with the evolution of the spirit, the growth of the spirit, the raising up of the frequency of the spirit that occupies a human body in this current time. So when you practice it in healing, why not practice it in dreamtime or waking time, because when you are healing, that too is during your waking time. So, it is about really noticing and finding the ways do to it more. This is very helpful, as well, to find the ways in which you can do them. For these things that you say you cannot do, find the ways in which you can do them! Then use that technique to carry it over, you see; and you will find yourself doing it in more places, being able to do it in more ways, and becoming aware of your ability to do it in more places. That also means what comes with that . . .

REBECCA: Sort of a little surprise extra package, if you will, is the responsibility to carry the practice over into *everything*. You understand? So, it does not come without a price. It would be quite delightful if you could all just gain these little magical skills and then flit about in the ethers and visit many destinations that you wish to go without having to spend any of that money of yours. Certainly, you can actually do that, and we *encourage* you to do that because it is a wonderful way to learn that you can do it and to experience these other things and other places.

Perhaps you might visit a place that you love so much you might decide to bring your body there with you later or something. Let us say this last thing: It is important to always, whether working in dreamtime or in any other things, recognize that these things are spiritual principles that are best used as spiritual principles. Of course, in your humanness, you will exploit them; they are at times being exploited, of course not always intentionally. Again, the human ego, the human self, in its fear and in its greed, often uses these things to substantiate the continuous seeking for self.

YVES: Yes.

THE COLLECTIVE: And so, we will take our leave . . . we bid you a fond adieu.

The Common Threads Between the Various Religions

July 10th, 2010 – Yves was recording and directing queries. This too was a long expanded session wherein two breaks were taken. During this session, Julie did not experience the same headaches as she had started experiencing during the longer sessions. It appeared that her physical body was adjusting to the extended periods of channeling as the group had said it would. She was able to drift in and out with much more ease between sitting periods.

THE COLLECTIVE: We thank you for your swift return. As a reminder, we will continue working with the container of the two of you, but specifically, with the vehicle whose voice box we now use to ensure proper vibrational frequency that is conducive to the transmission of the data that we have come to share with you this evening.

We see that you did not have any specific queries regarding the topics that perhaps you will reserve those for after we begin the topic, yes? First, we would like to start by saying that depending on the vehicle and the container, we are not sure how long this session will be or how many sessions these topics will need. With the current energy resonance, it may be necessary to move material around when you get to the final editing of it in terms of the places that it will fall in. Because again, we have not locked into the ideal resonance, so we will not be able to impart as quickly and concisely, as we would like, at least not at this point in time. But let us begin.

What we would like to say, firstly, is that some of what we will say tonight we have already said before in various different sections of the material, and we will likely say it again in other sections of the material. Religion, religion itself, is what you would call resultant from man's need to create law, and from man's need to create order. Now, we will not get into whether it was needed or not, because that is a matter of opinion oftentimes. You understand? What we will talk about is if you were to create what you call a timeline, prior to your popular religion of Christianity. When we say popular, we mean some of the most subscribed-to religions, those religions that have taken over most of the world. Christianity is one of those (as well as Judaism, Islam, Hinduism, and Buddhism) that are somewhat large and getting larger. But in your world, there are three major religions that are recognized; and again, they are Judaism, Christianity, and Islam. Those are all relatively new religions as well. Islam is the youngest religion followed by Christianity, then Judaism. Hinduism and Buddhism are much older religions. We could get into many other names, and there are those that have certain names now, which had different names before. We would like to point out to you that the Buddhists and Hindus will tell you that although they still have sacred texts, they are not a religion per se, but that instead, they define their practice as a way of living. Of course, other practices will tell you the same thing. When you reference the indigenous cultures of this land here, where you live currently, this is Native American spirituality, yes? They also say that within their culture, there was no religion but a way of life. What happened, however, is that in some of these other places, their way of life, their culture, their customs, and then their belief systems were all put into one pot, and that was then sifted. We could go on for eons about the many different decisions that were made, why and how, but we will try to keep this simple for your understanding.

Human egos have a natural tendency to look at others that are somewhat different than them and judge them. They believe that their way is right and the others' wrong. They think that they know the proper way for things and that others do not. What happened for several different reasons in different religions is that there was a need in their view of their practices to ensure that people towed the line, so to speak.

You see, there was a time when all of you who walked upon the earthen plane were all indigenous practitioners. Now, if you were to look in different areas of the world, we are talking about a time when the world was not only one piece of land but also, after different things that have occurred in the universe and the land was separated, you would find that there are different names used for similar things, right? Different names for different energies or spirits of things or what have you, yet all of the practices were ones that had to do with the world around you. You understand? So these different practices were connected with nature—and when we say nature, we are including the mineral and plants and such. Within that was your relationship with the Earth and all things upon it, because that was a time when there was an inherent understanding that you were all a part of the Earth and the Earth was a part of all of you. Therefore, there was a natural order or rhythm to things, and things naturally happened with no need to write them down in a book. At the time, you were born into this way of life, and it was so much a part of what people did that it was not necessary to be learned by studying a book. Now, one of the unfortunate things that still affect your world today is that there came a time when greed and power became something that the humans were seeking more and more of. Now we are not saying that this never occurred with humans; we are not saying that at all, because it did. However, it occurred at varying levels, you understand; but once people began seeing what power could give to them and what things it could give to them, they began to develop and design this system to maintain what you refer to as the "status quo." You begin seeing people beginning to mark themselves as different, separate, or special, in order for them to hold on to all that they had gained. Now, let us say you go back to, let us say, Judaism: Some of these teachings were practiced for a very long time before they were ever written down in books. Many events were written long after they happened. In the indigenous societies and cultures, in the indigenous ways, things were passed down by story, yes? What happened was, stories began being written down instead. Now these stories were often used to teach lessons, to show things, and they were not always literal things. You understand? When these stories were written down and as man was writing them, man then began tweaking the information to fit the need of the time. You had your scholars that began writing things down and realized that they could have quite a bit of power in the written word, in what they were saying. We are not speaking merely of the original writings of scribes. For the original writings were not as screwed up then as they are now. Some of them did write accurate information or wrote it in a way that it was obvious that they were stories that held meaning. In earlier times, not all people had the ability to write or read. So things were written, and then others read it to the people. As more came along up the ranks and learned how to read and write, they realized that they could say or write anything. Therefore, when things were not going as they wanted or planned, or if the teachings or stories did not look as believed, they would change them. They took pieces out of it, and no one knew. Now, if you go back over all of this time and you would think of the amount of times that new scholars took over writing, you can imagine how much has been changed. Still to date, it is changed. In Judaism—because we are speaking of Judaism currently—there are those scholars who still sit in their rooms and debate the meanings in the Torah or the Talmud, and you have different sects of that. You have some that say, "This is the written law. It is not to be changed." Others say, "There could have been some misunderstanding. Even now, we think that we are being enlightened to understand it a little bit better." And still there are others that say, "Well, we think this is kind of loose here, and we think that it was meant to be loose, these parts of it, so that it could change with the times." You understand? So at all times, if you look at how this is happening, who is to say that it was not happening all along? Because it was!

If you were to hone in on the geographical location, and the time period, and the situations that were occurring, well then, that is where they brought in their customs that then became their laws, and they began to say that they were God's laws. For some, it was their understanding of it; for some, there were prophetic dreams, or there was spirit interaction. But again, you must remember always that things have been changed, because people realized, when they began seeing the type of power that they obtained from holding these sacred texts, that they could make the people do anything, you see? So they coveted them in such a way that others could really get their hands on the material. So they would change it to serve them, sometimes for themselves, individually, but oftentimes for what they believed it to be. And when we say "them," we mean the masses at the time, what they thought would best keep them in control or under the control of those with power. What happened, then, is that the beginning parts of the Christian Bible, which were the original texts from Judaism, their stories were mixed in with their customs and the laws. Let us take, for instance, one of the things that they speak about in the Judaic tradition as well as in the Islamic tradition—that one is not allowed to eat swine. This is said as though it is a proclamation from God, that it is unclean. And it was unclean, you see? It was unclean to eat swine during that time or era. The other animals at that point in time were taken in and had been taken care of, but most swine were wild. We are talking about wild boar and such. That

247

was a wild animal that often was dirty. They knew that it would eat its own feces and that it ate garbage or whatever it needed to eat in order to survive; therefore, it could not be eaten. It was also meat that went rancid faster than others. You understand? Therefore, it was a custom and a practice that they then wrote into a book, you see? In your world today, the truth is that in any place that you go to that raises any animals; the swine is no filthier than the cow or the chicken or anything else. It is not that the swine is so much cleaner, but because the other animals are not taken great care of either in your bigger production places. You understand? Therefore, these are the types of things that began to weave their way into these written works. There were things written over time that began to contradict other things that were written. This is because in the original scripts or scrolls, there was certain information; and then, as people began changing things, they did not necessarily change it with consistency. Once questions came up that challenged the ruling class, they just changed something else in it. You need to remember that in those days, there were certain chosen people that were allowed to read and write. Women were not allowed to read the scrolls. Perhaps because it said so many detrimental things about them that the men who were in power were concerned that the women might make changes to the scrolls. There are many things in there that were written due to lack of a full understanding even of how things work and others lacking information on certain occurrences. For instance—and you will find this in every tradition with different reasons "why"—in every tradition, there is talk of women in terms of their monthly cycles, yes? You must understand that there was a time when people did not even understand what a cycle was, you see? Therefore, it was seen as unclean. They believed a woman should not at all be touched during this time because they did not understand what was happening. They wondered how a woman could bleed for that long and still be alive or be in good condition afterward. Some people believed it was evil influences on the woman; others believed that it must mean the women themselves were unclean or not pure. Therefore, there were many different versions along the same theme, depending upon the culture and their belief system at the time. You will find this is many of your sacred scriptures as well.

You may read that you are not to touch a woman when she is unclean, or that you cannot be in the same place as her, or that she cannot touch the food you will be eating, and many other versions, including some who say it is a "curse" from God!

When you look at all of these different versions, no matter where you go, you have to look at something and say there was something to this energy at one point; however, everyone changed it to suit their need or their practice or their belief. Whose belief? The people who were writing it down, of course! Often, there were still some who were passing this on verbally, unwritten. Considering this, it is understandable why there would be so many mistakes around this issue. For instance, let's say you, Yves, were to sit in your own village, and you were to listen to a lecture that your teacher, your Malidoma Somé were to give. After his lecture, if you were to go around the room and ask everyone to share what they learned from him, how many people would say the exact same thing in the exact same way?

YVES: Not many.

THE COLLECTIVE: Actually, none. No one will say the exact same thing in the exact same way. So if you are all sent out, if your Malidoma said, "Take this information and write it in a book and we will secure it," then if you had twenty people in the lecture, you would have twenty different books. Because as he is speaking and you are listening, you are grabbing on to what speaks the most to you. It is all going through your own frame of reference, or your own map of the world. If he is talking about a flying frog and you have never before seen a flying frog, then you might describe it all different ways. You could describe it as being a literal flying frog, or you could describe it as a parable and change it all around. You understand? You can come up with an entirely different lecture by the time you are finished. Additionally, if you were to take bits and pieces from each one, who knows what you would come up with by the end? You understand?

This is why we say to you that if you look in your sacred scriptures, if you look in your teachings from different religions and different practices, you will find if you were to weed it all out, that there are threads that are consistently the same. Now, one could ask, why are they consistently the same? How is it that there is a practice over here that is perhaps a little different but very similar to this practice over here and this practice over there? If all of these people were separated by land or water or culture or custom, how can it be the same? That is because those are the grains of truth; those are the strands of things that are true. The two of you were speaking earlier this evening regarding medicines and food sources. You talked about how at one time humans were in better communion with nature, with animals, with Spirit, and with the spirit of things, yes? Those things did not need to be taught then. They were just known.

What happened is that as greed began to set in for man, which in some ways was necessary greed (but we will not get into that), you began forgetting, you began doubting. Therefore, then, that removed your connection or your "eyes," so to speak. There was a time when man did not have to think about how he knew something. He just knew it. There are those of you who came here with certain things to offer to contribute to the tribe, or the village. You came with those abilities, and those were the abilities you used. Many of those things you just knew. The hunters knew how to hunt for food; the other food gatherers knew how to do that. The medicine makers knew how to make medicine; those who spoke to the animals knew how to do that. Those who spoke to the sky beings knew how to do that and so on. As more and more things began to interfere, those ways started slipping away. Therefore, others decided on a particular way of "doing things," for the community, and they wrote it down. Over the years and over-time, suddenly, it had become law; and for some now, it has become God's infallible word.

God does not actually use words. Ultimately, I suppose, you could argue that point and say, if we are all a part of God and we are using words, then God uses words. Well then, you would win that argument, of course. However, what we are saying is that the Divine Source is just that—it is the Divine Source. The Divine Source is broken off and incarnating in different ways and shapes and forms, but there is the very center of that that is non-incarnated. You understand? Therefore it does not, it cannot use words. Just as we do not use words either; we use her words *[referencing the medium]*, and we are very far away from that Divine Source.

It is important to note that, and we do not say this in any way to put down religions that people practice; but what we are saying is, if you are looking to move forward in your evolution, it is time to see religions for what they are and then to find the wisdom in them all. You understand? They can be utilized. Do that by all means. However, do not use them as the written words of God because they are not—they are not.

There were many who were prophets who would warn of difficult times to come, or they would speak of others too that would come later and share their wisdom because they needed more to share, to remind you all, because you had all forgotten. You understand? Those were their gifts.

These were people who would come, and they would share wisdom; but again, you must remember that they were still only people. Much of the information that they received was still written down by others. Most of the prophets did not write either. When we say prophets, we are not talking about the prophets of your Christian Bible; we are saying prophets in general. Many of these prophets were unlearned. After all, what did they need to learn? They were prophets. You understand? So they did not necessarily write down the information that they shared. Others did, and others after that and after that and after that and so on. Even within your many religions, there are "branches" or sects of those traditions that believed or interpreted the writings differently. There are literal translations and figurative translations, as well as the more mystical sides to each religion. Your mystical teachings tend to be a little closer to what the real teachings were, but they still are not the exact teachings.

What has happened is that religions have given people and governments so much power that we fear that it will be a very long time before people can turn back to these ways. These religious books have done nothing except serve to separate all of you more and more from each other. Your attachment to these books and these incorrect teachings have created war after war. You never stop to question or to notice that you are holding a book—and fighting over the words in a book—as you attempt to force it down another's throat.

There was never, never, any information ever given that told one human being that they should slay others or force others to accept their belief, to accept their god. There are those who will quote to you from any one of these books; however, we are telling you they are untruths. *These ideas are man-made. [Said forcefully.]* There are people out there believing that this is the word of their god and they will fight for that. Even if they're not fighting physically, they will try to convert people to their belief system, never stopping long enough to think and see the bigger picture. They believe that they're doing it to save someone's soul, yet they are really doing it for the powers that be that are over them and are merely trying to get more from those people. *They are pawns.* You have all moved so far away from the heart in you that knows. That is how these religions, religionists, and the powers that be manipulate the masses. Because people look for hope; they look for a connection. You are all craving it because it is your birthright. It was always there, and there is a part of you that knows that there is something in you that is missing. There are so many of you walking around, feeling lost and empty. You could have everything that there is to have. You could have a host of friends, you could have a huge family that is all very close, you could have all of these material things, and yet there is still a part in all of you that feels lost, empty, alone, because you have lost that connection. And so, when someone comes and they assist you in having perhaps a couple of moments of feeling connected, then it's very easy to buy what they're selling, you see, and that is exactly what they are doing—they are selling it.

[Long pause.]

There is more hatred, death, suffering, illness, and hunger, from religion, religionists, and their differences than from anything else.

Anything else! People use their religion to con-
quer others, to gain their money, their property,
and their alliances. Even now, in your world
today, there are many who complain about religions that do these things we mention, and yet
many times, they are of a religion that does the
same thing. You understand? Yet, they cannot
see it. Not enough people pay attention to the
history of things; not enough people think. They
do not connect the dots. You pick up any of your
sacred scriptures right now—anything written
in a book that says that this is the way, this is the
infallible one way—and one word of God, and
you will find inconsistencies. In this text that
you read, you will find inconsistencies, but we
have told you there will be inconsistencies; and
we have told you why. We have said we are not
the Divine Source, and that this material will be
limited not only by what we can access but also
by what you can handle, as well as what the
vehicles can manage to get through, yes? You
will find in other channeled materials, and there
is other channeled material out there, some very
valid and valuable material, and some may
conflict with some of this material. It could be
because it is meant to conflict, and there are
many different variables as to why that could
be. Likewise, religion, the customs, cultures,
and laws, when first being passed on to others,
were passed on to meet the people where they
were at, at that time. However, where people
are at now is just that they have gotten more

and more dumbed down. Because the religions, the religionists (we will keep saying that word, and when we say that word, we are referencing those who get a payoff from the religion, you understand?), they get a payoff. Maybe not just an individual person, but again, a country, or the religion itself, because they are all so . . . again, if you look at your major religions, then you will also notice there are often hierarchies. Within those hierarchies, there are all different levels of power and control. Anytime anyone thinks or believes that they can speak for God, that can become a very big problem. In your Christian religion, or *religions*, there are many versions of the Christian Bible. There is the New Standard Version, the New English Standard Version, the King James Version, and so on, because people translate them and say, "Well, this is a better translation," "Well, this is a better translation," and again, coming from something that was already translated improperly to begin with. Imagine what a mess it becomes. If you carry that book and you have all of these different versions, and then one thousand years from now it will be translated and retranslated to make better sense based on what people understand, now imagine, you could have a whole entirely different book. You understand? You have seen more recently, in your past century or so, that other books have been found, other scrolls, other texts—things that were taken out.

Perhaps they were not put in to begin with. This is not just limited to Christianity.

As individuals, when you read this text, you will pick and choose what to follow from this information based on what you are ready to do, yes? Again, you can read the same thing and, from that one person, may decide to begin to meditate; another will give up all her belongings and walk the world greeting people. Another will do something entirely different. Because, again, it will meet you where you are, but also—and very important to note—you will take it to where you are willing to go with it. You understand? We wish to be very clear about that because, again, human beings have a way of limiting themselves and then placing it outside themselves by saying, "Oh, but you said it would meet me where I'm at, and that is where I'm at," and what we are saying to you is yes, but you can go farther. You do not have to go farther; but again, in terms of the evolution of Spirit, you should push yourselves a little farther. And each of you that are reading this text now will know that whatever you read, whatever inspirational thing you read, each time you read it, you will understand it differently based on where you are in your life, what is happening in your life, as well as your own willingness to view yourself fully. So that is how things move through one's individual frame of reference. So we wish for you to begin to think, people. That is what we wish for you to do—begin to think. If what we just mentioned is true of now, then, of course, it was true then. Therefore, even if some humans wish to argue the point that the words in these sacred texts are the infallible word of God, you must understand it is not God that wrote them. So if you can agree—we challenge you here to do this—if you can agree, when you read something or when you hear something that you may hear differently, depending on what you are going through, then would that not hold true for all humans? Therefore, even with the scribes and translators, would that still hold true? So *think*; you must *think* on these things.

We will prepare to take a break, thank you.

[There was a fifteen-minute break. During break, a discussion was held regarding the material. And Julie, feeling as though her trance state was not very deep, expressed her concern over the level of trance, as well as the information that is coming through.]

THE COLLECTIVE: And so we would like to begin again by offering an opportunity for any queries or questions based on what we have shared of the information thus far on this your evening.

YVES: No, everything is very understandable.

THE COLLECTIVE: We would like to start by adding a short side note regarding the current process during this session. We have started out by increasing the concentration of our energy and raising the energetic frequency around you. Julie is accustomed to experiencing a certain level of our concentration. And because we have held back some of the concentration, her physical body does not feel the way it normally does when channeling; therefore, she notices the difference. Also, there are times when the information we share seems very basic to her. But you must remember—she must remember, rather—that since she is already linked in to us, then there are times when even if she doesn't know that she already knows, she does already have access to the information. It may not mean that she is walking around knowing it and hearing it all the time, but she has access to it, and so she has access to our energy. And our energy carries—we are thought form, you understand?—so it always carries all of that information and that knowledge. So it is as though there is a book on a bookshelf that perhaps she doesn't know is there, you see? And she may not have read the book, but somehow, someone mentions the book, and she happens to know the author's name but doesn't know how she knew. So that is some of it, and yes, some of it probably would not be new information to her anyway. However, we are not writing the book for her. We understand her concerns, and they do not so much come from that place of wanting us to write it for her but from her desire to have the material be as expansive as possible. Part of which is because she has a need—her ego-self has a need for some proof to herself over and over again that the material is valid, you understand, that all of this that you are doing is valid. She has a need to prove that it is not just a piece or a particle of her that is creating all of this. You understand? We only wanted to address that briefly.

We were discussing religions and the scriptures that are used within religions as well as their underlying purpose or what "spawned them into being," so to speak.

Let us readjust here. We are merely scanning what information we have already imparted.

So we have spoken about the religions that most people that live here on this Earth at this time of yours would be familiar with. We have spoken of some of the ways in which things have been twisted and turned. What we would also like to say is that this will always be or has always been true to some degree. From what we see currently, it will continue to be true for many human beings for some time. This is because in your humanness, when you include the ego-self, and taking into account frames of reference and things such as that, you will look at something or take a belief in something and put your own spin on it so that it works into your own agendas.

Additionally, this did not just occur with the onset of these three major or three better-known religions that we were speaking of, you see? In Hinduism, for instance, there are also many writings or sacred scriptures, and most of those who follow this religion understand that it is mythology. Also, when they talk of the many gods and goddesses, they see them as an aspect of a piece of ultimate Divinity. It is similar in some ways to how we talk of the over soul of the over soul of the over soul, leading to the divine over soul. That there are all these little particles and pieces of the consciousness; similarly, this is what they see—these many gods and goddesses—as the aspects of the over soul. You understand? Yet, even within that awareness, there are still writings within that religion that creates division and has been espoused that is a corruption of the original teachings. This teaching relates to the separation of people according to their "castes," as they call them. The separation of people in those castes denotes what a person is allowed to do for a living, who they are allowed to be with or not be with. Again, this is a cultural thing that is a custom that was created as a means for those who held some power to maintain that power. So even within this religion that many people in this area where your world are now turning to, there are faults. Meditation has become a practice here because of its practice there. You understand? So while, again, like anything, this religion or way of life holds within it benefits for many people, there are still ways in which others are oppressed by other aspects of that religion. So even though they will say it is not a religion, it is a way of living. There are still those within that way of living that created a system—you see—to maintain power and control over others. And although there are many great practices in that culture for opening your awareness, the teachings contradict each other. For instance, on one hand, if you are to go to someone's home, they are very welcoming people. They have traditions where they are taught to share all that they have, but at the same time that this is happening in individual homes and places, there are some places in which they still share, but only if you are of their same caste or higher. There are some, and this is not true for all, who believe that you may not share with someone who is lower than you or you may not drink from the same glass of someone who is lower than you. Not even necessarily because of what some may say would be hygienic reasons.

You will find this less so in Buddhism, but you still will find ways in which power and control permeates in some of the practices. There are some sects of Buddhism that will not allow women to participate in certain practices. Or other parts of it, where if women are engaged in certain practices, still in all the monks, the males always have the final say or the final rule. You understand? So, again, if you look closely, there are ways in which these things permeate all religious doctrines and teachings.

Now, if you go back in time to the practices that people refer to as indigenous practice or culture, those things that were natural to the place and the time before all of these other things came about, even then, and continuing now in some of those practices, there are individuals who vie for control. People who still do what they feel they have to do to exert power. So power and control and exploitation of principles do not belong to any particular religion but to mankind. Therefore, when people get into the argument that religion creates a division and propose that if the world were to rid itself of religion, then there would be no more war and there would be no more problems, we say to you, this is not the case. It is not the religion itself. It is the things that were put in place within the context of the religion based on mankind and the human mind and the human ego and the human desire to make a connection to divine source empowerment. When they fail to accomplish it, they attempt to achieve it through power, control, greed, lust, and all those things. You understand?

YVES: Yes.

THE COLLECTIVE: We will pause momentarily for any queries you have.

YVES: No questions, thank you.

THE COLLECTIVE: In your religions, again, we wish to go back to those strands of things, for having a historical perspective of things is not very helpful in spiritual advancement if we do not help you to find the ways to advance with that knowledge. Again, each of these sorts of containers of religious teachings holds bits and pieces of everything. And some people may interpret the teachings one way, and others will interpret them another way. Therefore, what you need to look for are the things within those containers that help you to become a better human being, to become more loving, more compassionate, understanding—things that help you to have more peace and to be more peaceful. So when you are looking at any practice within a container, these are the things you must ask yourself: Does this container hold this up for me? And if it doesn't hold it up enough, what are the things within the container that might? Then do that! And if that doesn't help, then you need to begin to look at some other containers. You understand? Now, here's the tricky part for the human who decides what is more understanding, what is more compassionate, what is more peaceful. You understand? Because were you to ask some people, they may tell you that through their religious practice, they become very loving and forgiving and compassionate, and they give money to charity, and this and

265

that; but what we are talking about is your day-to-day life. How are you living your life? Are you (and again, because you're human, you're not going to do it perfectly) moving forward to being a better person, to incrementally beginning to gain some of these things? Is it making you less selfish, less self-serving? Is it bringing you closer to humankind, or is it serving to separate you? So even that needs its own context to ask and answer those questions. Because some of those same people that will tell you that they do those things are also the same people who put others down who are in other containers, yes? Or who are others who speak other languages, or who have a different color of skin, or are from different parts of the world, or so on and so forth, who don't have nice enough cars—you get the picture, yes? Or perhaps they ignore people that need their attention. Perhaps they ignore the hungry person on the street. Perhaps they ridicule others. Because, you see, even within this container, you can have a group of people that still are trying to keep themselves above others, yes? Look at the people around you, that's where you look when you're looking in your container. Look around you: What are the people around you doing? What does that tell you about it? Now, perhaps they are only showing up at their meeting place once a week, and so perhaps you are not seeing those qualities in them that you would like to begin to improve upon in yourself. And so that may be, again, because they are only showing up, you see? There is a saying that we have accessed from Julie, "If you hang with dogs, then you will get fleas." You understand? And so it is important as well to look at the company that you keep. Are they supporting your moving forward? Are they walking with you? Are they living that? Are you modeling for them, or are they modeling for you? You understand? Because otherwise, then, you can just feed each other those same lies. So if you are in a container—whatever sort of, we will use the word *congregation* because it means people coming together, you understand. So, if you are in this congregation of sorts (of course, in an entire congregation not everyone is going to be headed in the same way right?), does it mean that they are not practicing certain principles because it's meeting them where they're at? So as long as everyone is moving forward— meaning going toward that spiritual evolution, becoming better, becoming more connected—if they are doing that, then each person may be at a little bit of a different place of it. But there will be some that are not; that is a "given," as you would say. However, if the majority is not, then you need to look at that. You need to ask yourself if it is the container or the people. Because where will you get your motivation from? You see, it will be very easy to become lazy, and if no one is ahead of you, where do you go?

Although we often talk of listening, with the heart and with that place in your stomach you refer to as the solar plexus, you sometimes need to use your physical eyes, which can be helpful for some things. You must look around you and ask yourself, "Can this container that I am currently in take me to my destination?" This is not a judgment on the container. If you need to cross the sea, then one of your army tanks will not get you there; likewise, to cross the desert or go through the forest, a ship is not the proper container. Therefore, it is important to assess and look at these things and take it even a step farther out from that container. Right now, we are referencing the container of your congregation, your religion, your practice, whatever it is that you wish to call it. You should also look at the other "containers" of your life. For there are many different places that you operate from. Now, for some of you, it may be important that you work in an environment where others are working toward the same cause or some of the same goals for your lives. For those of you for whom this is important, you must look at that container and use the same formula, ask yourself the same questions. Others may perform tasks in jobs where they work alone, so that makes it a little more difficult to assess. Perhaps you work in an office setting where you may have many different types of people so this may not be an area where you are looking to see. "Are these people helping me to move forward, or are they supporting who I am and my cause," and so on and so forth. You understand? However, you must take that same measuring tool to look at your friends. Who is in your circle of friends? You must apply this across the board because you cannot make it through the quicksand if you have cinder blocks tied to your feet. In other words, the farther you wish to go in your spiritual development and evolvement, then who you are and the principles that you practice needs to be interconnected. You understand? We are not saying that after reading this section you should go out and change everything all at once, but you should be moving toward having each of these places that you walk in begin to interconnect. When you are walking fully in the integrity of your path and purpose, it is then that you are aligning yourself with these spiritual ideals and principles that we have been speaking of. Therefore, there should be a likeness in all of these worlds that you are walking within.

Otherwise, it makes it very difficult for you to stay in one of them. Of course, the world will always throw things at you, so that as you are walking in this straight line, everything else in your life is moving with you, and that you can go in and out of them without having to change yourself. You understand? Without having to change. Of course, there are different settings and different environments, and there are social customs. So, of course, we are not saying that if you are naked in your shower, then you should be naked when you go to your work, for then that might be a problem, yes? However what we are saying is that *[slapping hands together with each word that follows]* who you are should not change. Because if you have to always change it, then that is not who you really are, isn't it? This is very important because this is where you really get down to the nitty-gritty stuff of spiritual evolvement. Because we have given you, and we will give you and we can give you and many people can give you, techniques or tasks; and all of those are things that assist the body, the mind, and the spirit. Those are all vehicles; they are tools. But the purpose of those vehicles and tools isn't just to have vehicles and tools; it is to get you out somewhere, yes? As we said earlier, you need to begin to become more compassionate and more peaceful if you are attempting to align yourself more with that which is a higher resonance with you than the average human, with that which is more evolved than who you are now, then you must get past just the daily tasks of it. What begins to happen as you are doing these things is that the layers of heaviness that have been built on you overtime, because of the way that your society is, you begin to take off these "layers of clothing," if you will. So that you become more genuinely yourself—you understand—and not based on the extraneous pressures of who you should be or what "someone who is successful does," or what they look like, and all of that. Because when you do these things, then you begin to take your shades off when you're looking at others. You see and can meet them where they are. And that separation starts; the separation isn't as wide at first, and then when that happens, you bring them forward, and then so on and so forth, and slowly—very slowly, we might add—this separation that exists between people, religions, races, and all of that becomes smaller and smaller and smaller. You understand?

Do you have any questions?

YVES: No, I think my question will probably come in the next session or after I have had a chance to listen. Actually, I am formulating some now, but they don't quite fall into what we're talking about. I am sure as you continue to speak, some of them will be addressed. If they are not, then I will bring them up at a later time.

THE COLLECTIVE: We wish to make a very strong point here in saying that the tricks of the trade are not enough. The idea behind this spiritual evolvement, of course, is that each of you has your own reasons that you wish to evolve. You have your own agendas, and that will always be, so long as you incarnate as human beings. But the larger agenda that, which your higher selves call you toward, is to bring you back to some, not all, of those ways of being. We spoke of when people had the ability to just know things. They were just so connected that they did not need all these rules and regulations

271

and details and directions in order to just move through life. But again, there is so much that has been built up on each of you that there has become this padding, iron gates, and cement walls around you all. And so, again, you are shedding these ideas and beliefs that don't fit anymore. They do not help you to move forward. You begin to shed all of the things that keep you stuck, that get in the way of your forward progress. Let us clearly state, we understand that at times in your humanness, this is a very difficult task. You become attached to ideas of things, to things themselves, or to people, places, jobs, duties, money, and what have you. It is difficult to let go of those things and those ideas; however, it is sometimes necessary to do this. However, it is these same things that make you believe that you are okay with them and won't be okay without them. They serve as the padding, the walls, and the gates. There are so many layers for each of you to shed.

Sitting down and meditating assists in raising your vibrational frequency. It assists in aligning the physical body with the spirit more; it assists in taking care of the physical body in some very important medical ways as well. It serves to slow the human mind down and assists in your becoming more centered in the body and spirit. Many people begin to meditate because they are in some uncomfortable situation or uncomfortable pain or whatever, and they are trying to get rid of their stress. The thought is, *Okay, if I learn how to do this, then all of this won't be so bad*, yes? And of course, if that is what you wish to do, then by all means, please do that. But again, if you are looking to move forward, to shed these layers, then meditation is only the beginning. It is something that you do to help raise your frequency to begin moving forward and to help keep everything in line as you are going forward. It also helps that you continue doing it, of course, to raise your awareness to some of those more subtle messages or energy shifts. To the changes in things around you and all of that, which then puts you more in line with Spirit and the potential for evolution. However, there are many people who have meditated for many years, and it does not mean that other than meditating, they have actually changed the way that they view their life, the way that they walk through their life, or even the way that they treat other people. You understand? Similarly, going to the meeting places of your religious orders does not mean that you will change those things either.

So, yes, it is important to have these tools and these vehicles, but it is also important, when using these, to begin to utilize them in such a way that you can begin to look in the mirror and see the ways in which you still keep yourself separate. See the ways in which you still keep people away. See the ways in which you still judge others. See the ways in which you still hold on to things that no longer serve you. This is not an easy task, we understand, when you are human. But for those of you who are reading this text, because there's something in you that is saying, "I wish to follow the call of my spirit; I wish to complete as much as I can complete of what I planned for this lifetime, to learn and to do," then you must do these other things. You must shed these layers no matter how difficult, no matter how much time it takes, no matter how painful, no matter how frightened you can get. You can always turn back if you wish, but for some of you who are reading this text, the turning back and turning away becomes more frightening than the letting go, or the changing, or the releasing of the layers, or the letting people in. You understand?

Even those of you who are attempting to return to some of the old ways, who are attempting to step outside of the box of what had been the more popular religions or the things that are accepted and all of that, you still, in many ways, are influenced by the culture, by the customs of now, of this time period. You understand? So if you still have this frame of reference, and you put those goggles on, and when you begin to look at these other things, these other technologies, these other practices, this other understanding through these goggles, well, of course, you are not going to get it right. You understand? Because you are using something that you are trying to get away from as your measuring stick. Yes. So many of you need to be shaken up. And there's much of that happening in your world right now. People have always been being shaken up. But many of you reading the book right now, if you look back over your lives, you will see these distinct points in time when you have faced hardships, which all people do, but they are the shake-up kind. And any of you who are reading this book now who have not, well then, be prepared, because—if you are moving forward, if you are committed to this, if you are committed to your soul's intent—that is the only way to remind you, to shake you up enough that you land on the ground, not knowing whether or not you want to dig your way all the way into the dirt and bury yourself there. For it is in those moments of desperation, when all feels lost, it is only by experiencing that depth (that when you rise above it you can begin to see that you don't need to hold on to these ideas, these perceptions, these things, or what have you) when your eyes open more to what's real, and to what is important. It is when you begin to understand that this life that you are currently experiencing as the person whom you currently are is not limited in this linear way, is not boxed in. When you begin to fully understand that it goes on and on and on, and these other things we have spoken about—about the other parts of yourself, yes—when you begin to understand that, when you begin to really fully grasp the idea that you aren't the only one that exists and that you are a part of a bigger part of you and that it goes on endlessly, then you begin to realize that there isn't so much to lose after all. Because, you see, you still have yourselves convinced that here is your life, here is what you have, here is what you must hold on to, and you have it in this little block. Because you are seeing your life in its totality, as the individual person that you are right now, as the goal. This is not the goal. The goal is much bigger and broader, higher and lower, inward and outward. And when you really begin to grasp that, you begin to understand the concept that there is nothing that you own; therefore, there is nothing that you can lose. But again, in trying to maintain this illusion of this linear life in this box, you attempt to hold on to things to define yourself as a separate, individual human being, that define you for who you are in this life or what you have done, and that is who you are. However, this is not. Your job is not who you are; it is what you do. Now for some of you, you may have jobs that you do because of who you are, and they become a part of who you are, but they still are not you.

When you are holding on to all of these things and you are grabbing these definitions of yourself (either your own or other's ideas of you, your wants or others' wants, and you always carry it), how can you possibly carry them all when your arms are already full? You must put your packages down. Be sure, as you do that, you do not stubbornly shove your hands into your pockets. Instead, open your arms. For what is placed in them you may find to be of more value in terms of your evolvement. Perhaps the package isn't as pretty. But you don't buy your gardening tools for the looks of them, do you? You buy what works, that you may plant the seeds. And likewise, when your arms are filled with weeds, they will strangle those plants, they will interfere, and they will block the sunlight. Now these weeds may not even be intending to block the sunlight; they're reaching for their own sunlight. You understand? But if you are to have a good harvest, then you must remove the weeds that are blocking the light. You must continue to tend to the Earth. You must continue to be sure that it is watered, that it is nourished. And so you must water and nourish yourself. Many people also get caught (and many do this in the beginning, and ideally, they change their circumstances, but many do not) in this fast-moving, locomotive action; and they decide that if they meditate three times a day, if they do yoga four times a day, and if they—you understand where we're going with this? They're checking off their little task list. And many times, what they're doing is they're still just running away from themselves. So, going back to that mirror: Look in that mirror at yourself and look directly into your own eyes. Look in them, not at them. In them—*in them*. Most of you will have quite a bit of difficulty with this. And if you do, then there is something that you are not revealing to yourself. You know, yes, that when you are speaking with another individual, when they do not maintain what you call eye contact, you say to yourself, "This person is not telling me the truth," or "This person is not trustworthy," or "This person does not want me to see them," yes? And so we challenge each of you—this is not a new challenge—to look into your mirror, to really, really look. And try it first for thirty seconds; many of you won't even make it that long. Some of you may feel emotions begin to come up, and then you'll stop. And we say let them come up. And again, it is important that you remember that you must look *into* your eyes, not at them, not around them, not at the outer parts of them. But just as though when you are looking at a loved one and you're looking into their eyes, look into your own the same way. And stay there with yourself. And if you continue this practice and you allow these things to come up, you will see the areas where you still need to work on. The areas where you need to shed those layers. The areas where your fear exists, the areas where your guilt exists, the areas where your pettiness exists, the areas where your judgment exists, the areas where your greed exists, and so on. If you have this as a regular practice for some time, those things, those areas that we just spoke of, they'll begin to come up even when you're not looking in the mirror. In a way, you are noticing the ways in which you are doing this as you are walking through your day because you know that at the end of the evening, you have to go back in front of the mirror and look yourself in the eyes. That helps you to begin to change some of that. And again, this too is a tool to begin processes. You understand?

There is much more that we have to say about this and much more that we wish to share about these practices of the religions, but for this evening, we must take our leave of the physical body. We will actually not be fully taking our leave. We will be staying with the physical body in the more subtle ways that we do. But the throat is beginning to become hoarse, and so we wish not to damage it as we will be in need of it again soon. And so, we ask first, before we go into anything regarding our next sessions, if there are any other queries that you have this evening regarding any of this that you feel need to be asked now and cannot wait to be asked at the next session.

YVES: No, everything in your discourse is clear, and I have no questions about that, no. Again, the questions that I have will have to wait until I have heard the whole discourse, and then I can address them.

THE COLLECTIVE: We thank you for your continued work on behalf of this text, and we bid you a fond good evening.

Meeting the Over Souls
in the Forest

August 14, 2006 – This session was conducted prior to starting the manuscript. Julie had been directed by Spirit to go into the town park in Schodack, New York, to channel Spirit. It was approximately 9:00 p.m. when the session started. This session was much different from earlier sessions as well as the sessions that followed. In this session, what was channeled was the over soul of Julie, and it seems as though Yves's over soul was also close by, assisting with the information. To date, this was the most mind-blowing session for Julie in terms of her "coming back" after a trance. (We now see this session as one of the hints that we received early on, that we were to work on this book together, for spirit.) The session was ninety minutes in length.

OVER SOUL: We see that you have listened and walked into the forest. We are pleased. Though it may seem a simple task, the walking in that you just completed speaks of something far greater. We called both of you here tonight mostly to see if you would heed that call. And you have. There are others here with me now, and we look with pride and pleasure over both of you. We stand at the helm of the greater ship to watch from the other plane of existence where many of us reside. I have watched you for some time. At times, I assisted in leading you forward by—as you would say in your language—dangling a carrot, which perhaps you did not even see at the time, and yet you stepped forward.

YVES: Thank you. Many times, I felt I was being led, and I was. But at the same time not knowing, and somewhat feeling that because I do not know, that I may step into something and be unprotected. But lately, I've been feeling that even though I do not know anything, I feel protected that you guys are with me, and so I am evolving very slowly in that respect.

OVER SOUL: Define *protection.*

YVES: Uhm, that I would do something that would cause—that may have some negative . . .

OVER SOUL: Define *negative.* You see, what you try to do instead is to walk forward and not have it affect anything and to keep everything static. When you walk forward, that cannot happen; it is an impossibility. So when you claim to be looking for protection, what you are really asking for is for everything to stay the same.

YVES: Okay, there will be obstacles. There will be adversities, and there will be enemies.

OVER SOUL: If you focus on the enemies, the enemies will grow larger.

YVES: Yes, I do understand that.

OVER SOUL: When you keep looking over your shoulder, you trip on the very small twig that is in front of your feet as you walk upon the forested floor. These petty, small things can be quite the distraction; and although oftentimes, yes, change occurs or things happen, that may not seem petty as you are living in this body. Yet from where we stand, the only thing we are concerned about is assisting you. Assisting you to accomplish what you decided to accomplish when you came back to the earthen plane. Therefore, you see, from the perspective of the human self—the embodiment—you may see things as being troublesome, or you may view them as being problematic and resultant from work that is done. Yet, what we say to you is that you are judging it based on the human self that is living in the illusion. For when you take away the stage that you are upon—because this life is a stage—when you take away the scenery and the set, what matters most is, did you make it across the stage?

And so you see, you are trying to make it across the stage but giving particulars about where the set should be. What we say to you is that while you are busying yourself moving around the sets for your comfort, you may not notice things as you are moving around, and you bump into the wall that had been moved prior. We understand that this is not something that is easy for human beings to grasp, and this is part of the struggle on the earthen plane. Again, I say to you that we stand at the helm. There are several of us who are here this, what you would call, evening, of yours. This is your evening; we have no evenings or daytimes. We have no time, nor do you really. In actuality, we who are standing here at the helm are nothing more than the bigger parts of the two of you.

YVES: I have an idea, yes.

OVER SOUL: We think not fully. We think that you may grasp some of that which we prepare to share with you; however, you must also understand that even in our sharing, there are still limitations, *currently*. The voice that is coming through the body right now is very similar to the voice that this vehicle uses, is it not?

YVES: Yes.

OVER SOUL: Now, let me explain to you why that is. Although you may hear some fluctuations from time to time with the energy as I speak to you, this will not be different beings coming through; in fact, the vocal box of this physical vehicle carries my energy in such a way because I am the same energy as the soul that resides in the physical vehicle. However, that is only a part of the many parts that make up the energy that I am. You understand? So you see, standing with me also is the energy that the part of the you that sits before that part of me today. It is that larger part of you. Now, understand that there are many parts. That while you are here talking to me, the energy that is here with me that is the larger part of you is directing your inquiries, but not too much to interfere. You understand about free will, correct? Yes. Many people have gotten lost in the idea of free will because they look at it only as though it is up to the entire universe. The free will and the laws of nature, which I will say are all true and valid things. You refer to us in this lifetime, in this incarnation, as over souls. We have a desire for the larger part of us to accomplish certain things. And so, there are parts of us that separate and incarnate; and although you have heard this concept before, we believe that the totality of it, the reality of it may be difficult for you to fathom or swallow at this moment. Because at this moment, all the lifetimes that you see as past or future are happening concurrently. And so, when we say that we stand at the helm, really, you might look at it as a hub.

You are one who enjoys communication types of things (your recording devices and your computer devices), and so if you were to view us as the central hub of the intelligence or the data bank and you tap in—I believe you refer to that as a network, and many people are on the same network and can access the different various files and programs that are on the network. Are you following me?

YVES: Yes.

OVER SOUL: And so too, many selves of you, are tapping into the network to access or input or upload or download information. We are more or less the central mainframe computer.

YVES: Yes, yes, that is a very good analogy. I like that. I am trying to access information, and I do have some information; but there is more information I am trying to access, but I do not know how to navigate to it.

OVER SOUL: Well, the navigation would not include hacking into the computer.

YVES: True, yes. I do not have clearance for it, for that, to have access to that information yet.

OVER SOUL: Correct. Also, the information is downloaded from the mainframe computer when the computer and the network have the capability to store the information. Just as when you are putting more information into your computer at your home or workspace, you may at times, if you have too many programs, need to expand its memory or enlarge its capacity or capabilities. Likewise, it is so for the human body, as you know it is very much like a computer. The brain is a computer. It stores information, and just like a computer when you program it, there are certain things that it can and cannot do. You cannot use an old program to have the computer do something new, store certain types of files, or access certain types of files. Likewise, the brain needs to be reprogrammed as well. The reprogramming often is completed through the various tasks that we remind you of either via other vehicles, voices, writings, or things that you read, or sometimes just by the blind dangling carrot. It is like a patchwork or road map that is created in the motherboard of your human computer system.

YVES: Yes, I do understand.

OVER SOUL: We are very pleased to be conversing more directly with you tonight, and we must say to you that not many are allowed the privilege of this direct communication. Many would abuse the information. One thing we wish to tell you is that it is more important for you—as you feel our energies tonight, the energy that is coming through this physical body right now—to take notice of that energy. This energy is also carrying some of the energy of your over soul because we are in a way intertwined in our energies, currently, as we are standing at the helm.

YVES: Could you explain that another way?

OVER SOUL: All energy, while it may be contained, moves in and out of other energies when it is free. And, therefore, just as you have others who come to assist at times, at times they have come speaking as many—not one, but many. Tonight, as I speak to you, there are two energies combined. Let me see if I can make this simpler for you to understand. The energy that is the source of that which watches over you and the many yous, that which is a part of the many "yous," your bigger self, is infusing my energy with thought forms and patterns and directions and programming that can then be disseminated down into the physical vehicle whose voice box is now being used for this purpose. Does that make sense to you?

YVES: Yes, that makes sense.

OVER SOUL: The one thing that we wish to advise you on is that it is more important for you to feel this energy as it is coming through because it is comingled with the energy of you, of the bigger you, so that you can know when you are connecting. It is more important that you begin to work on having awareness of its presence, and of the other "yous" that are present, rather than attempt to continually access it via other means. In other words, using the voice of another being. Because while this is helpful now in this moment, and while there may be other times that we come in (but I will say to you that there will seldom, seldom be times that we come in), we do enlist the help of others. Those you have walked with before on other paths, in other places, in other galaxies, in other moments of now. That they will step in to assist when asked, and we, of course, will always assist in guiding you; however, we will seldom use the voice box because that can create and command on us so much energy and so much responsibility to the point that we're no longer overseers, that we are now becoming gods to the puppet that you are. That is a mistake that was made long, long ago, if you were to count in the time in your world (we used the word time for easier understanding of what we meant). We say to you that there was a time when some of us roamed the Earth as our larger selves, and we then decided to work on these projects. At times, it can be very difficult because, you see, your evolution and your decisions also affect the evolution of us as a whole, because we are the bigger part of you.

YVES: Yes.

OVER SOUL: And so, for many of us at many different times or events or moments, it is very

difficult to not reach in and move things faster
or move things out of the way that we might be
benefited in the way that we see fit. For even as
we stand here at the helm, even while we are
the mainframe of information, there is something grander than that beyond us. We do not
have direct lines, such as you often have. We too
have the propensity of it, the largeness of it; it
just goes on, as you would say, "until infinity
and beyond."

In some of your sacred scriptures, as you
call them in this part of your present lifetime,
is written the concept that there is no beginning
and no ending. And people look at that still in
a very linear way, like the world did not begin
and the world did not end. In truth, what we
are saying is what those words really mean is
that there is no beginning and end because it
spreads out across forever. Everything is intri-
cately woven together and connected. That we
at the hub, even though we may be seen here
[gesturing into the ethers above], we are more here
[gesturing to the sides], and it spreads out farther.
But from us there is yet another hub in a different dimension, and from there and so on. You
see what I am getting to, correct?

YVES: Yes, it is quite, quite involved.

OVER SOUL: Yes, much too involved for—
if you'll pardon what seems to be perhaps

offensive; it is not meant that way—your tiny human brain to possibly conceive of its totality.

YVES: I do understand. Because again, I am having enough of a task feeling, being aware, as you said, of your presence. That is something that I am aware of that I have been trying to access, and feeling and accessing the direct information of you coming through. But at the moment, I am at a loss to feel it in its totality. At times, I feel . . .

OVER SOUL: You will never feel it in its totality. Even as you measure yourself up against someone else's measuring stick, the measuring stick that you see as larger than yours is still unable to see everything. So in other words, as I'm saying, if you feel as though you are moving out to here [*motions to one place in front of body*] and others around you are moving out to there [*motions beyond the earlier place*], beyond here still is endless. It is no more or less endless than it is endless from where you stand.

YVES: I do understand—I do, I do—that there's always more. It is like they talk about the big bang theory as to the universe is expanding, but it is expanding into something that is even more expandable.

OVER SOUL: That is correct. You say that you are beginning to feel, but you are not feeling it in its totality, which is why we say to you, you never shall.

YVES: Okay, maybe not in its totality, but as for me comparing myself to another vehicle, the vehicle that you are using at the moment, she is very . . .

OVER SOUL: Yes, well, that is silly, isn't it? For you see, if you were to measure, you are measuring only one thing up to that vehicle. You are measuring the ability, the connection, or the knowing; you are measuring only that against the being. Again, let us look at the "computer," if you will. Let's say that you have a mainframe, you have a computer that works at this, and you have a program that works at recording music (I will say because you are one who likes to record). Therefore, you have this program in there, and over here is another program; and what you are trying to do is to get your music program to do everything that this typing or word processing program does. So what that means is not that you cannot access the typing or word processing program, but, rather, you need to remember as well that there is the music program on the computer, and so the typing isn't the only piece, and the music isn't the only piece. You are seeing this as separate, as though this vehicle is something for you to move toward becoming more like it. Correct?

YVES: Yes.

OVER SOUL: Yes, and we say to you that that is preposterous. While you view this vehicle as being farther along than you, and that you are walking toward it, when what we are saying to you is that you are both in the place where we have brought you together. Because, together, as you walk, there are programs that you have as your own even while you will learn different things from each other, sharing with each other those programs that you have make more of the totality. If you were to get yourself to where this vehicle is, then you must leave behind the other essential pieces that *this* vehicle is missing.

YVES: I understand.

OVER SOUL: You spoke of that, you spoke of that. By the way, we are quite proud of the work that you two achieved in your last evening, but also we want to mention that we noticed that you spoke of your work together, and I believe you said teamwork. You spoke of the balance of you, and you spoke of the yin and the yang, and yet, I might add quite humorously, when sitting before the mainframe computer, your question is, "Why am I not more like this one?" When, by golly, certainly, certainly, one as curious as you would ask, although perhaps not receive, much deeper, more pondering questions than that when seated before the mainframe.

YVES: Yes, yes, I get it . . . I get it . . . yes.

OVER SOUL: You say that you get it, and we believe that you are beginning to see a better picture of it all. However, it is important to remember that part of this walk and the weaving together of your two energies (which is necessary for you to assist others, together) is going to lend itself to you not always "seeing." So what we want to say is that it is okay, but remember that rather than, you know, aiming for this goal of having the same abilities as this vehicle and thinking, *this is where I want to be*, or have this bar that you have placed for yourself to reach. We say that the bar that has been set by your *higher* self is *not* the same bar.

YVES: Okay, now that brings me to the question, what is my work, the work that I have agreed to?

OVER SOUL: *[Laughter.]*

YVES: *[Laughter.]* I know, I know.

OVER SOUL: There is no way. There is no possibility that you could ever achieve the work that you came to do, were I to tell you.

YVES: My work with Malidoma Somé you directed me toward him, yes?

OVER SOUL: You were drawn toward Malidoma, yes.

YVES: I was drawn toward Malidoma, okay.

OVER SOUL: Malidoma taps into that other self of you that exists, which helps to bring you closer to your other self. You have a deeper question about that. When you ask if we directed you to Malidoma, there is a more probing question.

YVES: I feel that Malidoma is . . . is one of the keys in me getting to my work, my work that I came to do on this plane as far as—

OVER SOUL: If we may interrupt and point out to you that you refer to your work on this plane as though you refer to your work when you get up and go to work from 9:00 a.m. to 5:00 p.m. It is as though you have tried to capture this work as though it is a career. Moreover, what we are saying to you is that sometimes the work is not what would seem to be work.

YVES: That is true, because sometimes, a lot of times, people do what they love; and it is called work, but it is a labor of love.

OVER SOUL: Again, even in that statement, you are trying to fit it in to the work mold. And what we are saying is that everything that you do here is work. It is not separate from you. It is all that you are, it is all that you think, it is all that you breathe, it is all that you do. That is your work. Again, you are attempting to find the place for it rather than walking into it and allowing it to come to you.

YVES: Yeah. I am trying to understand. How do I do that? It's like I was trying to learn how to feel; but then as you mentioned, I get instruction in many different ways, and I believe I was led to that book by you guys, and I got a somewhat a better understanding of what some of my fears are.

OVER SOUL: The best book that you have regarding that is your current experience. Therefore, when you ask the question, "How do I learn how to do that?" what we say is you walk—you walk forward. *You* walk forward. Sometimes you'll walk gently, sometimes you will walk roughly stomping, sometimes you will run, sometimes you will sit and dig your feet (or your heels) in, but you move forward anyway.

There is no secret code or a way to understand the heart, which is the heart center or the soul center or the part of the program that remembers what is programmed from the mainframe. You see, this is programmed often from the current cycle. This is programmed from the mainframe (must be pointing somewhere,

Yves could not recall where); and so in terms of knowing how to do that better, it's to not do it so well and then perhaps do it a little bit better and then not do it so well again. The point is that in spite of that, you should keep moving forward toward that which you are going. And mostly to stop trying to figure out this computer *[pointing to the head]* from this one *[pointing to the heart]* because they are on different networks, so to speak. The head or brain, is a useful computer. It is a kind of computer that they might use in your automobile repair shops, where they attach the automobile to the computer and they diagnose what the problem is. So this computer, the programming here, the brain, is very good for diagnosing what appears to be the problem. In that case, you are looking with your physical eyes, which are attached to that computer system (the brain). Yet this here and here *[pointing to heart and solar plexus areas]* is not connected to the physical eyes but, rather, to the third eye and to the memory of who you really are. This is connected to the hub. At times, we can access the brain by going through the heart or solar plexus, but it does not happen the other way around. You are trying to do it the opposite way.

YVES: Yes, I am coming down from the brain to the heart when I should be going from the heart to the brain.

OVER SOUL: Yes, yes, that is correct. We do not have much time here—not because we cannot stay, for we can; however, you cannot.

YVES: Yes, I can. I can stay longer.

OVER SOUL: No, you cannot.

YVES: Okay, you are speaking from a different point of view than I am thinking.

OVER SOUL: That is correct.

YVES: Okay. So I continue my work—the blending, the melding work with Julie. I continue my work with Malidoma and continue to open up my heart and come from there and, hopefully—no, not saying hopefully—and from there I'll have greater access to you which is . . .

OVER SOUL: Yes, however, do not be trapped into believing that now you have the formula. For it may change, dear.

YVES: No, that's the thing. That's one thing I have come to realize that I keep looking for the elusive formula. Yes, actually, yes, it will change because as I work with things, the equation will change.

OVER SOUL: That is correct. We prefer to say move through things as opposed to work—

because we feel you give too much weight to the word work. You are very task-oriented, which can come in rather handy as we have learned how to access that to get you to move forward at times by giving you tasks. For you are quite the good listener when it comes to tasks. You are getting better as well at listening to those things that draw you. Yet still, you should heed the warning to not allow that ability to close, for we see a pending potential that may attempt to pull you away from that place of understanding, that place of openness. This is similar to the many others who are in human form, but we are not at liberty to entertain that topic on this evening.

YVES: I do not understand.

OVER SOUL: You do understand. Nevertheless, you want us to tell you more information, which we are not at liberty to give. The only thing that you need to understand is that this part of you, this part of you that is beginning to open and to feel and to direct, is the part of you that is so new at doing this that it can easily be squelched by this and these *[pointing to head and eyes]* and what appears to be happening in the world around you. What this computer (the brain) tells you regarding what is happening in the world around you and what will happen as a result of that in the world around you, and all of the pictures of the world from here *[pointing to brain]*. You still have this free will. If you choose to return to the brain, you may do that, to only this brain. There were others who spoke with you last week. Yes, they are friends of ours, and they spoke with you and spoke of going into the proverbial forest and that while you may walk out of the forest, you cannot do so without leaving essential pieces of yourself behind. Do you recall this?

YVES: Yes, I do.

OVER SOUL: Yes, what they mean by that is that when you begin working from this computer *[pointing to the solar plexus]*, things begin to be input in *this* computer *[pointing to the heart]* as well, and it raises something. When you attempt to go back to the other computer *[referencing the brain]* and work from that place and make your decisions from the brain, then you must completely, at this point, seal that *[referencing the heart and solar plexus]* back up again. Because there is no way now, with your inner knowing opened up, for it to close without you sealing it or shutting it down. It is not like the camera whose shutters can open and close at will with no negative impact. Of course, there are those who choose to do that. Again, you certainly have the free will to do that. However, those who do this, walk around as though they are ghosts through the rest of their lives.

We must take our leave. We have one final thing to say that we wish for you to pass on. The one whose voice box I use. She knows of my existence; I have tapped into her many times. I would like her to consciously tap into me in her meditations, to listen and watch for my direction, but not just my direction, but to be aware that it is I—that it is she, I should say—that it is she here at the hub who is directing.

We will accept no further questions. We bid you adieu.

YVES: Thank you.

Julie's transition back from the trance was quite slow and much more difficult for her to manage than was customary.

After 10 minutes she began opening her eyes. Julie was having trouble knowing which was her reality. This, according to the Eighty-Second Regime was the result of connecting directly with her own Over Soul, thereby making it harder for her to come back to herself since she was with her higher self.

The conversation that follows was recorded after the session, between Yves and Julie. Included you will also find, further description from Yves after the recording was stopped.

JULIE: *[Sounding sleepy and almost child like.]* Are you here?

YVES: I am here, you are back.

JULIE: Oh my god, are you sure?

YVES: Yes, I am here.

JULIE: Oh my god, I just came back and thought I was here all alone and I didn't know where I was.

YVES: Mmm – Well, Seth[3] popped in.

JULIE: I know.

YVES: Toward the end they let him come in.

JULIE: I feel like I am not back all the way Yves.

YVES: Okay.

JULIE: I feel like you aren't real right now.

YVES: *[Chuckles.]*

JULIE: I am freaking out a little bit, because I can't 'feel' you. I see you but—okay let me see if you are real *[reaches out and feels around Yves shoulder]*—I feel like I am sitting on a blank piece of paper and then there is paper all around me—ahhhh bright lights—and none of it, it is

---

3   Seth is another energetic persona that speaks through Julie and is a part of the Eighty-Second Regime of Light Workers, but his function is different. He presents as a child and teaches about his own learning in the spirit realms and speaks through Julie to bring not only teachings of beyond "death" but brings much humor and innocence and in doing so lifts the spirits of others in attendance. He has informed Yves and Julie in the past that he has his own book to write for children. Seth is not the same energy as the Seth that was channeled by Jane Roberts.

all drawings around me, do you know what I mean?

YVES: Mhm, well they mentioned a lot of things.

JULIE: Is that mhm, like do you know, really...

YVES: No they did.

[Interrupting and talking over Yves, at this point Julie's responses seem to be slow.]

JULIE: ...what I mean?

YVES: Well, I uh...

JULIE: *[Pointing into the trees.]* Oh look, one of the hooded guys.

YVES: Really?

JULIE: Yeah

YVES: I am not even...

JULIE: *[Pointing again.]* See him right there between the two tree's? There is a tree and then a tree behind it *(which really describes the entire forested area but somehow these seemed isolated to Julie)*...right there, there is a hooded guy there.

YVES: No, I don't see him.

JULIE: Oh.

YVES: But, that's okay, I have been told to feel from my heart ...this is where everything is happening and that I am coming too much from my head with things and that I need to switch it around.

JULIE: You know what, Yves? I want to hear everything you have to say, but right now I probably can't absorb any of it, so you have to wait until I am off the plain piece of paper...

YVES: *[Chuckles.]* Okay.

JULIE: Because it is all just disappearing ink right now.

YVES: Wow, well that was some serious information that was imparted.

[Long pause.]

JULIE: I might be stuck here forever if I don't get up and move...say something grounding to me, like, you call me by my name or something.

YVES: Julie, come back to us, you are here. You don't feel like you are back yet but you are. Also the reason you feel this way is some high energy came through you, you were channeling some very high frequency. They say they don't usually…

JULIE: *[Interrupting again and loudly.]* Yeah, I'm seeing much too much right now, it's a little overwhelming.

YVES: Yeah, I can understand that, it is. It's a lot of stuff that came through.

JULIE: Like now I mean, not what came through, I mean now. I mean, holy shit, I don't feel like I am back yet…wait, am I talking? Am I…oh my god, my brain is going to explode.

YVES: It will not.

JULIE: *[Continuing over Yves.]* I don't know if I am back or if I am talking to you in a trance, but I think that I am awake, and I don't know if I am and I don't know if…

YVES: *[Places Julie's hand in the earth and puts dirt on it to ground her- about a minute elapses.]* Do you feel like you are back now?

JULIE: Kind of—but still in a different kind of trance… Oh look, a hopping gnome and there is this sphere like an Easter egg shape but bigger and in this sphere there is another sphere and another sphere and so on and it is going *[makes sound like a buzzing vibration]* and its not really touching the ground…but almost like bouncing off the ground, and all of the trees are breathing. I feel like I took acid.

YVES: Like the green lady right?

JULIE: Yeah like that, *[sounding a little bit panicky]* I really have to stand up, I really am getting kind of freaked out, there is just too much happening, there is too much I am seeing, I probably should close my eyes but then I will go back into a trance. There is too much information coming at me at once, too much, like visual not information, too much visual coming at me at once, whoa. Maybe I should just shut up (long pause) Thanks for keeping me safe and grounded.

YVES: You are welcome, thank you.

JULIE: Okay, I am really freaked out, I don't know what this is Yves. It is like thirty thousand thoughts a minute, and thirty thousand images a minute.

YVES: It's the energy that came through you are accessing all that stuff, because to them the past, the present and the future are all the same. It is all happening now, so I think that is what you are experiencing.

JULIE: Yeah, but I don't usually come back in their way, its like when Seth comes in, I don't come back in his reality, he comes in and he leaves and then I am like 'okay, I am back' I mean I might lay there and cough for a while but more or less I am just back.

YVES: Well there is a rewiring going on, and they say there is an interweaving going on between the two of us that has to happen. It takes us to a higher plane.

JULIE: Okay, but if I have to live like this from now on, I can't. It is just mega overload; just tell me it is not going to be like this forever.

YVES: It will not always be like that, Julie, it will not always be like that. Let's get up, lets walk. Let me get you up *[assists Julie in standing]*, I'm going to bring you back to this reality with me.

[Julie loses her balance.]

JULIE: Whoa... I feel like I am intoxicated *[stumbling as she walks]*.

YVES: Okay, come on let's sit you back down *[walks Julie to picnic table]*.

JULIE: I am okay just a little drunk *[stumbles more]*.

307

YVES: Okay...okay... let's sit you down...

JULIE: I wish we hadn't parked so far down the road...then we would not have so far to walk ...but if I sit. I don't know what will happen... *[looks at Yves]* you poor thing...I want to close my eyes for a minute but I don't want to go into another trance.

YVES: You won't.... you won't...because we have to leave so they are not coming back right now.

[Julie is looking around at this point trying to come back to her own awareness.]

JULIE: Okay, I can't look up at the leaves on the tree's its freaky. Wow. Now is the time I should look at the tree from the forest right? Just like what is right in front of me, like I can't take in the expansive view.... *[Yves turns on flashlight.]* Ahhhhh ...ahhhh *[Julie shields her eyes].*

YVES: I am going to stop recording now so we can leave.

We walked for some time and Julie needed to stop every so often to take things in more slowly, she was getting quite overwhelmed and anxious. We finally made our way through the park and toward my car, along the way she continued to experience bouts of vertigo and seeing things in the tree's and describing the surroundings much like she was seeing through it all. That everything was made of lines of light.

Upon arriving at the car, Julie asked how to open the car door, she did not seem to understand. Stating, "How does one work this machine." It was clear that she was still very much connected to her Over Soul, or the part of her that is not incarnated in her physical body, she seemed unfamiliar with the seatbelt and its use. I had to buckle the belt for her. On the drive back to her home, she continued to make occasional commentary on the surroundings. Seeming fascinated by it all as though she was seeing it for the first time, but still seeing through the illusion of it. I imagined her experience was similar to some of the scenes from the movie "The Matrix."

She continued to express concern that she would never get her mind back fully and feared she would be brought to a psychiatric ward. I continued to reassure her.

Upon arriving at her home, I walked her in to settle her and leave her in her roommates' capable hands. She apparently needed more grounding so her roommate suggested that she eat some fruit. Julie shared that she felt trapped in the house and made her way toward the balcony however she did not notice that there was a screen door there (that is always there) and walked right into it knocking it out.

She was then fascinated by the surroundings of the apartment complex and was leaning around and over the balcony so we decided she had better stay seated on the ground while her roommate fixed a plate of fruit to ground her back.

After another 30 minutes she seemed to be coming back more and was very tired, so I took my leave and her roommate assured me she would keep an eye on her.

The next few days, per Julie's report she was really drained but had finally come back to her normal waking awareness.

Till date, Julie has not had any experience this extreme during our sessions, but it certainly lends itself to much of the Eighty-Second Regime's teachings about our need to remain in the illusion some of the time even when we are expanding our awareness.

Epilogue

THE COLLECTIVE: There are many changes coming, and you must be prepared. There is nothing that you need to fear. There is nothing you have ever had; there is nothing you will ever lose. It is only as you begin to go through this world in your humanness, and begin collecting tokens, which you use to define who you are, that you then want to hold on to these tokens, or ideas and beliefs. However, part of moving forward, if you are to grasp the next pieces of growth, is to let go of some things that you are holding on to. You must let go. You have always had nothing, yet everything. The human being cannot hold a single thing. You may have the illusion that you are holding something in your hands at this moment, but this does not mean that it cannot break or fall. You think that these things are the only things you have. You humans hold on tightly out of fear. What you must understand is that if you would just let go, then you can embrace all of life—all of it! Most of you go through your life seeking, only seeking. Even when you are fortunate enough to begin to see a piece of the truth, you attempt to hold on to everything else that you know. It does not mean that you always must let go of it; however, if you are looking at the world with new eyes, you cannot see what is in front of you if you're busy looking around to the sides to make sure everything is coming with you or looking behind you to see that everything is still attached. The only thing that happens, then, is that in turning to what is behind or to the side of you, you bump into whatever it is that you are walking toward. When you bump into this, the force of it pushes you back, you see? There is so much that is waiting for each of you, and we do not mean only each of you as individuals— but as a people, a community, and as a world. There is so much that you run away from, and all you are ever truly running away from is the love that you are.

Each time you shut the door on what you have seen, each time you turn away from the mirror because of your fear, you have turned away from love. Each time that you make a decision out of fear, you have turned away from love. The way that your world is currently is because for centuries those who said they were the teachers of the truth told you that you were not divine. They told you that you were wrong, that you were bad. You were told so much that it is untrue. How could God be wrong? How could God mislead God?

There are many who have the mistaken idea that here in the ethers, there is always peace, quiet, and bliss. We say to you that there is this pain that all of you carry on your Earth that rises up to us. We call out to you, and so often, you do not answer. We beckon you to come closer. We hear your pleas and your cries—the ones you speak out loud and the ones that you hide silently in your spirits, for that is what humans have been conditioned to do now. We are the same as you, those whom you deem to be your enemies are the same as you, and those you deem to be the great wise ones, the leaders, are also the same as you.

They are all aspects of you, acting out your own divinity. When we say that you are all one, it is not merely a saying. Ultimately, in the central pole of the central most hub is the one—you. You are all it! You are not a piece or particle of it, you are *it*.

You are it, experiencing itself and its many different selves, its many different expressions of itself.

You are playing in the drama of your own production. However, it is not all written. You can rewrite the story. You can edit or change the scenery, you can use Wite-Out if you want, but do this: Change it! Often we speak of willingness. We speak of the difference between desire and willingness; and so often, it comes out in ways that it sounds as though the willingness just means are you willing to sacrifice anything? It sounds as though it is only about sacrifice, yet the next part of that question is, are you willing to embrace everything? It is easier to be afraid of the letting go than it is to admit that you are afraid of embracing greatness, of embracing your greatness, and of embracing the wisdom that you truly do have. It is easier than dealing with the fear of the repercussions or recriminations of others if you were to truly step into your greatness. You are great for you are Divinity. Remember this!

And remember this: That we who are here call to you from the ethers; we call to you from the sky. We call to you in the wind that moves through the branches of the trees as it rustles against the leaves as they hit the ground and crush under your feet. We call to you in the sound of the baby's cry and the mother's sigh. We call to you from the dirt and the muck and mire of the earthen plane. We call to you from the beautiful places, the peaceful places; and we call to you from the hellacious war-torn places. We call to you always. Will you, shall you, dare you heed the call? If you listen, you will hear us. We come not only when you ask. We come— sometimes gently, sometimes strongly. We come in every single moment in every single experience. We are present for all things alike.

There is not a time where there is a distinct difference in cases where we herald in and appear or not. The difference is you opening your eyes! You see? We exist always at all times, in all places. As do you. The saying "All life is sacred" does not only mean that all lives are sacred; it means that *all* of life is *sacred*. Each moment the wheel of life is turning, in every moment, every bit of it is sacred.

If you see these things differently, then you will always limit yourself, for you will always be trying to be in one place or another. Meet each moment with sacredness; see each moment as a gift from the Great Spirit that leads you. The Great Spirit that lives in you. The Great Spirit that comes in the calling of the birds or the rustle of the trees as the forest animals move through them. The Great Spirit who calls to you from the council fires, in the drumming, in the rain and snow, the sunshine and thunder. This spirit is called Great Spirit, for it is thus.

As this manuscript reaches its end, we continue to call to you. You will find us in your dreams; you will feel us in your heart when you feel the beat of Mother Earth beneath your feet as you walk upon her. Let that serve to remind you of our presence, and that all life is sacred.

We wish to thank those who have read and heard our words and guidance. We wish to say to you that although we have used this vehicle to impart certain information, we stand ready to assist you should you wish to be assisted. All that you need to do is call upon us, and we will lend the support that is needed.

We may not be those spirits that you are familiar with, but rest assured that if you have picked up this book and read it, in some way, on some level, we are connected to those who are connected with you. Elsewise, you would not have picked up this material. It is our hope that as you place down this book, you might think upon these things that we have shared. Think upon the ways that this might reflect in your own lives, or your challenges. How it might reflect in your own hopes, dreams, desires, and your own wisdom. For, we are here to serve humanity, now.

Therefore, we wish nothing more than to arm you with information that will assist you in moving through some of these tumultuous times that your world and each of you faces in different ways at different times and periods in your lives. You must know that you are not alone. You have never been alone, nor will you ever be alone. It is when you feel the most alone that, if you sit in the silence of that aloneness, you will feel us and others like us surround you and enfold you within the energy of our love

We are of the Eighty-Second Regime of Light Workers, and we are here to serve you.

APPENDIX A:
THESE CHANGING TIMES
CONCERNING THE YEAR 2012
AND BEYOND

April 8, 2010 – Yves and Patti were present and directing questions. Yves was on the recording device. The session was 119 minutes in length with no breaks. This was originally an earlier chapter in the book that has been moved to the Appendix due to its original title being dated. However due to the nature of the content that it contains it was decided to keep the information here as we believe it is timeless and the issues and principles contained herein remain relevant.

THE COLLECTIVE: This evening, we would like to start by greeting you both here. It is our understanding that there are some queries that you have posed.

YVES: There is much talk on this Earth of the year 2012. Some people believe it will be the end of the world; others believe that the end means a change in consciousness. Can you tell us about any changes that may occur?

THE COLLECTIVE: Let us start by stating that in saying "the world," you are referring to this earthen plane that you are familiar with, correct?

YVES: Yes, that is correct.

THE COLLECTIVE: Without going into it, there are many worlds. The world, this earthen plane, is not scheduled to change its form for quite some time. Allow us to clarify what we mean when we say, "change its form." What we mean is what *your* understanding would be as the end of the world. For even if the world were to end, really, it only changes form, you see? Just as in the death of the physical body, there is a form that is changed. If you take all of the energy, all of the living things on this planet of yours, even when these things die, the energy continues. Let us clarify something; there have been times in your world when what you would refer to as planets have ceased to be seen by the human eye—well, there are many that cease to be seen by the human eye, but you get our drift—that does not mean that these planets have "ended," so to speak. The energy is just moved elsewhere. But for the purpose of your question, there is, at this point in time, no sched-uled shift or changing of the world or ending of the world—to quote you, "of your world" for some time. You would not see it in this lifetime of yours; however, certainly, changes are afoot.

Now these are not things that will happen only when this year 2012 occurs. It is not as though, suddenly; you will see Earth and climate changes and consciousness changes and all of that. All of that is happening, all of that *has* been happening, and all of that will continue to happen. This is a marking of the new age, a new period or measurement of time when there are predetermined consciousness shifts that are *due* to occur. Are you following us?

As you are aware as anyone who is paying attention in your world, in the past decade, the amount of cataclysmic changes, have been increasing, traumatic events have been increasing, climate change is already occurring. It is not something to occur. You are seeing this "around the globe," so to speak, and you will be seeing more.

At this point in time, it is a necessary thing for several reasons, and again, we will do our best to address each of these things. We may pause from time to time because as we speak, there may be further queries about that which we are referencing. And so, either party is certainly welcome to pose queries on what we are speaking during the times that we pause.

Over time, in many of your different cultures, religions, and practices, there are many different ways that time has been measured, yes? When you look at some of your oldest religions, which are still in practice, if you were to go into the bowels of them, you will find that there was a time period in which "seers" (those people who would access beings such as us), would document the periods during which certain changes by design are set up to occur. Now, again, remember that in the bigger umbrella of all of this is that all of you are here on the one hand for your personal spiritual growth and for experiencing that on the earthen plane. We are going to stick to the Earth for ease of communication.

We have spoken before—but will not get into it tonight—of the over soul and how each part of you belongs to something higher and higher still, and that, that which is higher, is also looking to grow and evolve. Therefore, there is a process of not only the individual evolvement but also the more collective evolvement. As the collective is evolving, then that evolution is also seen here on your Earth. In other words, there are times when there is spiritual evolvement on the bigger scale, not the individual scale, and this is when you see physical evolvement. So there are these ages, these periods of time, where there is an intended jump in the evolution of the spirit—you understand—of the collective spirit. You are currently moving into an age, a "period of measurement," if you will, an intended purpose for further evolution. As we are moving into this age, changes begin happening before you get to that intended outcome, right? Just as in your own personal lives, when change is afoot, there is a buildup to that. In your own initiatory rites [*directing this at Yves*], it was not just the initiation; there was a buildup, the event, and then there is the continued extension of that initiation, yes? Likewise, that is what is occurring here, now. There is a buildup, not just in terms of climate changes, but also changes in how your world is operating. For instance, your own country (the United States of America) has been the model for many other countries, yes? Currently, the cards are being pulled out from underneath all of the other cards, and stacks are falling down. There is a shift and an awakening occurring in people here who are now looking to the places and the people that they were moving away from. There was this idea that the way of life here in your divided country or your land, that it was more "civilized," it was more "advanced," it was "better," people were "happier"; and all of this is a fallacy. There has been too much of an attachment to material wealth. So while, for some time, the rest of the world was looking at you, some of you here now are beginning to look out at the other parts of the world to see what works. There are many places in the world where there has not been "much" for quite some time, yet they have found a way through all of the suffering and all of the difficulties. You will find that in many of these places, people are still kind, they are giving, and they are loving. Now this is not all, of course, because there is strife everywhere, but again, we speak in generalities; if they have never had it, then it is not difficult to lose it. You understand? The world's power is beginning to shift, you see, because that idea of what is power or what is a powerful thing, is beginning to change. Unfortunately, at this point in time, the way that things are moving, from where we stand out here in the outer realms we say that more will need to fall apart, that more will be lost. This is the only way for your higher selves to see; for your awareness to be brought back to what matters, to what is important. There are many of you who have been "waking up," so to speak, but it is very difficult to do in this world. Because you are in ways waking up yet as you continue to walk through this world it is difficult to awaken. So in order to do that, you have to stay asleep a little bit, and you wake and you go back to sleep and you wake up and you go back to sleep. The only way to stay awake a little longer is to remove some of those trappings, yes? This will be very difficult for many.

YVES: Can you elaborate more on what will be lost?

THE COLLECTIVE: Again, we will attempt to water it down, if you will. As we are looking at your globe, in different places, there will be different ways that things change. If it is amenable to you, we will speak for this moment about the places that have the most capital, about the places that have the most power, about this country and about the people in other countries who have much wealth. Unfortunately, some of what will happen, and when we say unfortunately, we are saying it from the human perspective—it is not quite so unfortunate to us—many more will lose jobs, many more will lose homes; financial institutions, which are already crumbling, will continue to do so. There is, right now, a bit of a veil pulled over what is still occurring. It is just as when you have your Earthquakes, yes? There is the catastrophic event, and people can "see" the damages, following which, you have aftershocks. What people often think, because they judge that aftershock, compared to the magnitude of the earlier Earthquake, is there is no damage, but there is. You must understand that in the core of the Earth, in that place where the Earth quake occurred, where the aftershocks occurred, there is not a singular circular area where there is a quake and then an aftershock, and that it is limited to that area because what happens is that as these plates are shifting, *everything* shifts. You cannot have one part shift without affecting other parts as well. Now, the trick here to understanding is being able to understand that if all things are connected, then if the Earth's core is the Earth's core, then this Earthquake or aftershock in one place creates something that moves outward to other places, which in turn imbalances other places still.

Therefore, one thing affects the other, and now you have financial institutions that are collapsing, you have a government system that is bankrupt, and that same government system is loaning money to the bankrupt financial institutions, In your movie theaters, there was one such movie that still today, after many years, is very popular with children, and there is a curtain behind which is a man pretending to be a great magician. People fear this magician, people revere this magician, and people come to this magician for favors or works. No one opens the curtains because they would rather not know. For as long as they see the smoke coming out of the fake masked face and they hear the booming sounds and all of that, it is enough for them because it is difficult to pierce through that veil, through that façade. So with all of these things happening, aftershocks are occurring, and the people grab onto hope wherever they can. The problem is that their hope includes still relying on finances and material things. Human beings have gotten farther and farther apart from one another. It seems that until you must rely on your own survival, *until it comes to that*, you will not change. You sit comfortably, perhaps say on a beach, enjoying the sunshine, listening to the gulls overhead, perhaps hoping to see one of your dolphins jump by—it is picture-perfect until the storm comes. Then the same beach that gave you such peace and such joy suddenly becomes a place of terror. When you are in that place of terror and you have to survive, well, the body that wanted to laze around before suddenly jumps to its feet and runs or climbs or whatever it is that it does because it must. Likewise, the only way to raise your unified consciousness is to bring you to a place, and again remember you are bringing yourselves there, where you must begin to rely on something other than this curtain. Something other than your separated lives, your separated homes, and your bank accounts that keep you divided into little places that keep you from "walking to the other side of the tracks," so to speak. As people become aware that the money is not there now, let us qualify this and say that we are not saying to you that on the very first day of the year 2012, this is what will happen; it is not like that. Again, it is a period, a marked period of time. This marked period is about getting to the place of change, and where there will be either evolution or destruction. And so, again, depending on the movement of it, the time period can change. There are some traditions that measure in thousands of years, but time is very elusive, however. This is happening as we speak.

There are many of you who are now beginning to seek other ways, but the problem is that you are seeking the other ways to try to stop this process so you can still hold on to what you have. You tell yourselves that if you evolve quickly enough, then you will not have to lose it all, and one counteracts the other, does it not?

YVES: These catastrophic, cataclysmic changes would also involve some catastrophic geological changes? Because this world has undergone quite a few episodes of that ... these mountains that we see are resultant from cataclysmic changes. Would that involve some of that?

THE COLLECTIVE: We need clarification. Are you asking, will this involve some of this in the year 2012? Or will it involve it as part of that process?

YVES: As part of that process and even in 2012. For example, you mentioned Earthquakes. And Earthquakes happen in this part, but it involves the entire world. Will there be some movements of these plates occurring simultaneously along with the financial—

THE COLLECTIVE: *[Interrupting Yves's question.]* This is already occurring, so even as you are talking about geological changes or Earth changes, understand that it is already occurring. So what is happening here is that these things are moving now as we speak. You understand? Are you asking if anything will occur that will make an instantaneous change in the geology of the Earth? Is that what you are asking?

YVES: Yes.

THE COLLECTIVE: Not to the human eye, no. Again, we are answering you in terms of mountains springing up. You may see some land coming out of water that has not been seen in some time. You may also see other parts of land going underwater. You see, the Earth that you are on is a living, breathing organism. It is another piece of the breath, and since it is connected, there is no telling how a living, breathing organism will respond. Just as we might say to someone else that if they were to do something to Yves, then Yves may respond in "this" way or "that." We may have a general idea of your personality patterns. We may have a general idea as to how you might respond; however, we cannot say for sure because you are a living, breathing organism, and because of free will, you could at any time change your reaction.

So while we can say in generalities, we cannot say what will happen exactly. Again, this is because we are not sure if humans will change their wastefulness. If they will change their relationship with the Earth and about each other and depending on to what degree they do this. Due to this, we cannot tell you how the living, breathing organism that you are now living upon will react. We do realize we may seem somewhat vague in our answer, but again, it is very difficult to be exacting.

In the purest of teachings, you will find that there is never something that is guaranteed. If you go and you look into your holy scriptures, in many different texts, they will make prophecies. Those prophecies that have come along, you will notice, never gave a time line, and they gave only generalities, yes? What we can speak about, the most helpful things that we can offer to you, is "as things stand now" or "based on this action or that action." Unfortunately, we do not see a massive shift of consciousness anytime soon. While there are some of you that are being "called," the truth is that we need—and we mean all of the consciousness needs—more people than that to answer that call in order to make the changes that are necessary. Let us clearly state that the intention, ultimately, is not to keep the world from being destroyed ever. At some point, this world will be destroyed because, again, this is natural evolution. "Destroyed" is not always "bad," death isn't "bad"; however, the quickening of the destruction as a result of a lack of acknowledgment of the connectedness of all things is not necessary.

Let us say this: there is a veil of deception that all of you have placed around your own selves. You will be seeing more Earthquakes, you will be seeing more storms coming from the oceans, and there will be more fires in your forests. There will be floods and droughts that have always happened, but more of them will occur. More people will be destroying people. Again, we wish to *clearly* state to you that all that we are saying right now is that it is not in the year 2012 that you will see all these to occur.

328

We are saying that from where you are now, as you have seen these things increase, you will see them continue to increase.

There may come a time not too awfully long from now, but we will not give you the years, when your money will be useless, useless. As all of you already know, there is nothing behind that money even now, but no one has realized it yet, not fully. When the world suddenly realizes that there is nothing there, then there will be nothing there. In this country (USA), you have an opportunity to show the world something different. This is the opportunity you are being given. Now, many will do that willingly. There are some of you who may kick and scream, but you have an opportunity, yet this opportunity does not come without discomfort. The question is, do you want to teach by lecturing, or do you want to teach by leading? Do you want to sit and have deep conversations with others about the meaning of life and the uselessness of material goods, or do you want to demonstrate it? What of the usefulness of each other, of living in community? We will use, for example, there are certain spiritual communities with well-grounded intentions, but often, they have conflicting ways of going about building their community. It is like a tightrope because, you see, as they are attempting to build their community, they busy themselves trying to build other things. These are things that will be useful and are useful in many ways, but what of building relationships? What of building the spiritual part as opposed to "We will build this to get more people to come. We will build that to get more people to come, we will . . . ," and so forth. Are you following us? What healing are you bringing? This is a question for all those in community to ask themselves. This is not to say that such communities are doing nothing to help the world; let us be very clear about that. The bigger question is, do you really understand the purpose of creating a community; of being of *service* to the world; of demonstrating through your path a way of surviving, a way of living, and a way of communing? These are questions that all religions, all traditions, all communities, all families and friends need to begin to ask and really, really look at. *How are you walking through the world?* Do you stop to help someone only if you have time, only when it is convenient, only on those days when you happen to feel compassionate? What of all the other times? What of all the other people? Do you give someone a treat, a gift, or assistance because you had a good day? Why are you not doing it on the days when you feel you had a bad day? Perhaps you had a bad day because you did not give, because you did not notice, because you did not open your eyes. When we say "you," we mean the global "you." We will pause to readjust the frequency and to allow the opportunity for either of the two of you to pose any queries regarding this, for we know we have only touched the surface of this so far.

YVES: You mentioned some of these changes; catastrophic changes will come, as a result of financial disaster, which is currently occurring. From that, I get a picture of a return to a natural way.

Back to not too long ago where things were much simpler, where we did not rely on money, where you mostly rely on your relationship with nature, with things around you. Is that a return to that? To that way of life?

REBECCA: We are sifting through because that is a very difficult question to answer. Of course, there is always a yes and a no. The answer "yes" is the simple answer, but the other part of it is that even within that, ideally, there would still be some things that are done differently because while that was the way for some time, even then, there was the need for spiritual evolution. You understand? Therefore, what is important to point out is that those of you who are "beginning to wake up and are leading the people," so to speak, of course, from our perspective, the returning to that is not bad. However, it is going to feel bad, it is going to look bad; in fact, there will be times when it is going to be quite horrendous for many. So it is not that, sort of, smooth transition of living delightfully off the land and all of that, you see? However, there are those of you who might assist in that transition so that it is a smoother transition. Part of what will make it smoother is that the more of you that begin to make those changes now, the more of you that begin to learn these ways and rely on these ways—and not use them as merely a "Saturday hobby," so to speak—then the more you can show others. You can assist others in doing that, and you begin to assist us in striking a balance of the destructive tendencies toward the Earth and the nurturing tendencies toward the Earth.

As you nurture the Earth, it also begins to nurture. Therefore, due to current cause and effect based on what you have been doing, things will definitely have to change over time. How will they occur, how deep of an impact, and how much suffering will there be? That is a bit flexible or malleable based on, again, whatever the conditions are and what people do about it. For instance, you have some people who become "survivalists," if you will, but many of them are prepared to take off to the mountains, or perhaps they already have. What good are they to the rest of the world? They have separated themselves from everyone and everything else. Although we are not eliminating the possibility that you may have to take off to some mountains, what we are saying is while all of this is occurring; it is better to begin to practice new things. There is much you all need to learn about these ways. This does not mean that tomorrow you have to go build your own little hut in nature, although it is certainly supported, but what it means is that in addition to learning these things, you also need to be more compassionate toward the world and be more compassionate toward your fellow man, if you will. To risk all, to step out, to be willing to be "seen" for who you are and for what you are doing and how you are trying to live. How can you draw others to yourself and assist them if you are hiding behind a blanket? You understand? Then you also become the "man behind the curtain"; it is just a different one—yours is tattered and not quite as fancy as that of the magician's. Therefore, it is important to begin this now, and we are not saying that you have not begun.

COMPASSIONATE ONE: But what we are saying is that it is possible for you to begin to eliminate some of the sorrow. Catastrophes have occurred already; there is suffering already. It is all around you. Do not wait! There are dark clouds around so many, and they cannot see their way out. Judge them not. But reach; and if they take not your hand, then leave something there for them, a kind word, a loving touch, perhaps even something that they do not necessarily need. Perhaps they have plenty, and then you must leave behind kindness and love. That may not get them to follow you, but it may be the pinhole that allows the light, the remembering, to begin to come in. However, you must be willing to stand before them naked, standing in your own truth, standing in who you fully and truly are; even those who are blind will see that there is something. Something in you that is as clear and as pure as the divine. For that is what begins to awaken more and more in you.

All of you have seen certain people at times that as you look at them, there is something in their eyes, there is something around them, and there is something that just emanates off them. You are drawn, and you feel lifted just being in their presence. [Whispering.] This is because you recognize the divine; and if you can see it in them, it gives you hope that perhaps, some-where in you, it exists, and it does! If that exists in you, then all of these other things that you try to use to feel powerful to keep fear away are no longer needed because all of these trappings will keep you only farther away from the divine.

THE COLLECTIVE: The moment that you have a holding, or an owning, to any material things or to certain ideas, in that moment, you begin to separate yourself from that divine, from that energy, from that light, from that truth. There was a time when even here, on this Earth, all of you were connected to the Earth through her nourishment, and you began to slowly, and sometimes quickly, diminish her importance. Yet you still need her to survive. You muddied her waters; you polluted them. You began to take the food that grew upon her and tried to make it bigger. You polluted her trees, bushes, and plants with your chemical sprays and your wastefulness. Everything that you place on your body and in your body all came from her.

There are those of you who go eat organic foods or perhaps grow some in your yard, and yet there is still a disconnect. It *makes* you feel better to buy the organic food; it makes you feel better to have a little garden plot and say, "I am doing my part." However, oftentimes when you are purchasing your organic food or when planting your seeds and reaping the harvest, you still are not really connecting to the love that the Earth is offering you through that. Because when people ask you, you can say, "Oh yes, I eat organic foods, I have my own garden, I buy farm-fresh meats." We ask, did you connect with that animal and give thanks to it? Did you give thanks for its nourishment, for releasing its spirit that you might receive nourishment? Did you offer back your own nourishment of prayers and upliftment? You see, the connection still is lost. We understand that these are very difficult things to change, and we are quite patient, but natural order is not, cause and effect is not. So in order to begin to balance out the damages, you need to give back to the Earth, to the people, to the animals. Give them back their places to live. Of course, in your world, the population is much more than it was in the past;

however, some of that is being taken care of by nature herself.

There is a long road to follow; everything, everything has been pushed to the limit. Everything is overly abundant: the number of people, the number of buildings, the number of all things. This is too much for the Earth to contain, to hold and stay balanced. And again, this living, breathing organism automatically tries to find balance. So where there is an imbalance, it will react to create balance. Your physicians' work harder and harder, and researchers work harder and harder to find more and more cures, things to keep people alive longer. Death has become sterile and talks of it—taboo. You do this as though there is failure in a natural occurrence. These advances in your medical technology keeps more people alive longer, keeps people producing children longer. So nature has to come up with more creative ways to balance itself from all of the weight on its back. New diseases, new illnesses, new storms because it must shift, it must shake off. Just as we spoke of earlier about your own survival and your survival instincts, and this other living, breathing organism known as the Earth also has that survival instinct. You see? Only this [*pointing to the Earth*], this knows that it is all "interwoven," if you will. All of you do not, and so it works better; it's a stronger force. It is similar to one of your four-legged friends who has a bug or what you call tick upon its back. This four-legged will dig away at it, and it may even create a cut to try to get it out, you see? So it may harm itself in trying to keep it from harm—you understand— and so will the Earth. Because it too recognizes that all of *you* are a part of *it*.

[Long pause.]

YVES: This book we are working on is our way of raising the consciousness of the world through this dissemination of the teachings that you are imparting to us. Will the infrastructure be there for this book to be disseminated?

THE COLLECTIVE: We have spoken of this in stating that there would be people to read the book, the book would be out, and people would know when that occurred; so yes *[speaking directly to Yves and Patti].* Please do not be mistaken, however, in thinking that this project is what you are doing as your one contribution to the world, because there is much more that you need to do. This is one small piece. Of course, as you know, there is free will. And so, you can say no at any time, to any call. But understand that you're answering no to yourself!

REBECCA: *[Continuing to speak directly to Yves and Patti.]* It is very, very important that as you are creating this text with us, in tandem with us, you also begin to test out some of these things. That you begin to walk through these teachings.

You understand? Because it's important that . . . understand that we don't teach them just to teach them. We don't share them just to say, "Well, aren't we quite the smart ones." We share them because this is a way to live. And if you are seated here now, or if you are reading this text, then we are asking you to live that way. Again, we realize this isn't something you can just do overnight because there is so much that has to change and has to go in cycles, in bits and pieces, but we will say that intentional delay is not a good idea. Because there is much more that we need you for, that the world needs you for. There is much more that you need each other for, all of you, as a collective. This is where a collective consciousness as a collective group that can go in and out of other collective groups is needed; there is this nucleus that is attempting to plant little nucleuses of these collective groups around your earthen plane. That mainly comes to the places where people aren't changing, and then the nucleus in one place can spread out and bring in or carry to this other nucleus over here. You understand? And so that is how it begins to spread because, again, you cannot do this alone, and that is the whole point, isn't it? The point is in remembering your connection to all that is when you do this. Therefore, how would you do it alone? There are some people who may not gel in that nucleus, and some of you have already had this experience before. You must just let that fall away; let them fall away. It is not giving up on them, it is not looking away from them, it is walking toward what you need to do, and it allows them to find their own nucleus, you see? For to attempt to fit a square peg into a round hole doesn't really work, unless, you are good at what they call whittling. You can whittle it away, but that can be quite painful as well. It is easier to just let the square go to the square and the round go to the round and so on. You understand? So this is not to say that when one does not act in a way as you wish that you should, just discard them; but what we are saying is that there is a way of walking through the world, and when there are those that interfere with that, you need to let them do what they need to do, and you need to do what you need to do.

[Long pause.]

And for ease of Julie's physical comfort, we will be exiting in short order. We will not get to your other questions tonight, but we will need to impart more information regarding this question. As we move forward, we would like to continue along this vein. We do not want to spend an entire half of a book on 2012 because, then, 2012 will come and go, and people will think we are useless when certainly we are not. Is there anything that you feel is somewhat unclear in what we have just shared with you?

If so, then we would like to tie it up enough to be prepared to move from that.

YVES: So 2012 is not the end of the world, as we most people understand it. The world we know just disappears, but there are going to be some very cataclysmic changes . . .

THE COLLECTIVE: There will continue to be.

YVES: There will continue to be, yes, and some of it will involve the financial veil, which exists, which will make money useless. Earth changes will continue to exist; there is a call for a return to more natural ways, to acknowledge what the Earth has to offer . . .

THE COLLECTIVE: Are you writing your own version now?

YVES: I was trying to recap.

THE COLLECTIVE: *[Humorously.]* We are delighted you were paying attention; however, we believe we explained it much better than you. And so, our question to you was, are there any other queries regarding this that you need now to "sew it up," if you will?

YVES: No, it is all very clear. Thank you.

THE COLLECTIVE: And we have an assignment for each of you. We would like to ask you, if you so choose, that as you look at the data and the information that we have given you, we ask that you all begin to look at the ways in which you feed that imbalance. And we don't just mean a lack of recycling. But in all of these areas that we touched upon, where are you still feeding the imbalance? Where are you keeping things hidden behind the curtain? It is important that you begin to have this awareness of the places and the ways that you do this. For we understand that each of you is sincere in your desire to help others, to bring compassion and love and healing to this place. And in order to do that fully, you must continue to look at your own stumbling blocks. This is not to say that you have not done that or are not doing that, but it is to say that there is a call for more. Know that we will walk with you as you move through all of this. We bid you a fond good night.

APPENDIX B:
PARALLEL LIVES AND
MULTIDIMENSIONAL SELVES

> Date unknown in 2010. Yves was present and direct-
> ing questions. Yves was on the recording device. The
> session was in part of a more personal nature how-
> ever some of the information, seemed relevant to more
> worldly questions and therefore this bit of the session
> was preserved and is included for the reader to digest.

YVES: You have spoken of parallel lives in
other worlds, other dimensions, and other realities. Do people have other selves in the same
dimension?

THE COLLECTIVE: Ahh, that is a good
question. As with all questions, there are
answers that are seemingly very simple, and yet
they can become quite complicated, yes? While
that is possibly the case, and at times it is, let
us begin by explaining to you how that might
occur. We have heard about the other selves,
parallel lives, and how the over soul is at the
hub of all of this, giving directions like your "air
traffic controller," if you will. When your energy

from the over soul is dispensed into physical vehicles, there are certain allotted amounts of energy inserted. It is not as though the over soul has a formula—one part to one part to one part—but depending upon the intention of that piece of the life of that over soul, there can be smaller or larger amounts of the consciousness inserted. For instance, in those that you would deem your spiritual leaders, there would be more of the active consciousness of the over soul. However, let us clearly state that this does not mean that one has more or less of a "soul"; instead, it means that the overriding *essence* or intention may be stronger when it contains more of the over soul's combined intention of its many lives. In other words, there may be more of its awareness inserted in one body or another. Now this holds true across the board; this is not just in terms of if energies or beings are in the same dimension or the same world, for instance, on your earthen plane. So it could also hold true that this would apply in the other realms as well. Therefore, while it is possible, it does get a little bit tricky.

When you are in the other dimensions, there are those of you who can—and some who often do—connect with those other dimensions from time to time. And at times, that can be helpful, but it is not something that much time should be spent on. What can happen in this case is when too many "bleed-throughs," as we have referenced them, are occurring, the selves can get somewhat confused as to where they belong. And this can become problematic for obvious reasons. Therefore, when one incarnates, in more than one self in the same dimension, there are a couple of things that could happen that would be perhaps not so helpful to the soul's intent. One would be that it can become very confusing because if you are in the same dimensional realm, it is even easier to shift over to your other consciousness. There are some in your world that your physicians refer to as mentally ill. Some of them are those who can bend through dimensions and, hence, become very confused as to who they are. Therefore, they bring all of these different pieces of these personalities in, and they do not know which one belongs to them. They may shift in and out, or they may introduce themselves as someone else, perhaps one of your historical figures; and as one looks at them, they may say, "Well, that can't be."

And although at times we will say there is a bit of confusion about that, there are also times when that is, in fact, true based on their life within another dimension. Considering this, there is a greater risk of confusion when other selves of you are in the same dimension. For instance, if we are speaking of that which is the embodiment of Yves—who is seated before us currently—there are also the other parts of you, or of the over soul of you, who had also walked the earthen plane. These other parts of you are walking in the earthen world, but in a different dimension of it. When we say, "dimension of it," we are referencing your time zones. Therefore, while that scenario happens often, were there to be one or two or three other Yves's walking on the earthen plane in the same time zone dimension (while it can occur), it is even more dangerous. You see, if they were to come upon each other that could create a split or confusion in the individual personalities. However, at the same time, ultimately, if you have the over soul here that is at the hub of all of these personalities, what you must remember is that you cannot confine it to the over soul of Yves or the over soul of Julie or the over soul of your neighbor because that is only the over soul of individual energies that is a concentrated energy that then disperses itself into many different forms and forums and formats and so on. However, that over soul has been dispersed or dispensed from yet another overseer. So that there is this constant movement *[motioning upward above Julie's head]*. We are motioning going upward, mostly to make a greater understanding of how it works. Again, it is not so much a hierarchy as going up leaves one with the judgment of higher than. Although in the context of this, for your understanding, it is true to some degree. When we say higher *than*, we do not necessarily mean better than, although one thing would have more authority than the other would. But what happens is that this overseer is "stationed," if you will, to incarnate at will into things to oversee what is happening, to sometimes tinker a little without doing too much. That energy that is overseeing them would be the soul group. Again, we use this term only for your understanding. Soul groups are compartments of sorts. If you were to go into the ethers and see energies when they are discarnate, you would see these sorts of blinking lights, correct? Which is not the same as the ectoplasm from the physical body. The blinking lights in this case are the non-embodied energies. So these blinking lights are seen as very small, but they are much larger actually when they are concentrated. If you were to imagine or envision, these blinking lights are held within a womb or cocoon of their own, within the universal ethers, you see? So, if one were to draw a globe or a circle of something, this is the container which holds the energies of the universe; and then within that container, there would be sects and sub-sects of that and these little cocoons of energies that resonate together. Those energies then break off into the over souls, you see, that then break off into the individual incarnate energies in the physical dimension. And so it goes beyond and beyond and beyond until you reach that the infinite endless globe that encompasses all. We have spoken in the past about the shoots and offshoots and the wires that cross and all of that. Therefore, if you were to imagine that, it goes on and on like that. The ultimate overriding constant, never-beginning, never-ending energy, in order to be expressed, must constantly dilute itself into energy concentrated into many energies, concentrated into many other energies, until it trickles down so much that it is merely just a drop when it gets into you.

REBECCA: That, of course, can become quite complex as you begin to move in and out of those electrical lines and energies that exist. So going back to that, if one is in the physical world on the earthen plane at the same physical dimensional time frame, while it has occurred, and does occur, generally it's not in the best interest of that over soul. Now, there may be times when the over soul will insert more energy and then take out as a reminder that you will cross paths, that you will meet for a reminder. However, it is for a very short period of "time." This would be what some of you refer to as walk-ins, although the walk-in theory is not quite the way it is spoken of. The way it works, to use an example, is this: Imagine a bank robber who goes into a bank and runs in and backs out again and takes only what he needs in that moment and then quickly runs out again. This is what the over soul does when it inserts "more" energy in. It is important that you understand that ultimately, and here is where it can get a little deep in the human brain, you all are, in the ultimate sense, parallel lives of each other. So because if it is ultimately coming from that place of the "one source," that then shrinks down and down and down and down because it has to become smaller, then you are all ultimately a part of it. But if you were to recognize and realize that, well, then most of the fun is taken out of it because, then, this energy does not need to filter down to experience itself, yes? And so, while we are saying on the one hand the answer is no and on the other hand it is yes, that, of course, can be quite confusing to the readers. Therefore, we would ask you if, based on that which we have spoken to you about in this issue, you feel that there are further directed queries that need to happen to make that a little clearer for the readers. Because it is quite clear to us. But again, in your limited understanding, some of you will understand it at the base of it; and some of you, as we have said before, will be able to go a little deeper into that understanding. And others of you might just get quite a frightening headache from it all.

YVES: So there are not necessarily pleasant connotations of having the two selves in the same physical location. For instance, if I had my other self next to me right now, then that would not be a pleasant place to be because of the inter-actions of the two selves? The switching back and forth, which might lead one to be mentally ill if it lasts too long?

REBECCA: Again, this is very difficult to explain. You have the basic understanding of the standard practice of it. However, while we are speaking of the over souls and the soul groups and all of that, there are a couple more points to make. The first is to go back to what we were speaking of, wherein your over soul inserts some of your energy into someone else, and you may be right near each other, and you should be in order to remember. It may not be that this person is you *entirely*, but some of your energy is infused, just like our energy is infused in this vehicle currently. It does not mean they would be talking like you or anything like that, but there would be reflected either in their eyes or something they are doing where you are reminded of who you are and what you need to do. Now, of course, as we have always said, there is no hard-and-fast rule to any of this. Because on the one hand, there are those of you who are born as different parts of each other. Some refer to it as twin flames. Soul mates, by the way, are those who are generally in the same soul group. Twin flames are a different story. Oftentimes, the relationship can be combative, fiery, and smooth and a whole range of many different things. There are, at times, energies of two of you humans that may be entwined at the over soul level, so you are *sort of the same* but *not*. So it is sort of a "mixed cocktail," if you will—a lovely little martini that is mixed in together. But as you can see, if you partake of too much of it, then sometimes you can get quite drunk from it. So on the one hand, there are ways that are designed for where there is the "same self," so to speak, *but* it's the already "split-off self" that then incarnates and does that partly to bring it back together, and that is done generally when there is work to do on behalf of the universe. When there is work to do on behalf of the sort of "bigger" over soul, not just the stationary first-level over soul. The first-level over soul has things to complete to then bring it together and to bring it to the next-level over soul (or the over-over soul). There are times that the other (the *over-over soul*) will bring the energy down and split it here at the first-level over soul; and as it starts from here, it branches off and starts diluting and diluting and diluting. So the energies that those two would share are, sort of, like Siamese twins. So the over souls here on the first level are pieces of the same over-over soul, you see?

This is true for many people. It is not an unusual thing; it is a given thing that ultimately has to occur at some point in your "time." However, the bringing together of it in the concentrated form is something that happens when there is something that is to be accomplished within the realm of working with the energies out there, bringing awareness or enlightenment or truth and freedom to those who are incarnated.